Northwest Vista College
Learning Resource Center
3535 North Ellison Drive
San Antonio, Texas 78251

Children as Citizens?

INTERNATIONAL VOICES

Children as Citizens?
INTERNATIONAL VOICES

Childwatch International
Citizenship Study Group

Edited by

Nicola J. Taylor & Anne B. Smith

Published by Otago University Press,
Level 1 / 398 Cumberland Street
PO Box 56, Dunedin, New Zealand
Email: university.press@otago.ac.nz
Fax: 64 3 479 8385

First published 2009
Foreword copyright © Irene Rizzini 2009
Preface copyright © The editors 2009
Individual chapters copyright © The authors 2009
ISBN 978 1 877372 62 9

Editors: Richard Reeve, Wendy Harrex
Cover and page design: Fiona Moffat
Cover illustration: The star represents the citizens, the bird represents freedom, the water is calm and peaceful (bottom right corner), this shows balance between everything, (the axe) represents strength. (Australian Year 5 boy, aged 11 years)
Printed by Astra Print Ltd, Wellington

Contents

Acknowledgments 6
Foreword *Irene Rizzini* 7
Preface *Nicola Taylor & Anne Smith* 9
1 Children's Citizenship *Anne Smith & Håvard Bjerke* 15
2 Research Methodology *Nicola Taylor & Anne Smith* 35

Children's Perspectives on Rights, Responsibilities and Citizenship

3 Australia *Anne Graham, Brad Shipway & Robyn Fitzgerald* 43
4 Brazil *Irene Rizzini, Udi Mandel Butler & Nisha Thapliyal* 61
5 New Zealand *Nicola Taylor, Anne Smith & Megan Gollop* 81
6 Norway *Anne Trine Kjørholt, Håvard Bjerke, Gjertrud Stordal, Line Hellem & Pernille Skotte* 99
7 Palestine *Mohammed Shaheen* 129
8 South Africa *Rose September & Hazel Roberts* 147
9 Children's Perspectives on Citizenship: Conclusions and Future Directions *Udi Mandel Butler, Håvard Bjerke, Anne Smith, Brad Shipway, Robyn Fitzgerald, Anne Graham & Nicola Taylor* 169

About Childwatch International 185
Notes 193
References 197
Author Index 213
Subject Index 217

Acknowledgments

The members of the Citizenship Study Group gratefully acknowledge the encouragement and financial support offered by the Childwatch International Research Network to enable this research to be undertaken. We would particularly like to thank Jon-Kristian Johnsen (Director) and Pernille Skotte (Childwatch Secretariat) for all the assistance they have provided. Thanks are also due to the children, young people, parents and teachers who participated in the study across all six nations.

Finally, we would like to thank several people who have contributed to various stages of the study, but who were unable to remain involved throughout the life of the project: Natalie Kaufman (USA), Susan Limber (USA), Ingrid Willenberg (South Africa) and Jiri Kovarich (Czech Republic).

Foreword

This publication is the result of an important collaboration between Childwatch International members from six countries (New Zealand, Brazil, Norway, South Africa, Australia and Palestine). Childwatch International (CWI) is a network of child research centres in over forty countries which encourages collaboration between researchers throughout the world. Its research focuses on ways to improve the lives of children and promote their rights.

The history of this project began in 2003 when a group of researchers from seven research centres in Brazil, South Africa, New Zealand, USA, Palestine, Norway and the Czech Republic met to design a project that would allow a cross-cultural perspective on the topic of child and youth participation. We soon realised that we faced a great challenge, even within our small group, as we encountered difficulties in defining and finding a consensus about concepts such as 'citizenship', 'rights', 'responsibilities' and 'participation'.

We acknowledged the important paradigm shifts brought about by the framework of children's rights, in particular the United Nations Convention on the Rights of the Child, which recognised that children and young people are citizens and have universal rights. However, we were concerned that this claim often did not go beyond rhetoric. We also recognised the danger that terms like 'participation', 'citizenship' or 'rights' could be emptied of their meaning, or distorted, not reflecting actual practices on the ground.

We had a number of questions and doubts about undertaking such a valuable cross-cultural collaborative study. For instance, how could we create a common methodology that allowed space for the creativity and freedom of expression of children and young people in each country? How should we choose the groups of participants, whilst keeping some parameters for comparison between the countries? What contribution could a research network like CWI make to this ongoing debate? Although we were aware of the difficulties and challenges in relation to this project, we were confident that we had identified an extremely important topic to study.

We developed a methodology that emphasised the importance of listening to the views of children and involving them in debate about the issues. We also wanted to hear what their teachers and parents had to say about these topics. It was through eliciting the views of these different actors, living in different contexts and countries, that our study group felt it had a contribution to make to contemporary debates on children's citizenship.

Another challenge we faced was in selecting the groups to comprise our sample in each country. Beyond seeking the views of people from across the socio-economic spectrum, we felt that it was essential to include a group considered 'marginalised' from each society. The testimonies of 'street children' and children from the Landless Rural Movement in Brazil, and from refugee camps in Palestine, amongst others, revealed different dimensions of discrimination, which otherwise often remain invisible. Moreover, as we shall see, it is not uncommon that these groups are frequently overlooked in debates relating to citizenship and rights.

This book suggests that parents, teachers, carers, practitioners and policy makers can facilitate the authentic participation of children as citizens. To do so they need to be intentional, reflective and critical in their approach to concepts associated with children and citizenship. The work of our study group should therefore be welcomed as a resource for all those who live and work with children.

I particularly thank Nicola Taylor and Anne Smith for their commitment to seeing the research findings from the six contributing countries (Australia, Brazil, New Zealand, Norway, Palestine and South Africa) set within their international context and written up to form this book. Our study was important both to enrich the discussions in the countries in which Childwatch is situated and elsewhere, and to help to reinforce an interesting model of cross-cultural collaboration within the Research Network. We sincerely hope that this publication encourages others to conduct similar studies in the future.

IRENE RIZZINI
Rio de Janeiro, December 2008

President of Childwatch International Research Network
Director of The International Center for Research on Childhood (CIESPI)
Professor at the Catholic University of Rio de Janeiro (PUC-Rio)

Preface

Nicola Taylor and Anne B. Smith
Children's Issues Centre, University of Otago, New Zealand

Many lessons can be found in the real experience and practice of children. In societies throughout the world more could and should be done to create environments in which children achieve their optimum capacities and greater respect is given to children's potential for participation in and responsibility for decision making in their own lives – within the family, in school, in respect to their own health care, education, in courts, in local communities and in local and national political forums. (Jaap Doek, Chairperson UN Committee on the Rights of the Child, 2008, p. xvi)

'Citizenship' is a confusing and politically contested term, yet how this important concept is interpreted and put into practice shapes our experience in life. Being listened to, respected, and taken seriously tells us that we can stand up for ourselves and others, formulate plans and make a difference; and that we are not simply the helpless recipients of what other more powerful people do to us. With the recent global trend toward democratisation, dramatic economic, political and social change is occurring in every major region of the world. The participation and inclusion of all citizens, including children and young people, are essential ingredients in building strong families, neighbourhoods, communities, and democratic societies.

This book contributes to the theoretical understanding of citizenship. It also provides practical challenges and ideas to those who live and work with children, encouraging them to offer more opportunities for children to participate meaningfully in society. What sets this book apart from other citizenship publications, however, is its grounding in empirical research. We have not just explored the citizenship, participation and children's rights literature, but we have gone out and talked with a diverse range of children and young people about what these concepts mean for them in their daily lives. The findings from our collaborative international study will provide useful input into developing policies and practices to nurture the participation and rights of children and youth in their families, schools and communities. Research and theory on these increasingly relevant and much debated topics are examined critically in the chapters ahead. We reflect and build on this conceptual framework, in the light of the voices of children from six countries, who provided us with a snapshot of their experiences and understanding of citizenship in Australia, Brazil, Norway, New Zealand, Palestine and South Africa.

Our research sought to understand the meaning of citizenship for children in the everyday contexts of their diverse lives. We placed the perceptions and concerns of children at the centre of our research enquiry, but we were also interested in parents' and teachers' perspectives and how they helped children and young people to participate at home, at school and in their community. We wanted to contextualise citizenship from children's perspectives, by asking them to reflect on everyday experiences within their varied social, cultural and political contexts. In the research process we hoped, in a small way, to help the children who participated in our study to formulate their ideas and construct a sense of citizenship. We expected that the very different national and cultural settings in which the participants in our study were growing up would lead to an emphasis on different aspects of citizenship, and in this we were not disappointed. Nevertheless, even in such a diverse group of children, some common themes in their thinking were revealed, which closely resonated with existing theoretical explanations (such as Lister's (2007) theoretical outline of domains of citizenship).

Our research objectives were:

- To explore children and young people's understanding and experience of citizenship, and their views about their rights and responsibilities at home, at school and in the community;
- To examine children and young people's civic awareness and attitudes, the extent of their participation in families, schools and communities, and their construction of rights and other fundamental democratic concepts;
- To examine the role parents and teachers play in promoting 'good citizenship' to children and young people;
- To consider the impact of macro-level social, economic and political structures;
- To compare how children perceive and construct democratic concepts within and among different countries; and
- To develop ways of encouraging children and young people to increase their knowledge of citizenship, participation and involvement.

History of the International Research Project: 2003–2007

This was a cross-cultural and cross-generational international study, co-ordinated by the Childwatch International Research Network.[1] The research was undertaken in six countries in various stages of democratic development which each face a variety of economic, social and political challenges: Australia, Brazil, New Zealand, Norway, Palestine and South Africa. Child research centres from each of these countries collaborated on this project from 2003 to 2007 as members of a Childwatch Citizenship Study Group:

- **Australia:** Centre for Children and Young People, Southern Cross University, Lismore, New South Wales.
- **Brazil:** CIESPI, Pontificia Universidade Catolica, Rio de Janeiro.
- **New Zealand:** Children's Issues Centre, University of Otago, Dunedin.
- **Norway:** NOSEB, The Norwegian Centre for Child Research, NTNU, Trondheim.
- **Palestine:** Child Research Unit, Center for Development in Primary Health Care, Al-Quds University, AlBireh-West Bank.
- **South Africa:** Child and Youth Research and Training Programme, University of the Western Cape, Cape Town.

Following a preliminary meeting amongst interested researchers at the Childwatch Key Institutions meeting in **Bangkok** in 2002, Professor Natalie Kaufman, from Clemson University, South Carolina, USA, wrote a paper proposing a cross-cultural study of children and adults about what constitutes good citizenship, and attitudes and behaviours conducive to nation building. It was anticipated that this project would ultimately contribute to the *Childhoods 2005* conference being organised by the University of Oslo, Norwegian Social Research (NOVA) and the Childwatch International Research Network, to celebrate the University of Oslo's Centennial in mid-2005.

With the support of Childwatch International, senior researchers from five Key Institutions[2] then met in **London** on 14/15 October 2003 to form the Citizenship Study Group and to plan the research design. Agreement was reached on the research questions, timeline, sample and methodology. It was thought that semi-structured **focus groups** in primary and secondary schools, with children aged 8/9 years and 14/15 years, would be ideal to elicit their perspectives on citizenship, rights and responsibilities (Christensen & James, 2000). In order to compare teachers' and parents' perceptions of 'good' citizenship with those of the children, and to explore how these adults help children to understand concepts like democracy and community, a **questionnaire for parents and teachers** would also be developed.

The decision was made to use a focus group methodology, and the protocols for this approach were developed over time by the research group. Adaptations were subsequently made to the focus group protocols by the research teams in individual countries. This was necessary to ensure the questions made sense within each country context. Particular constraints, such as the amount of time which was available in schools for children to be out of class while they participated in the focus groups, also necessitated some changes (for example, to shorten the interview process to fit within the timeframe).

The Czech Republic unfortunately did not continue their involvement in the study group much beyond the London meeting, and the restrictions on research in American schools precluded the collection of data in South Carolina. However, the other study group members took responsibility for obtaining research funding to enable the study to proceed within their own country. The focus groups with the children and young people were undertaken in Brazil, New Zealand, Norway, Palestine and South Africa in 2004 and early 2005. The Australian Centre for Children and Young People subsequently became involved in the project when their affiliation with Childwatch was confirmed in 2005.

On 17/18 November 2004 the study group members met again at a meeting hosted by Professor Irene Rizzini of CIESPI in **Rio de Janeiro, Brazil**.[3] The children and young people's focus group data from Brazil, New Zealand (plus their parent/teacher questionnaire data), South Africa and Palestine was presented and discussed. The USA was experiencing difficulty in accessing schools for research purposes and so was unable to contribute any results.[4] Further important aspects of this meeting were the development of a study group work plan and the agreement reached on the format for the research report from each country in preparation for the Oslo *Childhoods 2005* conference the following year. In addition, Ziad Abdeen offered to develop a template for collating the data; the tasks identified for the citizenship symposium at the Oslo conference were divided amongst group members; and the collection of relevant published literature on citizenship and the group's publication plans were discussed. Presentations by study group members were also made at an International Seminar at the Pontificia Universidade Catolica in Rio de Janeiro.

The study group next met in Oslo, Norway, at the Citizenship Symposia during the *Childhoods 2005* Conference from 29 June–3 July 2005. Anne Smith provided a brief overview of the background to, and methodology for, the international research project on children's perspectives on citizenship. Papers were then presented which reported on each country's social and political context and their research findings.[5] The similarities and differences between the findings from the six countries were noted, and, during an open discussion session, conference participants addressed a number of key issues including: the difficulty in undertaking cross-cultural comparative research; the need to contextualise the data to the country within which it was collected; the lack of generalisability of the findings; the importance of feedback to the child and youth participants; and the role of human rights/citizenship education in the school curriculum.

Later that year, funding was obtained through the Norwegian Centre for Child Research and Childwatch International to enable members of the study group to meet again in **Roros, Norway**. This third meeting was hosted by Anne Trine Kjørholt and took place from 8–11 December 2005.[6] Following presentations by each country, the focus turned to the comparative data analysis which Ziad Abdeen had attempted via the construction of a template into which each country (except Brazil) had entered their key findings. It quickly became apparent that there were major difficulties with any comparative use of the data due to the different ways in which individual countries had collected, analysed and reported their results. The different cultural contexts also made it problematic to systematically compare the findings across countries and ascertain the degree of similarity in the strength, frequency and meaning of the children and young people's views about their rights and responsibilities.

The focus group methodology meant that it was impossible to quantify the responses in any meaningful way (for example, a reported comment may have been the view of the entire group or of just one or two of the children). The work plan written at this meeting was therefore directed towards a literature search of international publications on citizenship and the preparation of a collaborative research report.

Childwatch International funded the fourth meeting of the study group in **Dunedin, New Zealand**, from 13–15 August 2007. This meeting was hosted by Nicola Taylor and Anne Smith from the Children's Issues Centre at the University of Otago.[7] The meeting was used to conclude the first phase of the Citizenship project by finalising the chapters reporting on each country's findings and working collaboratively to write the final chapter of this book.

Despite the challenges involved in conducting an international research project of this kind, the very different social and political contexts framing children and young people's developing understanding of citizenship in the six countries participating in the study have provided a rich picture of children's perspectives on citizenship. Chapter One reviews the key components of children's citizenship reported in the theoretical and empirical research literatures. The focus group and survey methodologies adopted by the research team are described in Chapter Two, along with an outline of the international sample of 584 children and 312 adults. Each country then reports on their data and findings in the following six chapters. The book concludes in Chapter Nine where the similarities and differences in the findings from the six countries are considered in light of citizenship theory and previous research. Some of the implications of the findings for theory, policy and practice are also explored in the hope that our research might contribute to a better understanding of how democratic societies can promote meaningful and authentic opportunities for children and young people's citizenship.

1
Children's Citizenship

Anne B. Smith
Children's Issues Centre, University of Otago, New Zealand

Håvard Bjerke
Norwegian Centre for Child Research, NTNU, Norway

This chapter outlines some of the key components of citizenship for children found in theory and recent empirical studies. Since our project was initiated in 2003, the literature in this field has increased considerably. Citizenship is, in itself, a highly contested concept, and citizenship in relation to children complicates the issue even further. We do not intend to cover all aspects of this debate, but rather to present an outline of what we have found interesting and useful in the literature related to our study. We begin by looking at how children's citizenship can be defined and theorised, based upon some of the recent publications.

Defining Citizenship for Children

Citizenship can be defined as 'an entitlement to recognition, respect and participation' (Neale, 2004, p. 8). Citizenship for children is first of all a question of recognising the child as 'a citizen of today and the full recognition of this fact is one of the fundamental requirements of the UNCRC' (Doek, 2008, p. xvi). It entails belonging to a society, meaningful interaction within it, being heard and taken notice of, engaging, and having obligations and rights.

> *Full citizenship is made up of both rights (civil, social, political and, as some have more recently suggested, cultural or ethnic) and obligations that together are bound to the status of nationality. The parts of citizenship function together each bolstering the other.* (Cohen, 2005, p. 222)

Citizenship involves belonging to and interacting with other people in a group, community or society. Its nature is determined by the relationship between individuals and the societies in which they live, and the rights and obligations which are inherent in those societies (Ben-Arieh & Boyer, 2005; Sweetman, 2004). Implicit in the concept of citizenship is a sense of togetherness, connectedness, and a sharing of common interests, but also of difference and uniqueness (Heater, 2004). The more that children have the opportunity to connect with others in groups and communities, the more likely it is that they can behave as active citizens (Jans, 2004). Children's invisibility in the private sphere of the family removes them from public spaces (where they are likely to be seen seen as disorderly or at risk) and diminishes their power and opportunity for citizenship (Lister, 2008).

Lister (2008) argues that there are four main building blocks of children's citizenship: membership, rights, responsibilities and equality of status. *Membership* relates to children's sense of belonging, which is nurtured by reciprocal relationships, acceptance, and respectful treatment. Children's political identity, recognition as political beings, and sense of democratic responsibility is supported by their being counted as members of their communities and involved in individual and collective decision-making. *Rights,* especially participation rights, are of particular significance to children, in Lister's view, because children cannot express their views through the ballot box. While the United Nations Convention on the Rights of the Child (UNCRC) is not legally enforceable, moral and ethical rights should be enshrined in countries that have ratified it. *Responsibilities* to obey the law, and in everyday contexts, such as family or work, are another key component of citizenship. Finally, *Equality of Status, Recognition and Participation* are aspects of citizenship which are as important to children as to anyone else. We elaborate on these building blocks of citizenship more fully in this chapter.

The rights and duties of citizens are what make them full members of a community (Marshall, 1950, cited by Sweetman, 2004, p. 3). Rights for children are entitlements, interpreted and promoted or resisted differently according to the meaning they hold for people – most particularly for children and young people themselves, and the persons who have the most contact with and power over them. Responsibilities for children are both activities that adults expect and are obliged to carry out, and activities that children find important to take care of in their own or other people's interest. These expectations and considerations by both children and adults vary greatly in different societies and cultures. Children learn about rights and responsibilities through social networks and these are 'delicately negotiated possibilities' that have to be constantly worked through known relationships (Joseph, 2005, p. 1008).

Constructing children as citizens makes their influence and role in society salient, and contrasts with their previous invisibility, voicelessness and status as passive recipients of adult decisions made *for* them (Covell & Howe, 2001). If children are viewed as citizens, they are 'cast as full human beings, invested with agency, integrity and decision making capacity' (Stasiulis, 2002, p. 509). Agency and voice are complementary, with voice being an expression of agency. Both voice and agency influence children to try to make sense of their world, to 'grapple with serious questions' (Pufall & Unsworth, 2004, p. 9) and to act on their own behalf to modify the world that surrounds them. Being and becoming a citizen involves the acquisition of identity, through a reciprocal process of coming to share meanings, interests, values and a way of life:

> *As social beings, children are inherently agentive, and they voice their views in order to be heard, to persuade, to move others to action. As children*

act and ask to be heard, they are both building and experiencing their social reality and constructing their identity in the process. Neither their social reality nor their identity are elements in isolation from their social world. They are both parts of a mutual and ongoing construction. (Pufall & Unsworth, 2004, p. 9)

Citizenship implies participation though 'it is at first mainly local forms of participation which are within the reach of children' (Jans, 2004, p. 39). Children are social participants at home, school, in work and the community, and these settings provide them with the opportunity to practise citizenship. However, membership as citizens is not experienced by all, and people have been excluded in the past on the grounds of class, disability, gender and race. Given that children are 'a minority social group, whose wrongs need righting' (Mayall, 2002, p. 9), a 'difference-centred' theoretical model is relevant (Moosa-Mitha, 2005). A difference-centred model interrogates the hegemonic discourses and normative institutional practices defining mainstream culture. The process of inclusion and exclusion from normative social institutional beliefs and practices helps people to resist and make meaning of their own experiences, and is formative in defining citizenship.

This broader definition of participation as the expression of one's agency in the multiple relationships within which citizens are present in society is very important to a re-definition of children's right of freedom of participation as it recognises different ways of participating. (Moosa-Mitha, 2005, p. 375)

Libertarian models of citizenship predicated on sameness involve individuals and groups being excluded from citizenship because of their differences (e.g. ethnicity, gender, ability, age). Difference-centred models of citizenship emphasise the right of citizens to be different and equal, and are transformatory in nature. Instead of emphasising the 'less than' status of children and the individual nature of rights, a difference-centred approach acknowledges children's participation in multiple relationships and their voice and agency in these relationships. Moosa-Mitha sees children's rights of participation as crucial in allowing them to resist oppression and challenge the normative stance of assumptions about children within social institutions. Research that highlights children's views can therefore illuminate the gaps between their experience and their positioning in the social order.

Being, not Becoming, Citizens

The rhetoric of citizenship for children has traditionally centred around their potential for becoming citizens in the future, but recent conceptualisations of children suggests that children, while different from adults, are competent social actors and contributors to their own lives and society *now* (Davis & Watson, 2001; Freeman, 1996; James & Prout, 1997; Lister, 2008; Mayall, 2002; Roche, 1999; Smith, 2007; Smith, Taylor & Gollop, 2000). 'The constant referencing of children to their future potentials and possibilities belittles their present actions'

(Cockburn, 1998, p. 107). This discourse of children as lacking competence and requiring protection and nurturance, and in the process of becoming persons rather than persons now, has often been used to deny them agency and limit their citizenship rights (James & Prout, 1997; Oakley, 1994; Stasiulis, 2002). Conversely, conceptualising children as agents can be interpreted as denying their childhood and their welfare needs. Expecting children to behave and communicate like adults is not appropriate, and some change is required on the part of adults to accommodate children's differences (Lister, 2008). Agency and dependency inhere in the relationships between individuals and are not in opposition to each other (Alderson, 2001; Jans, 2004). There is no contradiction, therefore, in children being citizens exercising agency and continuing to depend on nurturance, support or regulation from adults (Alderson, 2001; Jans, 2004; Lister, 2008; Neale, 2004). If they are to exercise citizenship fully, children must be protected against abuse, discrimination, neglect and other ill treatment. Protection and participation rights are equally important and should be balanced in the promotion of children's well-being (Stasiulis, 2002). Agency does not imply autonomous unilateral individuals who lack connections to others in society, but involves a dynamic and reciprocal process of connecting to, and interacting with, other people.

Sociocultural Contexts

A sociocultural perspective is useful in theorising children's citizenship because of the link between agency and participation in social and cultural contexts (Smith, 2002). The ability to be a citizen does not emerge with biological growth, but is nurtured by social experiences and interactions with others (Neale, 2004). The opportunity to participate in 'progressively more complex patterns of reciprocal activity' supports ongoing learning (Bronfenbrenner, 1979, p. 60). For children to learn to speak up and voice their opinions, for example, it is important for adults to create participatory spaces and to provide support and guidance in partnership with children, in order to help them to formulate their views.

Sociocultural theory suggests that children become competent through participating in activities that are beyond their current level of skills or in their Zone of Proximal Development (Vygotsky, 1978). 'Children learn developmentally by doing what they don't know how to do' (Holzman, 1995, p. 204); they benefit from being viewed as competent learners and given the opportunity to learn in partnership with others. Joint involvement with others in challenging and engaging activities – feeling comfortable, accepted and tuned in to the other participants in a group (and group members being sensitive to you) – is likely to contribute to effective participation. Scaffolding by adults can engage the young person's interest in participating, draw attention to the goals and critical features of the task, and reduce task complexity. But there has to be social engagement before children can learn, gradually take on more responsibility, and enact their citizenship. As children become more confident and competent in their participation, there is less need for support and guidance from others. According to Jans (2004, p. 31), 'Citizenship is more like a learning process in itself than a predefined learning objective' so, if children or young people are isolated in separate communities, it is unreasonable to expect them in adolescence to be suddenly independent and behave in a socially responsible way. The emphasis in this social perspective on citizenship falls on the fact that it is not just a static state but an ongoing dynamic learning process for both children and adults.

> *The late modern condition allows children increasingly to present themselves as social actors, within as well as outside the family. The citizenship of children is based on a continuous learning process in which children and adults are interdependent.* (Jans, 2004, p. 40)

Thomas (2007) applies Bourdieu's concepts of 'habitus' and 'cultural capital' to explain why children have been excluded from social and political processes. Habitus is 'embodied history, internalized as a second nature and so forgotten as history ... the active presence of the whole past of which it is the product' (Bourdieu, 1992, cited by Thomas, 2007, p. 56).

> *... [Ch]ildren's subordinate status, and their assumed lack of concern with public affairs, are continually reinforced in subtle and not so subtle ways, through embodied habitus as well as the prevailing discourse.* (Thomas, 2007, p. 21)

Social interaction and discourse thus affect the dispositions of both children and adults to speak and act in certain ways which reinforce the subordination of children. Children also lack the social and cultural capital to enable them to be taken seriously. Thomas argues that, to achieve political change, it is important to understand not only institutional and legal contexts but cultures and the dispositions that frame them.

Adult Attitudes

Adults have a very important part to play in recognising and supporting children's citizenship, in how they construct childhood, and the extent to which they provide spaces for children to participate in joint activities. Children's silence, invisibility and positioning in the private world of the family out of society reflect the attitudes and practices of adult society (Roche, 1999).

> *Trying to change children's place in the world cannot occur without a shift in adult attitudes, values and behaviour ... weaving notions of children's citizenship into adult thinking so that it is understood to be as crucial to children's well being as their welfare needs.* (Neale, 2004, p. 179)

The more children are treated and constructed as citizens, the more likely it is that they will actively participate in society. However, as James (2004) points out, there are significant differences globally in beliefs about the role of children as participants in society, and differing opportunities for children to exercise citizenship. In many parts of the majority world, children make an active contribution to household income and shoulder major family responsibilities, but in the United Kingdom and the United States, according to James, children

> *are actively discouraged, and often legally forbidden, from participating in even quite elementary decisions about the shape and structure of their everyday lives at home and school (Christensen and James, 2001). Thus although the rights listed under the United Nations Convention on the Rights of the Child (CRC) might suggest that experiences of childhood are universal, the ways these rights come to be exercised and articulated by and for children in the course of their everyday lives vary extensively both within, as well as between, cultures.* (James, 2004, p. 25)

The UN Convention and Participation Projects

There is very little question that the surge of international interest in children's citizenship has been strongly influenced by the UNCRC, which 'confirmed an agreement that children and young people are citizens whose entitlements straddle moral, political and social agendas' (Matthews, 2005, p. 1). Since the Convention's adoption in 1989, there has been a global consensus on the importance of children's participation rights, including the right to express opinions freely and have them taken into account (Articles, 12, 13), the right of association (Article 15), and of thought, conscience, and religion (Article 14). Nearly all governments (including those of the countries participating in our study) have taken on the responsibility of providing the conditions necessary for children and youth to exercise participation rights. The UNCRC signals 'a remarkable international consensus on the nature and scope of children's rights … despite the varied political, religious, and cultural ideologies and beliefs held' (Helwig & Turiel, 2002, p. 254).

One outcome of the adoption of the UNCRC in many countries has been attempts to incorporate children's voices and participation into policy making:

> *There is currently an unprecedented wave of development of consultative work with children and young people by a range of statutory and non-statutory organizations. Every government department is now committed to the participation and planning of children and young people in the planning, delivery and evaluation of government policies and services.* (Marchant & Kirby, 2004, p. 93)

Some of these well-meaning efforts have been criticised. Kjørholt (2002, 2004), for example, finds that much of the discourse on 'children as participants' is characterised by universalising and normative assumptions about the self-evident value of children's participation. She underlines the need to scrutinise how particular projects are focusing on the actual experiences of child participants. Neale (2004) points out that putting into practice the ideals of children's citizenship involves a change in the cultures of adulthood and childhood, rather than one-off consultations. Neale argues that a preferable method of respecting children's citizenship would be to make everyday interaction with children in decision-making an integral part of the lives of adults and children. Davis (2007) also criticises 'participation projects' and analyses their problems such as lack of resources, lack of trust/respect and lack of access to real participatory processes. He suggests that it is necessary to create more effective long-term methods of creating dialogue with children that build on strong relationships and interdependence between adults and children. In order to provide the right kind of support for children, adults will need to think through new strategies and do things differently (Roche, 1999). Thomas (2007) points out that participatory structures modelled on 'adult' democratic structures are not useful to children because children do not have the vote, and at any rate such structures are often not particularly effective in engaging constituents. While there is a great deal of exciting, dynamic and engaging participatory activity taking place amongst children, Thomas emphasises that, paradoxically, this has no influence on 'real' politics.

Roche (1999) argues that it is important to avoid thrusting children into responsibility in ways not of their own choosing. Children may very well see that there is no point in participating and disengage, if agencies and people do not change or do things differently, so there needs to be a commitment to acting on children's input (Sinclair, 2005).

Perhaps above all else, adults need reassurance that approaching children in this new way is a worthwhile and rewarding enterprise. Showing respect for children will encourage a climate of mutual respect between adults and children. ... Bringing children's citizenship centrally into adult thinking and practice, then, will foster a climate of mutual respect and support across the generations that will bring benefit to all. (Neale, 2004, p. 180)

Summary

Some of the key components of citizenship for children we have identified include: entitlement to respect and recognition; opportunities for belonging and meaningful participation within groups and communities; the right to have their voices heard and express their agency; and the fulfilment of obligations and duties to others. The four building blocks of citizenship are membership, rights, responsibilities and equal status. Difference-centred models which can usefully be applied to children emphasise that citizenship is transformatory, allows the resistance of oppression, accepts different types of citizenship, and challenges normative assumptions. Citizenship for children is located in the present rather than the future, with children being recognised as social actors now. Concepts of children as citizens with agency do not imply that children are isolated individuals, because children also require continuing care and nurturance and their citizenship emerges and develops within social contexts. A sociocultural perspective implies that citizenship is not a static but an ongoing dynamic learning process in which adults and children are social partners and interdependent. This interdependence between adults and children is a key component of children's citizenship. For children to achieve citizenship, adult attitudes and practices have to change. While the UNCRC has had a global impact in encouraging the inclusion and involvement of children as social participants, more effective practices for nurturing children's citizenship are needed.

Research on Children's Perceptions of Citizenship and Nationhood

Having examined how children's citizenship is conceptualised in theory, we will now review recent empirical research (mainly qualitative) which is relevant to our international research study. In particular we are interested in children's understanding and interpretation of their status, rights and responsibilities as citizens. Our theoretical arguments in favour of promoting citizenship for children will be enriched by an understanding of what meaning these concepts have for children and young people. A construction of children as agents whose voice should be heard and taken notice of makes it essential to observe how today's children understand and interpret citizenship. Promoting children's citizenship will also be carried out more effectively if we start with how children are currently thinking about this issue. In the long term, research in this area is likely to help democratic societies promote effective participation by children and young people, and encourage the development of knowledge, skills, values, and attitudes that are critical in sustaining a democracy.

It has been argued that the theoretical debate on citizenship is 'conducted in what is virtually an empirical void' (Conover, Crewe & Searing, 1991, p. 801), and that 'very little is known about the realities of how different people understand themselves as citizens, and the ways in which this impacts on the different dimensions of their lives' (Jones & Gaventa, 2002, p. 28). Our investigation of the literature, however, uncovered considerable relevant material relating to children's perspectives on the meaning of citizenship, including questions of belonging and membership, children's rights and responsibilities. It has therefore been impossible to cover all areas completely in this introductory review of the literature.

Citizenship research involving young people is dominated by large-scale surveys focusing on political literacy, civic engagement and participation, and young people's political views and attitudes about issues such as racial prejudice and discrimination. Understanding the extent to which nations prepare young people to undertake the role of citizens in a democracy has been a primary focus (e.g. Torney-Purta, 2002). The research literature is also predominantly Western, both in relation to its empirical data and in its dominant theoretical perspectives. There is, however, a growing interest in including perspectives from poor and marginalised groups in democratic societies, including those of children and young people in different parts of the world (e.g. Hart, 2002; Kabeer, 2005a, 2005b; Melton, 2002).

The Meaning of Citizenship

Citizenship has an important meaning for many people, despite the fact that very few speak the 'language of citizenship' in their everyday lives (Lister, 1997; Manning & Ryan, 2004). Research with young people in Leicester, United Kingdom, showed that the topic of citizenship stimulated discussion of issues of great relevance to young people's lives and experiences (Lister, Smith, Middleton & Cox, 2003; Smith, Lister, Middleton & Cox, 2005). This study examined how young people perceived and experienced citizenship in their everyday lives: what citizenship meant to them, what enabled them to feel like citizens, and what restricted their feelings of citizenship. It was a longitudinal qualitative study where young people participated in in-depth interviews once a year for three years between the ages of 16 and 22 (1999–2001). Five models of citizenship emerged from the study. Moving from the most to the least articulated, these were: 1) Universal status (being part of a community), 2) Respectable economic independence (waged labour, pays taxes, has a family and a house), 3) Constructive social participation (abiding by the law, respectable practice), 4) Social-Contractual (rights and/or responsibilities) and 5) Right to a Voice (having a say and being heard). The participants drew clear distinctions between what it means to be a 'good' and a 'first class' citizen, and had greater difficulty articulating their rights than their responsibilities. This research shows that young people prescribed to a number of different interpretations of citizenship, often simultaneously. The extent to which the young people identified themselves as citizens reflected these models and their own life experiences.

Another British study explored children's understanding of three elements of citizenship: social and moral responsibility, community involvement, and political literacy (Hine, 2004). The sample consisted of 269 boys and girls aged between 7 and 15 years, all living in deprived areas. Social and moral responsibility and community involvement and political literacy were discussed in focus groups. Hine discusses the study's findings in terms of the policy implications for the restorative justice system for young offenders, community development, and education for citizenship. He argues that '[t]he most important learning point is that children need to have the opportunity to live and experience 'citizenship' in their day to day life in school' (Hine, 2004, p. 40). Children in this study demonstrated the same range of views and opinions as similar groups of adults might do. Even though their skills and articulation were not well developed, they were able to take part in conversations and put forward their ideas of complex issues.

An Australian study (Manning & Ryan, 2004) examined young people's perceptions and lived experiences of citizenship. The study involved focus groups of 92 young people ranging in age from 13 to 25 and a national survey (n=687). Participants were asked to discuss the meaning(s) of citizenship, the rights and responsibilities of citizenship, their educational experiences in civics and citizenship, and their own experiences as citizens in various contexts. Participants were then asked to comment on the results from the national survey, to identify how the major theories of citizenship related to their lived experience and perceptions of citizenship, to name what they saw as the underlying spirit behind the idea of citizenship, and to compose a definition of citizenship. Young people's perceptions fell into five broad categories: 1) national identity, 2) formal legal status, 3) participation, 4) rights and duties, and 5) belonging to a group. The study showed that young people hold varied, sometimes contradictory and often overlapping perceptions of what citizenship is, as did young people in the U.K. study (Lister et al., 2003).

Belonging and Membership

This section reviews studies which examine how children see themselves as members of a 'citizenship community' (national or local), their sense of national identity, and what it means to be a citizen of their specific country (Ireland, Wales, etc.). Nationality and citizenship are integrally related concepts, since citizenship takes place within the context of a national culture.

> ... nationality becomes a narrative, a story people tell about themselves in order to lend meaning to their social world, a story which transforms perceptions of the past and the present. (Howard & Gill, 2001, p. 89)

Membership can be defined in a narrow sense as the status of a citizen accorded by a community (for example the ancient city-state *polis*, the British Empire, the nation-state and the European Union). In a wider sense membership can be defined as the feeling and practice of citizens in different communities (local, regional, national and global). A nation is usually characterised by internal homogeneity and definitive boundaries separating one from the other (Stephens, 1997). These feelings of identification with, and differentiation from, fellow citizens are 'grounded in the common-sense world of everyday life' (Stephens, 1997, p. 9), and children have an important part to play in their ongoing definition and contestation.

Discourse about citizenship is increasingly prominent in Ireland, a country which like many others, has recently become more diverse and multicultural. Waldron and Pike (2006) talked to 10- and 11-year-old Irish children about the meaning of being Irish, using focus groups, drawing and semi-structured interviews. The research aimed at getting children to engage critically with their own ideas, opening with a brainstorm about the idea of Irishness and an imaginative scenario involving Earth being under threat and people being evacuated to the nearest inhabitable planet. Several themes were drawn from the data. First, the overwhelming focus of children's interpretations of being Irish was cultural, and referred to such issues as language, cultural practices, physical and behavioural traits. Many children wrote or talked about the material aspects of culture, such as food, transport, geographical characteristics and buildings. The more expressive features of Irishness – for instance language (especially the Irish language), music, dance and sport – also emerged as important. Children talked about the national traits and characteristics of Irish people, such as being friendly, caring, relaxed, liking Guinness, and having a good sense of humour.

The authors commented on the power of cultural clichés and national stereotypes in the children's constructions of Irishness, for example a focus on leprechauns! Only a small number of children embraced the idea of diversity and Irish people were generally seen as able-bodied, non-travelling and white. Despite media-based cultural ideas dominating children's thinking, some children did show evidence of actively negotiating contradictions, problematising national identity, and embracing diversity.

Sue Howard and Judith Gill at the University of South Australia have carried out a series of studies about how Australian school children understand themselves as citizens (Howard & Gill, 2001, 2005). One paper (Howard & Gill, 2001) describes how children talk about being Australian and position themselves in relation to constructions of national identity. The researchers observed and recorded ongoing conversations among 21 11- and 12-year-old children about being Australians. Children's responses fell into two main themes. Children generally took a practical approach and associated concrete things with being Australian. The first theme was symbols, stereotypes and icons: the flag, kangaroos, koalas, Australian beer and football, the Sydney Opera House. The second theme was everyday life, such as language (including accent) and a laidback relaxed attitude to life. Children regarded birthplace and a period of residence as significant to citizenship. They accepted that having a visa and a passport were important aspects of citizenship, but they favoured individual choice so that people who wanted to live in Australia could live there. The notion of citizenship was also allied with having a vote, working and owning property. Children were aware of different standards of living and religions, and their consciousness of being Australian seemed to have been influenced by recognition that they were not some other nationality (for example American). There was general acceptance that non-Anglo-Australians were also citizens.

Another paper (Howard & Gill, 2005) focuses on the affective elements of constructing citizenship. Howard and Gill conducted small group discussions with 250 11- to 12- year-old children from a range of rural areas in South Australia about how they felt about being Australian. Children's responses indicated a very positive feeling about being Australian, such as feeling good, lucky and unique. Common responses were that children felt safe, free and proud. The researchers point out that children's constructions of being Australian were idealistic and partial, often deriving from a perception of Australia not being war-torn, or a place where oppressive acts like summary arrest happen. One child felt an enhanced sense of being Australian after meeting Americans in another country and being told she had a strong accent. Children showed a ready acceptance of multiculturalism and believed that in Australia people were treated justly and equally as citizens. Children often developed their ideas by comparing their situation with what happened in other countries, especially where adversity like war was happening. The authors believe that before launching new curricula (like a recent package, *Discovering Democracy*) the present state of children's knowledge should be explored. They suggest that their study gives educators a sense of what children know and understand, which invites further investigation of how societies are organised and an examination of the rules and regulations necessary to maintain democracy and social justice.

In a study of the accounts of 8- to 11-year-old children on being Welsh, the racialised aspects of their accounts were analysed (Scourfield & Davies, 2005). Children chose identity label cards describing themselves, and discussed their choices in small focus groups. The cards represented a variety of nationalities and individual characteristics (e.g. Welsh, English, black, girl). The children's responses indicated that generally Welshness was associated with being white, being born in Wales, and with the Welsh language. The researchers found that children had a limited range of received ideas about being Welsh which 'derived from the dominant discourses of the nation' (Scourfield & Davies, 2005, p. 103). Nevertheless some children demonstrated agency in their dismissal of exclusive notions of Welshness and insisted on a multi-ethnic Wales. The authors found reasons for pessimism in children's construction of Welsh identity as narrow, exclusive and white, but also reasons for optimism in others contesting this traditional model.

The meaning of nationality for Canadian high school students has been explored by Lee and Hebert (2006). The written responses to questions about national identity by 131 non-immigrant and 95 immigrant young people were analysed in terms of themes of national identity, social and cultural belonging, rights, and political and civic participation. The non-immigrants were more passionate and confident than immigrants about their national identity, but both groups saw many positive aspects to being Canadian, such as freedom, security, education and opportunities. Young people (both immigrant and non-immigrant) expressed loyalty and pride in being Canadian, and thought that multiculturalism and citizenship were compatible. Many immigrants expressed multiple identifications but still had a strong attachment to their ethnic origins combined with their identity as Canadians, and did not fear public discrimination for this. The authors speculate that immigrant youth have learned the harsh consequences of racialised hatred and intolerance. They conclude that most of the young people were comfortable with diversity and multiple identity, and this had a positive impact on their feelings about being Canadian.

An innovative methodology was used in a study by Holloway and Valentine (2000) to look at how children imagine other nations. Children from 12 British and 12 New Zealand schools (aged around 13 years) emailed each other about how they imagined the other country, and what they thought a typical week and weekend day was like in the other country. Then they emailed each other back and corrected any wrong impressions. For example, some British children mistook Australia for New Zealand or thought of it as an offshoot of Australia. New Zealand children were quick to contest this misconception, and explain that New Zealand is a different culture to Australia and its indigenous people are Maori, not Australian Aborigines. This reciprocal process of exchanging information between outsiders and insiders was an unusual and revealing way of learning how children constructed other nations and their own. It also allowed for the possibility of revising views of nationality. Children drew on stereotypical sources of popular culture for information about the other, particularly the mass media. For example, New Zealand children expected British children to live in houses like those on Coronation Street with two storeys and no front and back garden. But both British and New Zealand children also thought that most aspects of their school, home and recreational life were similar. Some emphasised sameness in terms of race when comparing their cultures, but other children avoided this 'whitewash', instead imagining cultural diversity. The authors suggest that the global entertainment media and global cycles of consumption influenced how both groups of children understood their own and others' nationalities.

An ethnographic study of children in a Palestinian refugee camp in Jordan provides a contrasting picture of marginalised children who do not easily fit into national moulds (Hart, 2002). Hart considers the refugee children to fit into Stephens' (1997) definition of 'deviant children' because the sources of their national identity are ambiguous and multiple. The study showed that they did not confirm their feelings of belonging to any one single community, but rather to a variety of localised and clearly bounded communities and also to a wider transnational one. Children in the camp were the objects of discourse and action from three main sources – the Palestinian nationalist movement, the Jordanian state and the Islamist movement, each of which positions the young in particular ways. Muna, a 12-year-old girl, had a sense of being Palestinian and could describe the villages where her parents had lived before 1948, but did not want to be involved in Palestinian politics because she thought that they had destroyed her father. At the same time, she was religious and insisted on wearing a headscarf even though her mother and sister tried to persuade her to wait until she was older. Nevertheless Muna continued to enjoy television and pop music and saw a future career for herself as an engineer, rather than confining herself to the role of wife and mother promoted by Islam. Hart believes that the young people in his study expressed their agency in resisting and reshaping the contrasting and contradictory politics which influenced their daily lives.

A study by Jonsson and Flanagan (2000) fits into this section, and also the next section: it concerns children's views about rights and responsibilities but is also very relevant to membership in specific countries. This study compares the views of children from seven countries on rights, responsibilities and distributive justice. The study surveyed the views of more than 6000 children (from the 8th and 11th grades) from Australia, Bulgaria, the Czech Republic, Hungary, Russia, Sweden and the USA. When asked about social concern in their local communities, children in every country other than Australia disagreed that people in their local communities cared for each other. Children generally (except in Hungary) thought that there were equal opportunities for success in their country. The majority of students in all countries (with some degree of disagreement in Australia and the USA) did not think that teachers cared about their students, and many (except in Australia) disagreed that teachers wanted students to express their opinions. Particularly in Eastern Europe (Bulgaria, Russia and the Czech Republic), and to a lesser extent in Sweden, students tended to agree that teachers were only interested in the smartest students. When asked if students cared about each other even if they did not know them well, students in all countries (except girls in Australia) disagreed. Only in Russia, and to a much lesser extent Australia and Sweden, did children think that they had a say in how the school was run. The authors argue that if a school climate of care is important for socialising young people into the obligations of citizenship, these findings are alarming. Children were generally in favour of government support in case of need, but they also (especially in the USA and Australia) believed that state support undermined self-reliance, and that it is natural for some to be rich and some to be poor (there was very strong agreement with this in Russia). The authors showed that most young people were experiencing widening social gaps but believed that there was equal opportunity for success. The only country where children experienced a climate of care in their schools and local communities was Australia. Surprisingly, even Swedish children did not experience this.

Summary

Studies of children's perspectives on nationality were very diverse in their methodology and explored different aspects of children's sense of belonging and national identity. Most studies were carried out in the majority world and showed that generally children felt positive about their national identity and associated it with (often stereotypical) icons such as flags and other aspects of social and material culture. Some countries (Wales and Ireland) seem to be associated with more homogeneous racialised conceptions of culture than others (e.g. Canada and Australia). Global media and consumption affected all children (even those in a refugee camp), but children were also influenced greatly by the discourse and interactions of everyday life. In almost all studies there were examples of children contesting traditional constructions of national identity, and being comfortable with multiple identities and multicultural societies.

Rights and Responsibilities

As outlined in the first section of this chapter, rights and responsibilities are an important component of citizenship for children. Melton and Limber (1992), using 12 vignettes about rights with 5- to 13-year-old children, found a progression with age in children's understanding of rights from egocentricity towards an understanding of the universality of rights. They found, however, that most children had substantial knowledge of legal process and concepts (such as rights) by the end of the primary grades. Both socioeconomic status and cultural background had an influence on the level and nature of children's understanding of rights. For example, American children put more emphasis on the rights of freedom of expression and self-determination than Norwegian children, who were more likely to mention provision or protection rights. Children from more working-class backgrounds had less understanding of rights.

Morrow (1999), in a study of children's perspectives on rights, found that children appreciated being given dignity and respect, and felt that they ought to have a say in matters which concerned them. Children felt their voices were seldom heard and, if heard, usually discounted. They felt that they lacked autonomy and inclusion in decision-making, even with regard to mundane everyday issues. There were ethnic differences, with Pakistani children less likely to emphasise their right to have a say. Even children as young as nine years were quite coherent and able to articulate their ideas about rights. Many children would have liked a say in decision-making – not necessarily to make the decisions, but to be heard in the process of decision-making. In contrast to the fears expressed in some adult discussions of children's rights, children were not rebellious or disaffected, or asking to take over decision-making from adults, but rather wanted to be included and be able to participate. Half of Morrow's secondary school sample had heard of the UNCRC and could recall working on it in school.

Covell and Howe (1999, 2000) believe that it is important for children to have an understanding and respect for their own and each others' rights. They argue that the most logical place to start teaching about rights is with children at primary school. Hence, they decided to develop and test primary school curriculum material about children's rights for grade 6 level children (11- to 13-year-olds). They encountered some resistance from teachers about introducing this new curriculum material. For example, teachers thought that it might encourage children to disregard adult authority. Covell and Howe used methods of teaching which encouraged peer interaction through group discussion and exploration of opinions and values in an open way, such as through role-playing. They showed that when children had participated in a children's rights curriculum, they were more tolerant, aware of, and respectful of the rights of others.

How high school children understand their rights at school – particularly their right to participate, their right to protection from physical and mental violence, their right to healthy environments and their right to recreation and play – was examined in a New Zealand study (Nairn & Smith, 2002; Smith, Gaffney & Nairn, 2004; Smith, Nairn & Gaffney, 2004; Smith, Nairn, Taylor & Gaffney, 2003; Taylor, Smith & Nairn, 2001). One paper (Taylor et al., 2001) compares adults' and young people's knowledge, priorities and awareness of rights issues. A postal survey of 107 secondary schools in New Zealand targeted ten 15/16-year-old young people and five staff members, participating in each of the survey schools. A total of 721 students and 449 staff responded to the survey. Most staff and students understood the meaning of rights, and defined them in terms of entitlements. Only 15 per cent of students were aware of the UNCRC, but 85 per cent of staff said that they knew about it. Students and staff showed different priorities in terms of which rights they thought were important to young people. About two out of every three students prioritised participation rights, while around a quarter prioritised provision rights, and only just over one in ten prioritised protection rights. Staff were relatively evenly spread in their views of which rights were most important to young people, with just over a third prioritising provision rights, a third protection rights, and just under a third prioritising participation rights. The right to be treated as social actors with views that should be heard respectfully by others was salient for young people in New Zealand.

Nairn and Smith (2002) found that most students thought that they had a right to feel safe at school, but almost a third of them did not feel safe. About two thirds of the students, but a much higher proportion of staff (93 per cent), acknowledged that verbal bullying took place at school, while about half of the students thought that there was physical bullying (compared to 83 per cent of staff). Almost half (45 per cent) of students said that they had been bullied, with 12 per cent reporting that they had been severely bullied. Despite the staff acknowledgement that children's article 19 (the right to be safe from all forms of physical and verbal violence) was not being implemented, students were unlikely to seek help from teachers if they were being bullied. This reluctance to seek help from teachers seemed to be due to a lack of confidence that teachers would be able to help. The study suggested that schools could more effectively implement children's safety rights if they consulted students about effective ways to combat bullying.

Smith, Gaffney and Nairn (2004) found that in every area of health rights, students saw information and advice as less accessible than did staff. Most staff and students identified mental health problems such as depression as a source of concern in schools, but only a quarter of students (compared to half of staff) thought that this topic was covered during class-time. Students in lower income schools reported the school environment as less respectful of their health rights than did students in high income schools. The paper concludes that schools and policy makers should seek the voices and opinions of young people in order to improve their effectiveness in catering for health rights. Most students thought the main barriers to implementing their recreation rights (Smith, Nairn & Gaffney, 2004) were restricted access (e.g. age restrictions or not being chosen by the teacher), too much school work, student attitudes and motivation (e.g. lack of confidence), and cost. The study suggested that social relationships had a major part in students' recreational life, and that friends were a key ingredient in their quality of life.

Joseph's (2005) study of children in Lebanon showed that children were nested in webs of family relationships, and that their rights and responsibilities were influenced strongly by who they were related to, and who they knew. '[That] children's rights and responsibilities were delicately negotiated possibilities which had to be constantly worked through known relationships was everywhere evident in practice' (Joseph, 2005, p. 1008). Joseph observed children in Lebanese villages in an ethnographic study and found that they were included in the many social visits made by their parents. They listened to, and participated in, almost all conversations during such visits, and engaged in after-visit reflections and commentaries. Such social interactions were a huge source of education for children, giving them important information about who had what, who did what, and who knew what locally. A 12-year-old, Fleur, helped the researcher when her tape recorder broke down, as she knew who had a tape recorder and offered to borrow it for her. 'To have rights, the children knew that they had to know who had the resources, skills, and services to offer them rights' (Joseph, 2005, p. 11). Children were learning to exercise their rights and responsibilities in this Lebanese context through social relationships and processes in everyday contexts. The research suggests that children have to be part of such social processes if they are to become active participants and understand their rights and responsibilities.

Canadian researchers have examined the development of children and adolescents' understanding of nurturance and self-determination rights (Ruck, Abramovitch & Keating, 1998a; Ruck, Keating, Abramovitch & Koegl, 1998b). They looked at the influence of different types of situational or context-specific knowledge that children use, and found that these were more salient than age or stage differences. According to Ruck et al. (1998a), two major findings emerge from their study. First, the reasoning of children develops differently for nurturance and self-determination rights, with priority being given to nurturance rights by young children. With increasing age, children were likely to espouse both nurturance and self-determination rights and to be more aware of the universality of rights. Second, their findings do not give support to a strong global stage interpretation of children's reasoning about their rights. Instead, children's understanding 'appears to be strongly affected by both the context and the content of the specific circumstance they are asked to judge' (Ruck et al., 1998a, p. 413). According to their data, children's responses are more in line with how subjects of all ages view rights in their own lives. For example, even participants from the oldest age group (16-year-olds) stated that their rights could be taken away, in contrast to previous research suggesting that they, at this age, should understand that rights are not revocable by authority.

Casas and his colleagues (Casas, Saporiti, González et al., 2006) carried out a large-scale survey of 10- to 13-year-old Spanish and Italian children's (and their parents' and teachers') views about children's rights. Children were asked if they knew what rights were, whether children had rights, and what children's rights were. They were also asked for their views about 16 dilemmas involving rights in everyday situations. For example, children were asked if parents should be able to make them take part in an out-of-school activity which was not one that they preferred. (Not surprisingly more than two thirds of the Spanish and Italian samples thought that this was unacceptable.) There were few differences between the Catalan and Molisian children. More than 90 per cent of both samples thought that they should be consulted about where their family went on holiday, agreed that a girl should not be excluded from a group activity even if it disrupted the activity, and thought that a boy should not miss school to work in a family business. The vast majority (94 per cent) of both samples believed that children had rights, but a smaller number (around 88 per cent) knew what a right was. Most children recognised that rights were universal, with only very small numbers (less than 6 per cent) thinking that rights were for specific groups only. Having their opinion taken into account on matters affecting them was very important for about two thirds of the sample who, for example, felt that it was unfair if they had to move to another school away from their friends. The results suggest that these Catalan and Molisian children had relatively homogeneous views about practical situations in their daily life related to rights. Rights related to provision of education, basic needs, privacy and participation were the most commonly recognised by children. The authors believe that their findings fit well with those of Ruck (Ruck et al., 1998), who suggested that contextual factors are very important. Children want to be consulted on matters affecting them, but how strongly they feel about this is influenced by how important the decision is and whether their parents act considerately to children.

In a review of research on children's concepts of rights, Helwig and Turiel (2002, p. 255) criticise 'the assumption that rights should be studied in situations that place them into conflict with other social concerns'. They argue that a common model underlies the interpretations in this research where 'civil liberties and rights are seen as abstract, genuine, or principled only if they override other social and moral concerns in contextualized judgements' (p. 256). In their view, conclusions about concepts of rights in many studies present only a partial picture and underestimate children's understandings of rights. They conclude that considerable research demonstrates:

> *that children affirm their own rights and autonomous decision-making in many situations. The model of shared decision making implied in the U.N. Convention appears to be endorsed (Melton, 1991) in many of its fundamental aspects by children themselves.* (Helwig & Turiel, 2002, p. 266)

This finding held even in non-Western cultural settings, such as Druze villages in Israel. The review suggested that children are well able to apply their concepts of autonomy, voice and personal choice to diverse social contexts including the peer group, family and school. They tend to endorse democratic decision-making over other forms, and believe that autonomy and rights are valued features of social life that should be honoured and upheld. The authors agree with Ruck (Ruck et al., 1998) that global models of reasoning do not explain the research findings well; rather, children develop early nuanced understanding of rights which are contextually specific and are increasingly co-ordinated with other social concepts.

The research literature on children's understanding of responsibilities is much more limited than the literature on rights, and much of it focuses on children's responsibilities for household work within the family (Bowes, Flanagan & Taylor, 2001; Brannen, Heptinstall & Bhopal, 2000; Cheal, 2003; Cohen, 2001; Martin, 2006). We will not cover this literature in detail but, generally, the research suggests that children are active participants with a strong sense of social responsibility in the tasks of family life, express their agency through negotiating their responsibilities with parents, are able to take the position of the other and respond to others' feelings and needs, and often have an indispensable role in sustaining family processes and activities.

Such and Walker (2004) looked at children's perspectives on the concept of responsibility. The authors point out that children and young people are constructed as free from the responsibilities of the adult world yet are frequently blamed for being 'irresponsible' or anti-social. The study involved open-ended discussions with 9- and 10-year-old children in small groups of up to three, about 'helping and looking after'.

Children had responsibilities at home that were understood as an inevitable and 'normal' part of daily life. Children described the basis of 'being responsible' as underscored by the values of honesty and fairness, and indicated that responsibility was a crucial part of their moral worlds. Being responsible, doing responsible things, and doing things responsibly were an important part of children's thinking. For example, 'owning up to things' was important, and if children did not own up, they felt a sense of guilt and shame. Meeting parental expectations was a vital component of accessing responsibility, freedom and power in the home. For the children, being responsible was an avenue to power and autonomy which opened or closed opportunities for other things. Children's moral understandings were, however, malleable, mediated by child-parent relationships and constantly being negotiated and renegotiated in the home.

A dominating theme in the literature on children and citizenship is education and the question of how children can learn to be responsible citizens, both at school and in formal and informal volunteering and community work. Some of this literature recognises children as citizens and argues that citizenship education is most likely to be effective if children can learn and experience through good practice (e.g. Bartlett, 2005; Osler & Starkey, 2005). Surprisingly little attention is given to children's own understanding of the responsibilities they have at school, and what their contribution means in their own life, now and in the future, as well as what they believe their school work means for the society (Qvortrup, 1995). More attention has been given to children and young people's social responsibilities. Based on a study in Sheffield of the meanings and experiences of citizenship among a group of 50 working-class young people aged between 14 and 25, Alan France (1998, p. 108) argues that 'young people's willingness to undertake certain forms of responsibilities both within the local community and in the labour market has been undermined by experiences of exclusion and exploitation'. He asserts that the lack of rights affects young people's willingness to fulfil certain social responsibilities and that they need more opportunities in both the community and employment.

Summary

This review of recent research on children's understanding of rights and responsibilities challenges traditional assumptions both of the carefree existence of children and their unawareness of the nature, existence and universality of rights. The research generally supports the view that most children, even quite young children, have an understanding of rights and their universality, especially if these are discussed within the specific contexts of their everyday lives in environments with which they are familiar. Most children are conscious that they are entitled to respect, recognition and participation: in other words they believe themselves to be citizens. Younger children put more emphasis on their right to have their needs provided for, but they increasingly come to view freedom of expression and self-determination as important. Children's growing understanding of these constructs appears to be deeply embedded in the social interactions that are part of their experiences, suggesting that opportunities to participate as valued social agents, and to take on responsibilities and experience rights, are critical ingredients in enriching children's knowledge.

Conclusion

This chapter has explored the theoretical framework of children's citizenship and examined the international literature on children's perceptions of citizenship and nationhood which is relevant to our own research project. The key components of citizenship for children were respect, recognition and participation, together with a set of rights and obligations. Children constructed themselves as citizens, different from adults but capable of making an important contribution to society. The construction of children's citizenship emerges from, and is practised within, ongoing dynamic interactions among children and others in their social and material worlds. The meanings of belonging to a nation were elaborated on by children in many parts of the world in the research reviewed. While influenced by global media and consumerism, children were active critical interpreters of the meaning of their membership in their own nations, but drew on multiple discourses, often resulting in diverse and pluralistic interpretations of nationality. Rights and responsibilities were freely discussed, negotiated and understood by children in familiar contexts. The research supports the view that an understanding of citizenship in a democratic society was characteristic of childhood in many societies. The present study builds on existing theory and research to explore further how children and young people understand and experience citizenship.

2
Research Methodology

Nicola Taylor & Anne B. Smith
Children's Issues Centre, University of Otago, New Zealand

The focus of interest in this qualitative study was on how children understood and experienced citizenship in six different countries, and how adults supported the enactment of children's citizenship and rights. Qualitative research is situated activity which locates the observer in the world, makes that world visible, and attempts to understand it in terms of the meanings people bring to it (Denzin & Lincoln, 2000). It is built on the assumption that human action is constructed, not caused (Cresswell, 1994), so it does not rely on large samples but on the variety of interpretations that people have about events in their lives. Qualitative research tends to be theory-driven, so samples are purposive rather than random in order to select cases which will provide rich data (MacDougall & Fudge, 2001).

Our research was framed by the paradigm of Childhood Studies or Sociology of Childhood, which positions children as experts and social actors in understanding their worlds:

> *Here the focus is on the child as agent, as participatory in constructing knowledge and daily experience; an important issue is children's own views on their daily experience, and these may be sought in order to construct an account of childhood.* (Mayall, 2002, p. 22)

This theoretical perspective has changed the way that researchers study childhood, and moved away from conducting research *on* children to instead undertaking research *with* children:

> *The transition from viewing children as objects to viewing them as social actors is not simply a matter of ideological reflection, it has a real impact on the conduct of research practice – on the initial choice of topic, the nature of design, and the type of methodology. There is an imperative to engage with children at an active rather than a passive level.* (Robinson & Kellett, 2004, pp. 86–87)

Qualitative methodologies are ideally suited to research where children's perspectives are being ascertained on events in their lives. They allow the expression of children's voices and place children in the position of active subjects rather than as passive objects of concern or attention. Children's voices were rarely heard in the past because of their lack of political and economic power and civil rights and their assumed incompetence (Morrow & Richards, 1996). An overly-protective stance towards children has also had the effect of excluding them from research (Powell & Smith, in press). Since the advent of the field of Childhood Studies there has, however, been an explosion of research recognising children as competent social actors, such that it has become 'somewhat of a new research orthodoxy' (James, 2007, p. 26).

James (2007) is nevertheless critical of some current childhood research because it does not address important conceptual and epistemological problems relating to representation, authenticity and diversity. She suggests paying more attention to children's conversations, focusing less on the dialogue between researcher and participant and more on the interaction between children themselves. This, she argues, would lend greater authenticity to childhood research. James (2007) also urges that the use of children's voices be tempered by acknowledgment of their particularity and the cultural contexts of their production. The voices of particular children cannot be used to speak on behalf of children in other parts of the world. The children from the six countries contributing their perspectives to our study enabled us to explore the significance of social and cultural contexts, and to create opportunities for the children to discuss their rights, responsibilities and citizenship amongst themselves through the medium of school-based focus groups.

Focus Groups

Focus groups grew out of 'focused interviews' in the 1950s (Madriz, 2000). They are a productive means of recovering the voices of marginalised groups because they provide 'a safe environment where people can share ideas, beliefs, and attitudes in the company of people from the same socio-economic, ethnic and gender backgrounds' (Madriz, 2000, p. 835). Focus groups are particularly useful for children (in comparison to individual interviews) because they reduce the power and control of the interviewer, are fun and stimulating for children, and encourage and support emotional engagement. They also allow the researcher to observe the social interaction and conversation between children, which reduces the problems faced by the researcher of bridging the generation gap (Robinson & Kellett, 2004).

Focus groups are discussion groups, centred around a particular topic that is the theme of the conversation. They usually include eight to twelve participants and are facilitated by a leader, who promotes interaction and ensures that the discussion remains on the topic of interest. Focus groups are similar to other qualitative research methods in that they enable researchers to have access to the opinions, viewpoints, attitudes and experiences of individuals. Focus groups offer several advantages as a qualitative data collection technique. They enable a larger number of participants to be included in the research, promoting greater discussion and idea generation than would be possible in individual interviews. While the competency of the moderator is important, the influence this person has on the participants is decreased in a focus group. Participants have more freedom to move the discussion at their own pace and in the light of their own knowledge and interests (Madriz, 2000). This more dynamic process encourages spontaneous responses from members of the group and avoids a 'question and answer' format. The choice of focus group interview methods in our international study also had the advantages of being appropriate to the questions we were asking, faithful to our theoretical perspective, and feasible.

The Survey

Surveying parents and teachers to ask about their views of children's citizenship was important as a means of providing some triangulation to the study. Triangulation involves using data from a variety of sources (in this case focus groups and questionnaires) and different perspectives (parents and teachers as well as children) to produce a constellation of evidence and lend validity to the data (Eisner, 1991). The survey provided a quick and realistic procedure for examining parents' and teachers' views on children's citizenship, rights and responsibilities. It also explored the extent to which children's agency as citizens was constructed as important within family and school contexts, and how well adults supported these processes.

Development of the Methodology for this Study

Following the preliminary work undertaken at the 2003 Childwatch International meeting in London, the international research team members further refined the study's methodology by email as they developed the focus group protocol, interview schedule and parent/teacher questionnaires.

It was expected that nine to ten focus groups would be conducted in each country with approximately eight participants in each group. Children would initially discuss their understanding of key concepts like rules, rights and responsibilities, and then consider how well these were being enacted in their own country. Next, the children would be asked what it might be like to arrive in an imaginary country to discuss the rules, rights and responsibilities needed in this new land, and ponder how these might differ from the country in which they currently lived. They were also asked to name the new country and draw a flag to represent it. The focus group protocol was later adapted for use in the six different countries and translated into relevant languages.

The focus groups worked well in terms of stimulating the children and young people to share their understanding and experience in a spontaneous fashion. Explanations and prompts from the skilled focus group leaders were, however, necessary to clarify the concepts under discussion. In most countries, two researchers worked together in each focus group, with one person taking responsibility for leading the group while the other took notes. The researchers explored how the children and young people understood citizenship, rights and responsibilities and what it meant to be a 'good' citizen in their own country. They then asked children to think about how rights, responsibilities and citizenship could, or should, be in an imaginary country.

Each country obtained their own research funding to undertake their component of the study, and sought their own Ethics Committee approval. School, parent and child consents were all in place prior to the research commencing in each locality.

Sample

Children and Young People: Children (aged 8/9 years) and young people (aged 14/15 years) were recruited through schools in Australia, Brazil, New Zealand, Norway, Palestine, and South Africa. Information about the project was provided to each school principal and their consent obtained for students to take part in the focus group discussions. Information and consent forms were sent home for parents, and the children and young people also signed their own consent forms.

The aim was for each country's sample group to consist of 100 children across the two age-groups, with approximately equal numbers of boys and girls, and a mix of children from high and low socio-economic backgrounds and urban/rural areas.

Groups of marginalised children were also sought in each country – for example, young people from the Movement for Landless Agricultural Workers in Brazil. However, this was not always achieved in the other countries, reflecting the perceived vulnerability and increase in gatekeepers to protect marginalised children. Marginalised groups, however, were sometimes included within their school sample (e.g. in Australia where children were recruited from schools with large Aboriginal enrolments, and in Palestine from schools in refugee camps).

While it did not prove possible to achieve the sample size of 100 in most countries, the sample did comprise 584 children and young people across the six countries (see Table One).

The focus groups varied in size from around three to twelve children/young people. Most groups were single gender groups, but some included a mix of girls and boys. The researchers were of the view that children would be more comfortable with other children of the same gender and similar socio-economic status. About half of the focus groups were from low socio-economic status backgrounds and half were from high socio-economic status backgrounds. There were also similar numbers of boys and girls.

Parents and Teachers: The parent/teacher questionnaires, designed by Professor Anne Smith, were administered in four countries: Australia (where completed questionnaires were received from 28 parents and 4 staff), Brazil (69 parents and 24 teachers), New Zealand (40 parents/caregivers and 31 teachers), and South Africa (43 parents and 73 teachers). In total, 180 parents and 132 teachers completed the questionnaires (see Table Two):

Table One: International sample of children and young people

	Australia	Brazil	NZ	Norway	Palestine	South Africa	Total
8/9 year old boys	27	25	20	10	44	28	154
8/9 year old girls	30	21	12	18	39	28	148
14/15 year old boys	9	27	11	10	55	28	140
14/15 year old girls	9	24	23	15	43	28	142
TOTAL	75	97	66	53	181	112	584

Table Two: International sample of parents and teachers

	Australia	Brazil	New Zealand	South Africa	Total
Parents	28	69	40	43	180
Teachers	4	24	31	73	132
TOTAL	32	93	71	116	312

Data Collection and Analysis

Details of data collection and analysis procedures are discussed in the individual country reports, but it must be acknowledged that our procedures varied because of the constraints on the research and the participation of children in different contexts. Some countries (e.g. South Africa) recorded and transcribed the data, but in other countries (e.g. Palestine) children were unhappy with being audio-recorded. Other countries used note-takers, or asked the children to provide written records of the outcomes of their discussion in the focus groups. In New

Zealand and Australia, children were divided into smaller groups and wrote their responses down on large sheets of paper.

Time was a particular constraint on methodology, so if children were only allowed out of their school classrooms for an hour, we had to limit the length and comprehensiveness of the discussions. Expense was a further constraint, with few countries having funding to employ interviewers or transcribers and several having to rely on senior university students to assist with collecting, recording and analysing data. Accessibility of participants for recruitment into the research was not easy, and one country (the USA) was forced to withdraw from the study because of lack of access to child participants in schools.

Research Questions

The key research questions underpinning this study were:

1. How do children and young people understand citizenship?
2. For children and young people, what does it mean to be a 'good' citizen?
3. How do parents and teachers encourage and support children and young people's understanding and enactment of citizenship?
4. How, and to what extent, do children and young people participate in civic life? (What motivates them to participate? What factors contribute to meaningful participation?)
5. How can we encourage meaningful participation and citizenship among children and young people?

The six following chapters review the key findings in response to the inquiry into these research questions in Australia, Brazil, New Zealand, Norway, Palestine and South Africa.

Children's Perspectives on Rights,
Responsibilities and Citizenship

3

Australia

Anne Graham, Brad Shipway & Robyn Fitzgerald
Centre for Children and Young People, Southern Cross University,
Lismore, NSW, Australia

Introduction

This chapter reports on the key findings of the Australian component of the Childwatch International Research Network project exploring children's perspectives on rights, responsibilities and citizenship.

We commence with a brief overview of existing curriculum in the state of New South Wales (NSW), Australia, related to education about rights, responsibilities and citizenship, and outline key issues emerging in citizenship curriculum development and delivery in Australian schools. This is followed by a discussion of the dissonances between what the curriculum currently requires children in NSW to be taught, and what young people have to say about rights, responsibilities and citizenship. The chapter concludes by considering some implications for future teaching practice.

Context

Significance of citizenship for children and young people

The importance of children and young people's understanding of, and their participation and inclusion in, civil society is well illustrated by the burgeoning literature analysing the relationship and connection between participation, citizenship and children (Davis & Hill, 2006; Lansdown, 2001; O'Toole & Gale, 2006). In recent years, the idea of children as citizens has grown from a broad understanding that their citizenship refers to membership of a particular community or nation towards connoting more specific responsibilities and rights. In the latter construction of children's citizenship, the development of children's knowledge, skills, values and attitudes is considered crucial to preparing and engaging children in adult decision-making by teaching them about democratic processes and practising some of the related processes and procedures (Archard, 1993; Davis & Hill, 2006; Flekkoy & Kaufman, 1997; Kaufman & Rizzini, 2002; Limber & Kaufman, 2002; Lister, 2005; Smith, 2002; Smith, Taylor & Tapp, 2003). Such debates draw attention to the importance of conferring on children the right to receive respect and to contribute to decision-making associated with citizenship, without necessarily attaching all the responsibilities of adult citizenship (Lister, 2005). This connection between the rights and responsibilities of citizenship has been described by Davis and Hill (2006, p. 12) as follows:

> *Preparing for later decision making, contributing views and taking part in actual decision making processes may all be seen as forms or stages of participation. Education programmes have mostly focused on helping children learn to be adult citizens, but some promote the idea of children as current citizens, with rights and capacities to contribute to the improvement of schooling for themselves and others in the present.*

Further, including children as active participants in civil society in ways that recognise them as citizens is consistent with Article 12 of the UNCRC which asserts that all children who are able to voice their views and opinions must be provided with opportunities to participate in decisions that affect them. Hence, a prerequisite of civic engagement is that students have a working understanding of their rights and responsibilities and of the value and significance of their current participation in civic life.

The educational context of Australian citizenship

Notions of citizenship in Australia are somewhat elusive. For instance, the *Australian Commonwealth Constitution* (1901) defines citizenship only in terms of how it is acquired, while the *Australian Citizenship Act* 1948 (Cth) does not detail the legal consequences of citizenship. Interestingly, the preamble to the *Australian Citizenship Act* 1948 (Cth) does not define what a citizen is, but rather defines what citizenship represents by way of obligations, rights and entitlements:

> *Australian citizenship represents formal membership of the community of the Commonwealth of Australia; and is a common bond, involving reciprocal rights and obligations, uniting all Australians while respecting their diversity; and persons granted Australian citizenship enjoy these rights and undertake to accept these obligations by pledging loyalty to Australia and its people, and by sharing their democratic beliefs and by respecting their rights and liberties, and by upholding and obeying the laws of Australia.*[1]

From the 1960s until the late 1980s, civics and citizenship education in Australia experienced a steady decline. This was attributed to the introduction and subsequent rise in popularity of social studies as a subject in the school curriculum, along with aspects of the social revolution in the 1960s that focused more on themes of change, prosperity and new values, as opposed to citizenship and national identity (Print & Gray, 2005). However, by the late 1980s interest in civic education was being revived, particularly at the Federal level of government. Senate inquiries in 1989 and 1991 voiced concern over the lack of civics education in Australian schools, and in 1994 the Federal Government established the Civics Expert Group (CEG). A seminal report by the CEG indicated an alarming level of ignorance among young Australians about the role they play as citizens in a democracy.

In 1997 the Federal Government announced its national civics and citizenship education program, *Discovering Democracy*. This was a significant initiative, with AU$18 million of Federal funding allocated from 1997 to 2000 to design and implement the program, with a further AU$13.6 million released from 2000 to 2004 for its consolidation and evaluation (Thompson, 2004). The central instrument of the initiative was the *Discovering Democracy Teaching Kits*, which were supplied to all schools, one for middle and upper primary, and one for lower and middle secondary. The teaching kits were organised around four main themes:

(i) Who Rules? (the exercise of power in a democracy, the rights and responsibilities of citizens);
(ii) Law and Rights (the rule of law, constitutions, parliaments, courts);
(iii) The Australian Nation (democratic institutions, changing civic identity);
(iv) Citizens and Public Life (participation and effecting change in society).

Implementation of the *Discovering Democracy* program was slow at first, possibly due to resistance from some areas of the teaching profession, as well as constraints in accommodating the initiative within an already over-crowded curriculum. However, a concerted focus on professional development and the release of new syllabus documents referring specifically to civics and citizenship in the late 1990s enabled the initiative to gain further ground. Further endorsement was received in 1999 when all State, Territory and Commonwealth Ministers of Education agreed to the *National Goals for Schooling in the Twenty-First Century*. Two of these three goals were specifically concerned with civic knowledge (the study of democracy) and citizenship (the development of social skills, attitudes, beliefs and values). Since then, civics and citizenship education has become a notable feature of the educational landscape in Australia.

Curriculum requirements for children in NSW concerning rights, responsibilities and citizenship

The content area of rights, responsibilities and citizenship is a clear and early inclusion in all Australian States' curriculum documents. For example, in NSW, 'Social and Civic Participation' is identified as one of three key syllabus skills to be taught across all year levels. Stage One students (5–8 years old) engage with this content through examining their own roles, rights and responsibilities at school and home. At Stage 2 (9–10 years old), students examine the rights and responsibilities of citizens at the local government level, and begin to explore the concept of civil action in more detail. By Stage 3 (11–12 years old) students not only learn about the functions of the various levels of government, but are also encouraged to compare different systems of government in terms of 'fairness and socially just principles and human rights' (NSW Board of Studies, 1998a, p. 37). Stage 3 students also investigate basic human rights, with an explicit focus on the relevant United Nations Declarations,[2] especially in the area of child rights (NSW Board of Studies, 1998b, p. 132).

However, despite the clear provision for an early and detailed treatment of civics, citizenship and human rights in the various State syllabi, there remains a recalcitrant gap between the curriculum concepts and the reality of young people's lives. This gap is particularly evident in the content area of human rights, which is by no means a high-profile feature of Australian civics and citizenship education.

Evidence of classroom reality not meeting curriculum rhetoric can be found in the Australian national report, *Citizenship and Democracy: Students' Knowledge and Beliefs*, which provided a picture of the effectiveness of civics and citizenship education in Australia.[3] While some significant strengths in civics and citizenship education were noted, it was also found that a number of fundamental problems persist, particularly in the students' understandings of human rights. For example:

- Australian students were significantly below the international average on measures of civic engagement. In other words, Australian students do not endorse action by citizens. Rather, they believe that a good citizen 'votes and shows respect for government representatives', and that historical and political knowledge and discussion were 'relatively unimportant';

- Two-thirds 'support the importance of promoting human rights' while only a little more than half of the students thought it 'important to participate in peaceful protest against a law they believe to be unjust' (ACSA, 2003, pp. xviii–xix).

In an effort to ensure continued attention is paid to the area, a portion of Federal Government funding for schools has now been tied to a national assessment program for civics and citizenship. Students in Years 6 and 10 (12 years and 16 years of age respectively) will be assessed against national benchmarks for civics and citizenship knowledge (National Assessment Program, 2004).

Key issues emerging in citizenship curriculum development and delivery in Australian schools

There is an ambiguity that underpins the profile of civics and citizenship education in Australia. On the one hand, there is no doubting the increased visibility it has gained within the educational landscape – Civics and Citizenship has now joined the areas of Literacy, Numeracy and Science as one of only four curriculum areas that are nationally tested. On the other hand, with the *Discovering Democracy* initiative coming to an end in 2005, the area of civics and citizenship education in Australia is now in a transition phase. In terms of emphasis, the Federal initiative is set to segue from 'Democracy' to 'Values', as the Federal Government establishes its *Values Education Framework*. This shift to partnering citizenship with 'values' raises many questions, including how a 'values-based' conception of citizenship will move towards the involvement of, and consultation with, children and young people in policy-making institutions and processes, based on recognition of children and young people as important and distinctive rights-bearers and stakeholders (O'Toole & Gale, 2006).

While it remains possible that the 'values' initiative will expand the current conceptions of civics and citizenship encountered in *Discovering Democracy*, such conceptions will need to go beyond merely embracing socially acceptable roles. They must encourage students to reflect on the (in)congruency between the rhetoric of civic values and the reality of the way lives are actually lived.

It was against this backdrop of key developments in the civics and citizenship education debate in Australia that the Centre for Children and Young People was invited to participate in the Childwatch International research project. It appeared very timely to be turning attention to the key questions underpinning this study: What are children's understandings of rights, responsibilities, and citizenship? What perspectives do their teachers and parents hold on rights, responsibilities, and citizenship? How do teachers and parents understand children's perspectives on rights, responsibilities and citizenship?

Research Methodology

The Australian research team adapted the focus group protocol developed by the New Zealand team. The research instruments were then piloted by the Centre for Children and Young People's youth advisory group, *Young People, Big Voice*, and amended accordingly. This procedure follows the Centre's commitment to developing research methodologies that are child and youth inclusive. The research instruments were comprised of:

- Class-based focus groups;
- Individual student questionnaires;
- Teacher questionnaires;
- Parent questionnaires.

The school-based focus groups were selected according to the following criteria:

- Gender – male/female;
- Age – 9/10-year-olds (Years 4 & 5) and 14/15-year-olds (Years 9 & 10);
- Socio-economic context of the school community;
- Government/non-government status of the school.

All schools selected were in a regional area of Australia on the north coast of NSW. One school was chosen on the basis of its large indigenous student population. The younger focus groups were single gender groups, while the

Table One: Australian child participants in the citizenship study focus groups

School Pseudo-nym	Govt/ Non-Govt School	Socio-economic Status	Age of focus group(s)	Gender of focus groups	No. of students in the group	Total no. of students
Mountain	NG	Low	9/10 yrs	1 female 1 male	11 9	**20**
Midtown	NG	Mid	9/10 yrs	1 female 1 male	10 9	**19**
Hilltop	NG	Mid	14/15 yrs	2 mixed	9 9	**18**
Riverside	G	Low	9/19 yrs	1 female	9	**18**

older groups were mixed. A key sampling criterion was that the classes had undertaken specific work on civics and citizenship, from either the NSW curriculum, or the Federal *Discovering Democracy* Kits. These classes were identified by the school principal, in consultation with teaching staff. Actual participants for the focus groups were those students from the available classes who returned the required consent forms. A total of 75 students participated in the study – 36 boys and 39 girls. Table One provides an overview of the sample.

Eight focus groups were conducted in the four participating schools between December 2004 and April 2005. Each focus group took approximately one hour and was facilitated by experienced senior researchers.

Parents and teachers in the eight schools were also invited to participate in the study by completing a brief questionnaire: 28 parents and 4 staff participated. Overall, there were 29 adult female respondents, and 3 males.

Researcher notes from the focus groups were entered into a qualitative data analysis software package (N6)[4], and coded by question. The data was then cross-coded by school, and individual focus groups. The four researchers then analysed the data independently and submitted the main themes they identified arising from the focus groups. These analysis documents were then also entered into the software, and cross-coded first with each other, and then with the original data (surveys, focus group transcripts and students' artworks). Tape-recordings of the focus group sessions were used to check and verify the accuracy of notated comments and quotes by the students in the focus groups.

Key Findings

The focus group participants were asked to discuss their citizenship rights and responsibilities in Australia. They were requested to think of an imaginary country where the members of their group were the Government. Participants were then asked (i) to think of the rights, responsibilities and type of citizen they would like to see in 'their' country, and (ii) to design a flag for 'their' country that represented what life was like for 'their' citizens. Students were then invited to compare the situation in 'their' country with the rights, responsibilities and citizenship roles they *currently* have in Australia.

Rights

The students in this study conceptualised rights primarily in terms of *enabling aspects* (i.e. as an entitlement to determine one's own behaviour and control one's own possessions) as distinct from *constraining aspects* (i.e. as a means of directing appropriate action towards an individual).

The younger age group (9/10-year-olds) principally defined rights as an '*allowance*' and indicated what rights do or do not provide for by giving examples:

To be free, to be able to say.

To (an) education, to go to the doctor.

While the older age group (14/15-year-olds) also defined rights as '*an allowance*' they further identified basic rights as something that accrue by virtue of our humanity and are not earned. In other words, they realised that some rights are universal:

What you have no matter what you do – (for example) water.

So everyone is equal to everyone else.

Additionally, some of the older age group identified tensions inherent in the relationship between possessing and exercising rights:

Some people can do things that they shouldn't be allowed to.

In terms of the students' perceptions of rights in Australia now (their actual or lived rights), there was confusion when they were asked to *name* rights, even though they had earlier been able to recognise the difference between a right and a responsibility. For example, when asked what rights they have in their homes, some younger students gave the example *'to wash up'*. It was particularly notable that few students were able to name concrete rights that they currently possess in Australia.

The rights which the younger and older students identified were linked to everyday activities (a right to 'do' something) and everyday principles and underlying entitlements (a right to 'be'). The younger student groups named a number of concrete rights: '*to education; not to starve; to say things; to feel or be safe and to go to school/receive an education; to play sport; to be respected; to be involved in the community; to expect your parents to care for you.*'

The older students also identified the following additional concrete rights: '*to health – stuff you absolutely need; to recreation – skate parks; to socialize with whomever you want; to work and get jobs; to freedom of religion.*'

Some younger students also named things that they do at school or home as concrete illustrations of the rights that they have:

to play songs;

to be ourselves;

to sleep;

to cuddle pets.

Neither the younger nor older students named many of the legal rights that they possess as young people in Australia (for example, employment and unfair dismissal rights; occupational health and safety rights; the right not to be discriminated against; rights when stopped by police or security guards in public places; right to leave school at 15).

However, the older group did note the reality of the limitations of rights – that is, that rights are not absolute and that the opportunity to exercise rights varies according to different contexts:

The right to privacy exists in all homes – but some don't respect it;

Depends on home – some young people have no rights and some have full rights;

No rights at school!

To express your opinion and thoughts to a certain degree.

Responsibilities

In defining responsibility, students described a relationship between possessing responsibility and trust – responsibility was identified as arising from actions and attitudes in relation to caring for people, their homes and their schools. There was almost unanimous recognition by both younger and older students that they had a responsibility to care for the environment. A significant number also identified a responsibility to care for the elderly in their communities. Consistent with the data regarding limited knowledge of rights, a strong theme that arose from all focus groups was that the young people were unsure what legal responsibilities they have.

The younger students regarded responsibilities as linked to actions – the things that they were required to do. They gave examples of personal responsibilities that were largely tasks they had to perform at home and school:

Feeding chickens;

Chores for pocket money;

If you make a mess you clean it up;

If you buy a dog you have to look after it.

Some younger students viewed responsibilities as earned, for example, being trusted to do things alone. The older students, in addition, perceived a relationship between possessing responsibilities and exercising the choice whether or not to fulfil them as an expression of individual morality:

Obligation – don't have to do it but should do it if you have good morals;

Being responsible for the actions you do … being trustworthy.

The older students were also able to express the relationship between responsibilities and civic order/control. For example, one Year 9 student (aged 14 years) observed: *rules that everyone has to abide to so there won't be any fights*.

The responsibilities that all students identified (apart from '*to care for the environment*', which was perceived more generally) arose from actions and attitudes in relation to:

1. Caring for themselves or others:
    To care for myself and keep safe.
    To care for younger kids.

2. Caring for their immediate home environments:
    To eat your tea, rinse and stack the plates; pick up the dog poo; wash up; to have a shower; to help dad bottle his beer.
    To care for parents and other things around you; to obey parents.

3. Caring for their school environment:
    Be responsible for my books, pencil case.
    Computer monitor, prefects, captains, flag monitor, bell monitor.
    To set an example for younger students.

Two of the younger groups and the older students also identified responsibilities that extended beyond their home and school domains into the community:

Respecting teachers, parents and elders.
Taking care of the land.
To show respect in the community – that we respect law and order; to protect wildlife.
To fit in (to the community); to participate; to take part in sports if you sign up at the start of the season.

The older students also acknowledged the relationship between rights and responsibilities, for example, *to protect your family from dangerous people, but to respect the rights of those people*.

In the adult questionnaires, parents and teachers strongly agreed that children and young people should be allocated responsibilities across the home, school and community that were in accordance with their developmental level and individual abilities. At home, the responsibilities identified by parents fell into the two main categories: (i) young people contributing to their share of the household duties, and (ii) young people contributing to a harmonious family life by treating parents and siblings with respect.

At school, parents and teachers again identified two main responsibilities, namely (i) being conscientious students and completing their work, and (ii) being respectful and mindful of the teachers.

Parents' examples of the responsibilities that young people should have in the community centred around either charity work or some other form of community service. The theme of young people using their spare time to assist the elderly in the community was raised frequently by parents, teachers, and the young people themselves.

Citizenship

Citizenship was a difficult concept to define for most of the participants. Although both younger and older students perceived that citizenship is both internally (attitude) and externally (action) driven, no clear and consistent definitions emerged. Despite this, students did identify factors that would assist them to be effective citizens in both actions and attitudes. These factors can be described as:

- involving young people in decision-making;
- modelling citizenship and mentoring young people;
- adults' supporting young people to be active citizens.

Interestingly, these factors were drawn from vicarious experience in the students' imaginary country, rather than their actual experience in Australia.

Across all groups of younger children three key traits of citizenship emerged, although no single group amongst either the younger or older students identified all of the characteristics:

1. It is principally a moral or lawful characteristic:
   A good person. You don't steal or hurt anyone.

2. It signifies membership of a (mainly local) social group:
   Joining in properly.
   Part of a community and town.

3. It entails possessing rights and responsibilities, including the entitlement/obligation to participate:
   Having rights and responsibilities for your country.

It is also significant that students could not comprehensively identify what their *actual* rights and responsibilities are in Australia, yet they found it quite easy to articulate many rights and responsibilities in their 'imaginary' country. Many of the rights identified in the imaginary countries were rights that currently actually apply to young people in Australia – though many students did not realise this. However, it must be emphasised that this finding does not, in and of itself, mean these young people had a poor capacity to *understand* their rights. Some quite complex understandings of rights and responsibilities (and the role these play in societies) were revealed as the young people spoke of their 'imaginary country'. The challenges emerged when they tried to apply these complex understandings to lived realities.

How could adults assist the children and young people to be citizens?

The issues identified by the younger students focused on: (i) involving young people in decision-making, (ii) modelling citizenship and (iii) mentoring young people in their roles as citizens:

Role models and leaders can help.
Right examples, small jobs at first.
Involve young people in making decisions.

Students also explained that it would be helpful if adults clearly articulated the rules and used plain language while encouraging a sense of personal responsibility:

Not talk jibberish – big fat long words – our language not theirs.
Look after and care for family members and younger children.
Look after nature, learn from past mistakes.
Help them abide by the law; accept positive criticism or feedback.

The older students responded to this question by focusing on the need to provide young people with authentic opportunities to participate in a meaningful way:

Participate in clean-up Australia days.
Fundraisers to help local hospital or to meet a need in the community.

A number of the students clearly resisted being forced into participation:

Nobody does want to (do stuff). Some people do, but it's not good to force people to do stuff.

Both the younger and older students identified helping the elderly as a means by which young people could be assisted as citizens:

Being respectful to elders; put on entertainment for the elderly; to respect old people.

Parent and Teacher Questionnaires

All the teachers, and 26 out of 28 (93 per cent) parents,[5] agreed that young people should be thought of as citizens, and that this citizenship began at birth. All the parents agreed that meeting one's domestic responsibilities (such as doing chores) was an important way that young people could exercise their citizenship, and all but one parent believed that children and young people should have an input into family decision-making processes.

All thought that citizenship at school could be demonstrated by taking on certain responsibilities (such as caring for younger students), and taking student leadership positions within the school (such as 'Monitor' of sports equipment, or School Captain). In addition, the parents and teachers were agreed that taking responsibility for one's self (e.g. completion of schoolwork, accepting the consequences of one's actions) was an obvious way that citizenship at school could be exercised. Singing the National Anthem and learning its meaning was also a dominant example used by both parents and teachers to describe how young people could exercise their citizenship at school. This type of participation at school was cited as important by 23 of the 28 (82 per cent) parents, and was universally emphasised by the teachers.

Two parents took care to emphasise that their schools could do a much better job of providing their children with more opportunities to take on meaningful, as opposed to token, responsibilities. One teacher agreed, emphasising that young people should:

Be more involved in decision-making at all levels – in order for them to 'own' the decisions, they need to be contributing to the 'making of them'!

Parents and teachers unanimously thought one of the best ways for young people to exercise their citizenship in the wider community was to take part in public commemorative occasions and environmental projects, such as ANZAC Day and '*Clean Up Australia Day*.' Respect for the traditions of their nation was cited as one of the most obvious characteristics of good citizenship in young people. Comments such as '*be patriotic*' and '*show respect and be a giver to society*' indicated the clear expectation from parents and teachers that a good young citizen is a respectful individual who is willing to make a positive contribution to their society. However, only one parent referred to a more active mode of citizenship, one where young people can be on the look-out for opportunities to use their '*own initiative*', and '*do things [in the community] without being asked*.'

Parents and teachers agreed that treating young people as citizens could increase their children's confidence in participating in the wider community, and could ensure that future society is more fulfilling for them. Three parents saw the quality of their child's future community life as being linked to treating young people as citizens:

They will grow up feeling that they are respected – one gives respect when one receives respect.

They will have a happier and more fulfilled life.

[They will] gain a sense of ownership and responsibility.

In an interesting contrast to some of the imagery found in school curriculum materials, only one parent believed that qualities such as heroism and patriotism could emerge from treating young people as citizens.

When it came to the perceived disadvantages of treating children as citizens, the parents and teachers were divided, both between themselves, and across the two groups of adults. Two parents strongly believed that there was no 'downside' to treating young people as citizens in the wider community, provided that young people were taught the necessary skills to enable them to participate. When asked, they saw the disadvantages as:

None, provided expectations are reasonable given age and maturity.

None, if given the opportunity to prove they are polite, respectful of others and property, especially if adults recognise and acknowledge when they do the right thing.

However, another parent expressed concern about how young people might deal with what could be required of citizens, as they learned more about the adult responsibilities that accompany being a 'good' citizen. The concern was that, if not handled in an expert way, young people could become *'scared of wars and national service.'*

The teachers were similarly divided on what the disadvantages were to treating young people as citizens (it should be noted that there were no teachers who saw no disadvantages). Half the teachers were not sure if there were disadvantages or not, while the other half saw the potential for some students to abuse the opportunity to participate. These teachers thought that treating young people as citizens could be problematic if young people used new-found knowledge of their rights in an inappropriate or immature way:

I guess that if they didn't understand that in the end adults have to make decisions for reasons the children are sometimes not privy too.

Sometimes they become too outspoken.

Discussion

Family and school are key contexts for children and young people exercising rights and responsibilities

Both the younger and older students were able to name the rights and responsibilities that they possess at home and school with relative ease. They found it much more difficult to name rights and responsibilities that they possess in the community (apart from a responsibility to the environment and the elderly). Interestingly, even the rights and responsibilities that children could name in the contexts of home and school included no mention of specific legal rights (for example, in relation to corporal punishment, their employment rights, their right to have the best interests of the child considered in family law matters).

Schools have a key role to play in improving young people's knowledge of their rights and responsibilities

There are significant gaps in young people's knowledge of the rights and responsibilities that they actually possess in Australia. Although a large number of older students in particular could identify some of the rights that young people have under the UNCRC, these rights were not, on the whole, named as rights that they actually possess. Furthermore, there was no notable differentiation between the conditions of their lives that were commonly allowed by adults (such as a room of their own) and the rights that young people possess.

The one exception to this was the universally identified right to feel safe, not to be threatened or harmed in their community, school or home. This was the first and most explicit of the rights the young people mentioned in the focus groups. Beyond this, the most common thing that young people interpreted to be their right in Australia was a freedom of choice in respect of choosing their friends and the type of music they listened to. The right to a form of 'sanctuary' space that was private from, and respected by, adults was also mentioned frequently, such as the young person's bedroom.

Clarity concerning factors that assist in being a citizen

Both the younger and older students were quite clear about the factors that facilitate a sense of citizenship. These included (i) involving young people in decision-making, (ii) modelling citizenship and mentoring young people, (iii) requiring compliance with clearly articulated rules (expressed in plain language), (iv) encouraging a sense of personal responsibility, and (v) providing young people with opportunities to participate authentically and voluntarily. That both younger and older students identified helping the elderly as a means by which young people could be citizens signals that this is an area of community service that Australian school students participate in and/or that young people feel they have something particular to offer.

In relation to parents' and teachers' perceptions of the rights that young people do, or should, possess, the parents and teachers surveyed unanimously indicated the importance of acknowledging that young people have rights in the home, at school, and in the wider community. For parents, the most significant right for children at home was that children should have the right to spend time with their parents. The importance of listening to the feelings and opinions of their children was also emphasised.

In terms of young people having rights at school, parents and teachers concurred on the need for young people to have the opportunity to participate in the leadership of the school at a variety of levels. However, parental responses varied in relation to the ways parents sought to support the rights of their children at school. The parents' responses indicated that they were confused about the procedures for lodging grievances with the school, and conflict resolution between parents, teaching staff, and students.

On the subject of rights in the community, there was some variance among parents and teachers on the degree to which they were aware of, and agreed with, the UNCRC. Parents who were cautious of supporting the Convention mentioned that they were concerned that an over-emphasis on children's rights could be potentially divisive to the family unit and suggested instead an emphasis on family living standards as a more useful option.

Scaffolding rights and responsibilities

Students identified rights and responsibilities in terms of assuming responsibility in accordance with individual capacity. They sought greater opportunities for social participation that increases in scope and responsibility as they mature, allowing them to '*take small steps at first*' and to '*practise before the real thing.*' Students' sense of their rights and responsibilities changes as they develop. The younger students appeared to accept that their rights were entirely circumscribed by their parents regardless of whether or not they liked the range of rights and responsibilities they had. The older students, while acknowledging adults' more extensive experience, clearly identified the desire for opportunities to exercise rights within limited contexts. They did not seek ultimate control over what their rights should be, but rather sought to be consulted and heard in relation to the rights they wanted to exercise, and to have their views acknowledged even if these views were not adopted in the final decision.

The students frequently referred to how critical it is that they are '*stepped into*' taking on more responsibility – '*just small jobs at first.*' Younger students stated that they '*need practice for bigger responsibilities when you get older*' while older students noted '*it's fair enough that everyone helps so that we learn about responsibilities.*' All groups suggested young people take on more responsibilities at a younger age than is currently the case; however, they also acknowledged the importance of having their input '*filtered*' by adults.

Underestimating young people's capacity for understanding and participation in the nuances of citizenship

As mentioned earlier, one focus group activity involved students designing a flag to represent what life was like for the citizens of 'their' country. This activity generated some rich data. The flag illustrations and the explanations provided by the students revealed sophisticated nuances young people possessed in their understanding of the nature of citizenship and democracy:

58 *Children as Citizens?*

The star represents the citizens, the bird represents freedom, the water is calm and peaceful, (bottom right corner) this shows balance between everything, (the axe) represents strength. (Year 5 boy, aged 11 years).

My stars represent, like, the people being together, and working together, and being equal ... (the stars are supposed to be the same size), I was going to make that (the chequerboard) pink and black to show that you don't get paid out ... they can feel free to wear what you want or live how you want... (the trees) they show the wildlife, and that we won't cut down all the trees ... (the fire) shows that we are strong and we don't give up, so long as it keeps burning ... (the fish and rabbit) shows that we treat all animals the same, like, we don't kill some and keep others ...(the cross) you don't do the wrong thing, and we're trying to keep everybody happy, and take away terrorism and stuff. (Year 5 boy, aged 10 years)

These examples, along with many others in the data, reveal that the capacity of young people for understanding ideas such as participation and citizenship is nuanced and thoughtful. Indeed, a claim might well be made that there is a curious contrast between a fine-grained understanding of rights in the imaginary country and lack of knowledge of rights in their real country, which points to the civic capacity of young people being underestimated at home, at school, and in the wider community.

Despite the relatively small sample, the findings of this pilot phase of the research support those of the much larger IEA *Civic Education Study*, which also found that young people still have a poor grasp of how they may go about participating as citizens in a democratic society. Mellor, Kennedy and Greenwood (2001) surveyed 90,000 participants and focused on students' understanding of concepts such as democracy and citizenship, national identity and international relations, and social cohesion and diversity. The study analysed the students' knowledge of content, skills in interpretation, understanding of key concepts, attitudes and expected actions. Significantly, it found that:

> *Australian students are not strong in their understandings of what constitute their civil rights ... Australian students have a strong sense of natural justice and equity, but they lack clarity about the theoretical precepts of democratic models and structures.* (Mellor et al., 2001, p. 4)

The findings from our study indicate more work needs to be done both in capturing the views and perspectives of young people in relation to rights, responsibilities and citizenship, and ensuring initiatives introduced into schools take account of the creative and complex ways that young people apply their understandings.

Conclusion

There is clear evidence that the civics and citizenship education of young people in Australia has made considerable progress since the mid-1990s. However, despite its prominent national profile, there remain disconcerting gaps between the conceptual knowledge that students hold and the practical application of those concepts in real-life situations.

There appear to be three key issues that significantly contribute to the gap between the rhetoric of curriculum and the reality of practice in civics and citizenship education. These are:

(i) a general underestimation by teachers, parents and the wider community of young people's understanding of their rights, responsibilities and their role as citizens.

Young people clearly expressed, through their individual questionnaire responses, group discussions and artwork, a sophisticated and nuanced understanding of the different facets of being a citizen. At the same time, they also expressed the view that their opportunities to exercise citizenship at home, school, and in the community were not commensurate with their level of ability or understanding. This gap in expectation did not appear to be recognised by parents.

(ii) a lack of, or delayed, emphasis on human rights in the Federal curriculum.

That the young people in this study were unable to transpose their theoretical, or utopian, understanding of human rights onto the terrain of their daily lives reflects the late examination of human rights in the *Discovering Democracy* kits, where they are examined explicitly in middle secondary school (15–17 years – the oldest students in this study being 15 years of age).

(iii) a lack of opportunities for students to exercise the 'social action' component of their civics and citizenship learning.

A narrow range of civic participation activities was discussed by both young people and parents. In addition, the nature of civic participation mentioned by parents and teachers (singing the anthem, attending ANZAC Day), was quite different to that discussed by the young people (caring for the environment, helping the elderly). The teachers and parents conceived of more passive forms of civic participation, whereas the young people's examples were more active and required greater commitment and deeper engagement.

As a result of these issues, the findings from the study raise the following questions for future research:

- How can we utilise what students have told us to develop a curriculum that is more responsive to their knowledge 'gaps', their extant sophisticated understandings, and their daily lives?
- How can teachers and parents be encouraged to experiment with more meaningful opportunities for social action and civic participation and ensure these are included in the curriculum?
- How can educators best gauge the relationship between current education initiatives about rights and citizenship and Australian students' actual understanding of these and develop a best practice approach to rights and citizenship education in the Australian context?

Given the considerable expenditure on civics and citizenship education in Australia over the past ten years, the persistent gap between curriculum ideals and students' working knowledge, and the current state of transition from 'civics' to 'values' at the Federal level, the above questions seem more than worthy of further investigation. Moreover, if the answers to these questions are ever to gain any purchase at the 'chalkface', the importance of finding these answers through research that utilises the perspectives of children and young people cannot be underestimated.

4

Brazil

Irene Rizzini, Udi Mandel Butler & Nisha Thapliyal[1]
The International Center for Research on Childhood (CIESPI)
Pontifical Catholic University, Rio de Janeiro, Brazil

Introduction

The present study involves societies in different stages of democracy and development facing various economic, social and political challenges. Brazil is a country with great social inequity: a consequence of one of the worst income distributions in the world and also of the absence of consistent socio-economic policies. This is also the reality of the city of Rio de Janeiro. The streets of this city, and one of the Landless Movement's settlements, were considered to be important sites for the research, along with schools in the city of Rio de Janeiro itself.

Brazil is, however, also a country with one of the most progressive laws for children's rights anywhere in the world. The *Statute on the Child and Adolescent* (1990) emerged out of widespread concern about the violence against children on the street, black youths and other marginalised groups of children. The movement for children's rights has radically transformed the ways in which ordinary Brazilians, policymakers, police and politicians think about children. Despite the persisting gap between our laws and practices in the child protection sphere, children are no longer considered '*menores*'[2] as in the past, but rather as subjects with rights. The current representation of youth protagonism (*protagonismo juvenil*) refers to the multiple abilities that adolescents develop following their childhoods, some of which have not previously been valued or recognised by the adult world.

Along with this transformation in popular opinion, youth activism and involvement in socio-political action in communities, schools and families has increased. In particular, school is a place in which children and adolescents spend a large part of their lives. It is one of the few spaces in which they come together across differences. There is an opportunity to learn about diverse cultural representations and ways of living. The participation of children in decisions concerning their education is being debated around the world. Research suggests that this kind of participation is vital for children to become involved in larger social and economic issues in their society and country (Hart, 1997; Hart, Newman, Ackermann & Feeny, 2003; UNICEF, 2003). Through this kind of participation, children confront problems and learn to devise solutions in collective and dialogic ways. Similarly, opportunities to participate in family and community decisions on a day-to-day basis are essential to their all-round development. The act of including children in decision-making in a truly participatory way instills not only a sense of belonging, but also of ownership and responsibility. Children can develop a sense of themselves as actors who have the power to influence the adverse conditions that shape their lives. They develop confidence and learn attitudes and practical lessons about how they can improve the quality of their lives. By describing the ways in which children and adolescents think about rights, responsibilities and citizenship, this research project hopes to inform systematic efforts to cultivate and nourish youth activism for deeper social change.

Contributions from the Literature

Encouraging children to express their opinions and feelings about their own lives and events in their community, and to participate actively in the world around them, signals a respect for children as human beings (Morrow, 1999; Weithorn, 1998). Critical to children's meaningful participation in a civil society is an understanding of their rights as individuals within their family, community, and society. A growing research literature is examining children's understanding of their rights and their role in society.

Unfortunately, opportunities and mechanisms for children's participation remain limited (Rizzini & Thapliyal, 2006). For instance, schools have begun to spend more time talking about, instead of providing opportunities to engage in, democracy. Citizenship education tends to focus on civic virtues/values and/ or moral/character education and avoid deeper discussions about democratic cultures and institutions (Davies, 2002; Davies, Gorard & McGuinn, 2005). It has also shown a tendency to encourage young learners to conform to authority and existing political structures (McCowan, 2006). The few viable extant democratic structures for child participation, such as school-based student councils, have largely focused on managing limited aspects of school life – little real power or responsibility is given to students (Davies & Kirkpatrick, 2000; McLaren, 1989).

The study of young people's conceptions of rights and citizenship is critical for a number of reasons. First, it is important for setting an agenda for advocacy, because it may illuminate the most critical problems that children perceive in implementing their rights. Asking children to describe the extent of their rights – and the impediments that they perceive in exercising such rights – may be an important first step in determining an agenda for action. The success of efforts to promote children's rights will depend on children's (and adults') attitudes towards, and knowledge about, rights and citizenship.

Second, this information may be useful in designing structures and procedures that are necessary if children are to perceive that they, in fact, have rights. If children do not believe that their rights will be enforced, they are unlikely to exercise them as citizens.

Other research indicates that participation in their everyday living environments as citizens with rights is important to young people understanding that they have rights (Melton & Limber, 1993; Morrow, 1999; Taylor, Smith & Nairn, 2001).

While popular and legal conceptions of childhood differ globally, it does appear that the more children are treated and constructed as citizens, the more likely it is that they will actively participate in society. The research literature suggests that children's understanding of their status, rights and responsibilities as citizens is likely to facilitate their participation in society and is therefore fundamental to sustaining a democracy (Flekkoy & Kaufman, 1997; Kaufman & Rizzini, 2002; Limber & Kaufman, 2002; Smith, 2005). Stimulating children's thinking about citizenship, and its associated rights and responsibilities, should encourage their support for democratic values, including just laws and tolerance for the rights of others (Butler, Princeswal & Abreu, 2007; Melton & Limber, 1993; Torres, 2006).

Research Methodology

In this study, citizenship is understood as the awareness of and ability to exercise one's rights and duties. Underlying this definition is an assumption of the possibility of creating adequate conditions to promote actions of participation and transformation that are not limited to attaining one's social rights. The Brazilian research team worked with focus groups of children and adolescents in different contexts and socio-economic strata: in public and private schools; and with those living on the street, in institutions and in settlements of the Landless Movement (MST).

Our goal in this qualitative research project was to organise the activities so that they could be carried out with the involvement and collaboration of the schools. Among other things, this meant we had to determine what time of the day and week would be devoted to the focus groups and which students would participate. We therefore spent some time discussing the objectives of the research with the deans of the selected schools. We also discussed how the data collected would be relevant to understanding how Brazilian children and adolescents think, and the importance of the participation of the school in gathering the data. The activities were designed with the age of children kept in mind. Thus we had slightly different sets of activities for the two age-groups. In addition, how these activities were carried out was determined by the conditions in each setting.

Activities with groups ranging from eight to nine years of age

Phase I: The map of the world was shown to them. The children named the countries, pointed out their location on the map, the continents they were on, differences in climate, languages and habits, ethnicity, differences and similarities in landscapes, flags, games, and so on. The book *Children Just like*

Me from UNICEF[3] was shown during this activity. The children also examined the map of Brazil and talked about the origin of their families, landscapes, distances, habits, ethnic diversity, popular culture, games, and the size of Brazil compared to other countries.

Phase II: The children were questioned about their understanding of different forms of social interaction as well as the meaning of rights, responsibilities and citizenship.

Phase III: To create a new country: name, place on the map, landscapes, people, animals, habits, flag; to determine the forms of social interaction and participation of each person in this country.

Phase IV: The children were asked to draw the new country taking the Atlas and the book *Children just like me* into account (landscapes, people, flag, map, etc.).

Activities conducted with adolescents from 14 to 15 years of age

Phase I: Arrival at a new country. The adolescents were given an individual number that was used as an access code to the new country and a name tag on which comments were written throughout the activity.

Phase II: The name of the country was chosen – this was a group decision. Each participant wrote the name of the country on his/her name tag.

Phase III: Three boxes were placed in the middle of the room. In each one of them there were questions related to the subjects discussed, as described below. Each participant took a question in order. The questions were answered and discussed by the group.

Phase IV: Creation of the document of the country. This document was written on a sheet of cardboard and encompassed the answers on rights, responsibilities and citizenship in the new country.

Phase V: Each adolescent was asked to read his/her number aloud – the number given at the beginning of the activity. This action marked the return to the reality of our country.

Phase VI: Evaluation – how can the adolescents adapt the situation of their recently created country to the place where we live? What can the adults do? What can the children do?

Phase VII: Each participant wrote a motto on his/her name-tag that would represent the discussion brought up in the activity.

Table One: Brazilian child participants in the citizenship study focus groups

SCHOOL 8/9 Years	Boys	Girls	Total
Public School	8	8	16
Private School	8	8	16
Street Children	4	-	4
MST (Landless Movement)	5	5	10
14/15 Years			
Public School	8	8	16
Public School	8	8	16
Private School	-	6	6
Street Children	8	2	10
MST (Landless Movement)	3	-	3
TOTAL	**52 boys**	**45 girls**	**97 students**

Participants (sample)

The field activities were started in May 2004. The CIESPI team conducted discussions with 13 groups of children and adolescents, which included two mixed groups with both boys and girls as a way to broaden the comparative results. In total, there were 97 young people involved in the focus groups. Of these, 46 were 8/9 years old and 51 were 14/15 years old (see Table One).

We selected three municipal schools that predominantly had students from lower middle class backgrounds who were living in the *favelas* (slums). We also decided to include students from two private schools that are generally regarded as providing a quality education. Since these schools charge high monthly fees, the students that attend them usually come from the middle and upper-middle classes. Two focus groups each were also conducted with, respectively, children and adolescents living on the street and the children of the Landless Movement (MST). Twenty four teachers and 69 parents completed questionnaires.

The Research Settings[4]

Coelho Alceu Municipal School: A public school, in the Jardim Botânico neighbourhood, in the southern zone of Rio de Janeiro. This school had seven classrooms and served 272 children – 1st graders to 4th graders. It also offered a special class with nine students.[5] The children in this school lived within the same community or in nearby communities. These were either poor communities or *favelas*.

Two groups were conducted in this school, one with girls and one with boys. The school let us use their library. We were not interrupted and the children showed a lot of interest in the discussion. The activities were almost concluded, except for creating the flag for the new country, one of the final steps of the planned interview.

Carmo Castro Municipal School: A public school in the Jardim Botânico neighbourhood, in the southern zone of Rio de Janeiro. This school had eight classrooms with 301 students from 5th grade to 8th grade (11 to 17 years of age).[6] The school was part-time, with students attending either in the morning or in the afternoon. Most of the students came from a *favela* in the vicinity of the neighbourhood.

The pedagogical co-ordinator and the dean's office had previously contacted Ciespi with the desire of developing projects in partnership. After we had contacted the school a few times, the team approached the school to describe the research. The idea was promptly accepted by the deans, reminding us that the Political and Pedagogical Project of the school was in consonance with 'educating citizens'. The dean's office and the teachers helped to conduct the groups. Unfortunately, we did not have enough time to finish the activities, so we set a new date with the school and the participants. On our return, we noticed that the students' level of interest had changed. At the first session, there had been a very interested group of students and a somewhat uninterested group. At the second meeting they had exchanged places and the previously uninterested group was eager about our return. Fifteen days later, one of the Ciespi researchers ran into one of the participants. The adolescent said that she was waiting for her turn to get to the 'new country' and that the group was waiting for the team to revisit the school yet again so that they could keep discussing the subject. This feedback showed the interest of these adolescents in participating in discussions about their reality.

João Novini Municipal School: A public municipal school in the Botafogo neighbourhood in the southern zone of Rio de Janeiro. The school had 18 classrooms and 704 students from 5th to 8th grade.[7] This school was chosen because it served students of various types who lived in several neighbourhoods and lower-income communities and other *favelas*.

Two mixed-gender groups were conducted in this school. When both groups were starting to build their new country, their activities were interrupted by the school lunch offered to the students. After the break, one adolescent demanded that 'decent' lunches should be offered in all schools and that the students should be able to eat as much as they wanted.[8] Consequently, the biggest demand was gastronomic abundance and the excited adolescents talked about sweets and dishes that they could eat in this new country! It is likely that they had never tried many of the foods they desired.

Deus Nosso Pai School: A private Catholic school in the Botafogo neighbourhood in the southern zone of Rio de Janeiro.[9] Founded in 1926, it provided the community with primary school services. In 1952, it started vocational courses and offered chemistry, electronics, nursing and secretary courses throughout the years. To meet the needs of young people who had to work during the day, a night course was created. The vocational and night courses, however, terminated in 1985. The school presently works with Infant Education (until kindergarten) for children from 2 to 6 years of age, Elementary School (from the 1st to the 8th grade) for 7 to 14 year-olds, and Secondary Education for adolescents from 15 to 17 years of age. Students are drawn from the middle and high-middle classes.

Two focus groups were conducted in this school, with 16 students – one group of eight boys and one group of eight girls. Both groups were conducted on the same day. The activities were intense, despite the amount of time available (only 1 hour and 30 minutes). The boys' group was a bit excited as they had come straight from their lunch break. After running on the courts, they were tired and needed some time to catch their breath and calm themselves down. Even so, they were still a little excited! At the end of the activities they were exhausted by the amount of questions asked, but they finished their drawings.

São Tomas School: A private school in the Cosme Velho neighbourhood in the southern zone of Rio de Janeiro.[10] The school has existed since 1959. It was initially directed only to boys, but in 1968 it adopted the co-education system. An elementary fast-track night course was started in 1973, which is today called Youth and Adult Education. This is a religious school run by the Brazilian Province of the Congregation of the Mission (PBCM – Vicentians or Lazarists priests and friars). Their philosophy of education follows the recommendations of the National Confederation of Brazilian and Latin American Bishops. During the 1968 conference in Medellin, the participants proposed an education capable of questioning social reality and changing oppressive social realities to promote a more human and democratic interaction.

The fast-track night course from 1st (where reading and writing is taught) to 8th grades was the school's response to the challenge of an 'education for all' (*educação para todos*). One of the qualities of the educational environment of the school was the range of cultural activities conducted throughout the year – theatre, choir, radio, magazines, excursions and student council, as well as sports and pastoral activities from the Graúna Citizen's Action Committee.[11] The school assists children, adolescents and young adults from a higher social stratum, from 1st to 9th grade, ranging from 7 to 18 years of age. At night the school offers the fast-track course for lower-income adolescents and young adults.

Some setbacks occurred on the day scheduled for conducting the focus groups. We were initially planning to conduct two groups with 16 adolescents divided by gender. We arrived at the school at the appointed time to discover that the boys' group had left. Some of the girls had also left, since they studied in the morning, while the group was set for 2 p.m. in the afternoon. We also had to wait for the pedagogical co-ordinator to come back from lunch, as the discussion was going to be conducted in her office. This wait took time from the focus group session. The group was finally formed by six girls – two less than the number previously decided. This group was also non-standard for other reasons: the selected girls were class 'leaders' or 'representatives', which was different from the other groups. The pedagogical co-ordinator remained in the room during the entire session, and made several interruptions as the girls spoke to ask questions and state her opinion on what was being said.

Group with homeless children (street children): To schedule the focus groups with homeless children, or those who spend a lot of time on the streets, we relied on a social educator[12] who was also a member of the *Rede Rio Criança* (Rio Child Network).[13] The meeting was in a house in the Tijuca neighbourhood in the northern zone of Rio that is currently used as a training centre and a place for meetings between social educators.

Two groups with children and adolescents of both sexes were scheduled. Only four children, from 7 to 14 years of age, came to one meeting – three siblings and another boy that the oldest sibling said he cared for. Before the discussion started, one adolescent was telling the others that his father had been stabbed during a fight and was at the hospital. The children were curious about the size of the knife that had been used and they started arguing and hitting each other. The research activities started after they had calmed down. The oldest boy and the oldest girl tried to answer the questions seriously and sadness was noticed in their eyes.

The second group was formed by ten adolescents – eight boys and two girls, ranging from 12 to 16 years of age. They had all participated in two social projects co-ordinated by the social educators that brought them. This group showed great interest in participating in the research. At the end of the activities, the group expressed how important it was for them to participate in this discussion. They said it was a chance for them to be heard, to speak their minds and that, unfortunately, not all children have this opportunity. According to what the boys and girls said, most of them live with their families. Only two of them declared that they lived in shelters, but all of them, from both groups, said they had lived in the streets.

Movement of Landless Agricultural Workers – *Movimento Rurais Trabalhadores sem Terra* (MST): MST continues a historical process of popular struggles, developing a social organisation directly connected with reality and guided by the political practice of their organisational principles (such as collective management, discipline, the connection with the base and study). Eighty representatives of peasant organisations that fought for land and saw the need for national articulation of their movement founded the MST in 1984. The first National Meeting identified the common experience of peasants from different states. This meeting defined the ideology followed by the movement and helped establish it as an independent organisation of rural workers.

MST's struggle for social transformation is widely supported. Since the beginning, more than 200 awards have been dedicated to the movement and agrarian reform became a well-known and highly important issue in society. Today, the movement counts on around 350,000 settled families and another approximately 160,000 families living in camp grounds. Considering the average size of a Brazilian family – i.e. four people – MST active members reach close to two million people. The settlements are liberated, and are an incentive for the struggle to continue. Not a single child is hungry or out of school in the almost 5000 MST settlements.[14]

There are more than 500 production, commerce and service associations; 49 co-operatives for meat, dairy and agricultural products (CPA), with more than 20,000 associated families; 32 servicing cooperatives, with 11,174 direct associates; two regional cooperatives for trading; and two credit co-operatives, with 6,521 associates. There are 96 small and medium-sized agro-industries, which process fruits and vegetables, dairy, grains, coffee, meat and sweets, as well as arts and crafts. These MST economic enterprises generate employment, income and revenues which indirectly benefit 700 small municipalities in the Brazilian inlands.

This production is connected to education. Around 160,000 children attend elementary level classes at the 1800 public schools at camp grounds and settlements. The education sector also works with infant education (newborns to 6-year-olds), counting on 500 educators. The MST develops a literacy program with close to 30,000 adolescents and adults. Seven hundred and fifty active members of MST are studying in universities, of which 58 study medicine in Cuba.

The CIESPI team contacted one of MST's leaders in Rio de Janeiro to schedule the focus groups. They recommended that we visit one of MST's camp grounds in Rio. We tried to set up interviews at a camp in the Santa Cruz neighbourhood, two hours away from downtown Rio. This camp was created four years ago and the 72 families living there were waiting for the ownership of the lands they are holding to be legalised. One of the communication co-ordinators of that camp said that it would be interesting if our team visited another camp in the city of Mangaratiba, three hours away from downtown Rio. This camp was six months old and held 300 families.

We agreed to visit the first camp and to visit the one in Mangaratiba later. The focus groups were conducted inside the camps' tents. The children's group was formed by boys and girls aged 8/9 years of age. The adolescent group was formed by three boys – two 15-year-olds and one 17-year-old. According to one of the camp's culture co-ordinators, they did not know about our visit and, therefore, did not communicate it to the adolescents. He added that, since the camp is close to a big city, the adolescents usually do not remain there on weekends.

We expected to interview children and adolescents involved with political and social matters who might therefore have a clearer notion of citizenship. However, since the camp was settled recently, its members had not come through a process of 'awareness' – as it is called in the MST – and our expectations were not met. These families had left their former communities only six months ago and, thus, their culture was the same as that seen in other groups. Aside from this, it was a valuable experience for our team to conduct these interviews at the MST.

Key Findings

The children's and adolescents' perceptions on rights, responsibilities and citizenship were explored in three settings: home, school, community.

Rights

Respect from others seemed to lie at the heart of adolescents' conceptions about rights. They also talked about rights as things that are achieved through work, the amount of money earned, and fulfilment of their responsibilities. Our participants thought about rights as the freedom to make choices:

> *It means to be able do something, because you have rights. It means to be able to express yourself, to do something.* (15-year-old girl; Private School)

The adolescents complained about the lack of communication among family members, and with adults more generally. For instance, adolescents considered it important not to have restrictions concerning the time they got home. Beyond the level of family rules and expectations, adolescents felt that their opinions were generally not respected because, in most relationships between parents and their children, parental authority is unquestionable. They said it was difficult to be neither child nor adult. In one discussion in a Public School, the issue of the authority of parents and teachers was raised. The adolescents questioned the fact that these adults have more rights than them '*just because they are older, studied more or have more money.*' These comments revealed how these adolescents dealt with the authority of adults.

The idea of collective rights was frequently discussed by all the children, although they were not always clear about the difference between rights and responsibilities. The younger participants said the following:

> *To respect. Not to steal. To educate.* (7- and 8-year-old boys; Private School)

> *Children have the right to work. I work with my dad at the market.* (8-year-old boy; Public School)

> *It means the right to live a good life.* (8-year-old girl; Private School)

> *It means the right to have lunch and dinner.* (7-year-old girl; Public School)

It means the right to play and to eat well. (Group of street children and adolescents)

The older children spoke about the right to study in a good school, to receive proper nutrition – mainly at school – and to have efficient health services.

It means to have your own house. (Adolescents from the Landless Movement)

It means not to be treated with prejudice. (Mixed group of adolescents from 14 to 15 years of age; Public School.)

It means the right to learn, to get on a bus and go to school. (14-year-old girl; Public School)

It means the right to go to the bathroom. Some schools do not have a bathroom, because the people at school don't have anybody to clean it and so it stays closed. (Mixed group of adolescents, from 14 to 15 years of age; Public School)

It means the right to sleep. (Group of street children and adolescents)

In these utterances, adolescents showed that they were more likely to think that the state was responsible for the existing social structure and for supplying the needs of the population for education, health services, housing and transportation. Inequality and injustice were not connected to the individual, but rather to the government. Most participants thought that the state did not do what it should do.

Responsibilities

Responsibility was mainly perceived as being synonymous with obligation, but not necessarily as some kind of personal commitment. Responsibilities such as house chores fell into this category, and most participants agreed that doing homework was a responsibility.

My dad told me: 'The only responsibility you have is to study, leave the rest to me.' (14-year-old adolescent; Public School)

Public school students talked a lot about the necessity of being constantly alert about their personal belongings since stealing was a common occurrence. To have responsibilities meant to take care of personal belongings for most of the participants:

Not to lose my school material. (7-year-old boy; Public School)

To arrange one's own things. (14-year-old girl; Public School)

Most of the children also agreed that it was the responsibility of adults to provide for the family and to take care of the children. A minority of the children and adolescents understood responsibilities as a collective concept – that is, as something having to do with the well-being of everyone. For example:

To share things. (14-year-old girl; Public School)

Responsibility for the physical environment was linked most of the time to problems of pollution and garbage disposal, such as in the following comment:

If we pollute the sea and it rains a lot, this pollution clogs the gutters. If that happens, there can be a flood. (8-year-old boy; Private School)

Citizenship

The word 'citizenship' confused most children and adolescents. This was no surprise as it continues to perplex adults who have for generations been engaged in defining and re-defining its meaning. Some young people understood citizenship as a right, others as a responsibility, and others associated it with the city and the city government:

The citizen worries about the rights of all other citizens. (14-year-old adolescent; Private School)

In many cases, the definition of citizenship was linked to work.

To be a hard working person that respects others and is also respected. (8-year-old boy; Private School)

A citizen is someone who works. (14-year-old adolescent; Private School)

Slowly, throughout the focus group activities, groups began associating rights with responsibilities and participation, and came to the conclusion that citizenship is all of that.[15] But what does it mean to participate? Participation was mostly talked about at the level of the individual and in terms of enjoying some activity – for example, participation in community projects that gave children access to cultural, sports or leisure activities. There was a general sense that the children and adolescents felt that they did not know how to claim their rights or to demand that they be fulfilled. Some mentioned the right to vote as a responsibility of the citizen to choose a representative who will make the necessary changes in society. However, most children seemed sceptical and did not believe that politicians would be able to solve social problems.

Many children believed that nothing depended on them and that their participation was not important in the process of transforming reality. For instance, when they complained about the situation of public schools, we asked them what type of participation on their part could change this situation. They responded as follows:

> *I think that it is the government's obligation to bring things to us. They complain about the public school. It has been two months since they should have fixed that bathroom. When you try to turn on the sink, you can't, there's no toilet paper, no mirror.* (15-year-old adolescent; Public School)

When we asked the group about the participation of the student council[16] in demanding their rights, a response was:

> *Student Council. This is not the type of participation where we discuss issues in order to change things. It is too lazy here. I've never even seen most of the people of the student council. I'm only going to get to see one of them today because there's a meeting at the Regional Education Coordination (CRE). It's not the kind of participation with the objective of helping one another to make things better.* (14-year-old adolescent; Public School)

On the other hand, some children felt that they were participating actively through donation campaigns and/or sponsoring children or serving as surrogate families:

> *My mother ... works in a public hospital with children who have AIDS and I help her. I work with the children's families (...) there are always celebrations there, at Christmas, Easter and we always help. I sort of sponsor one of the boys and each month I give him something, like school material, pencils, a backpack, and toys for him to play with. It's not a responsibility, I'm not obligated to go to the hospital every month.* (15-year-old adolescent; Private School)

Key Distinctions between Contemporary and Imaginary Countries

The participants chose names for the imaginary countries which reflected their feelings that there was a need to change reality: *Country without Violence, Aremida Deluz, Solar Pole* and also *Country of Unity, Country of the Children, Brazil, Brazil II, Happiness* and *Home*. The names of these new countries reveal the hope of most children and adolescents to live in a welcoming, equal and just country. Even the group who gave their new nation the name of *Brazil* and *Brazil II* emphasised the changes that would be made in the imaginary country. In the process of creation, they raised issues related to events experienced in the daily lives of people that generated anxiety and insecurity, such as chronic urban violence. In addition, they expected that most of their imaginary countries would have good schools, abundant food, health and dignity for all.

One group created a country where only children could live. There would be no adults in the *Country of the Children*. Social rules would be enforced through the law. Justice would be the foundation of this country, so that everybody would live in harmony. Order would be maintained and punishments would include public humiliation, banishment, and death by electric chair. The children in this group drew prisons, fortresses and other ways to control criminality, which was their greatest concern.

Some of the other groups conceived of justice as something that had to do more with equal conditions of life, such as the groups that created the *Country without Violence*, the *Solar Pole* and *Aremida Deluz*. The name *Aremida Deluz* was created out of the letters of the words made by the group. In order to make the name selection process democratic, the children agreed that each one could pick one or two letters. Furthermore, they decided that these words meant '*a happy, fair country with high spirits.*'

The group that created the *Country of Unity* was very concerned about food and wanted to ensure that nobody went hungry. Their punishments would be varied, but they even admitted the use of dialogue to '*bring people back*' that '*didn't toe the line*', such as occurred with the *Solar Pole* and *Aremida Deluz* groups.

One of the groups mentioned sexual abuse by adults, especially in the case of elders and children. Some examples of sexual harassment were also brought up by several girls. That kind of behaviour would not be accepted in the new country.

At least two groups talked about housing issues. In the new countries of *Happiness* and *Home*, everybody would have the right to a house.

Rights vs Responsibilities

Most young people in the focus groups confused rights and responsibilities. For example, when asked about their rights at home and at school, it was common to hear some children and adolescents say that to do their homework was a right and not a responsibility. However, as groups reflected further on the matter, those who had made the mistake were corrected by their school mates throughout the focus group. For example, when asked which rights the children had at school, one girl answered:

> *To do your homework.* (8-year-old girl; Public School)

In response, another girl said:

> *Teacher, they're talking about responsibilities.* (8-year-old girl; Public School)

> *Responsibilities are what we are obliged to do and rights are a sort of free time. The rights are a reward for the duties.* (8-year-old girl; Private School)

Yet, other examples illustrate the confusion between rights and responsibilities such as the answer:

The right to respect one's elders. (Group of street children and adolescents)

Participants also distinguished between the rights and responsibilities of children and adults:

Ours is to study and play and theirs is to work. (8-year-old boy; Private School)

While we're at school, they are working hard to give us everything we want. (8-year-old boy; Private School)

Talking about Differences

We raised a few issues with the children and adolescents about differences and similarities between gender, age and social classes. In terms of recognition of responsibilities, we found significant differences between boys and girls. For example, most boys stated that domestic chores were exclusively girls' responsibility. When we asked what the boys' responsibilities at home were, some said they fed the pets and took out the trash, but few admitted to washing dishes, sweeping the floor or cooking, even when for oneself:

Boys don't have to wash the dishes. Women do, right? (14-year-old boy; Public School)

That comes from long ago: women work at home and the men go out to work. (15-year-old boy; Public School)

Many boys also considered that preventing pregnancy was a responsibility of the girls. Some even said that they wouldn't take responsibility for a child they didn't desire. When asked about their role in conception, their responses were ironic: they joked around and said that the girls should worry about it. The risk of sexually transmitted diseases was raised alongside the fact that they said they did not use contraceptives. The boys responded with evasive answers, such as '*man, what kind of woman is that?*', where they once more exempted themselves from the responsibility. The girls also gave their opinions on the use of condoms:

There are boys that, when they are going to have sex, say: 'You don't need this. It's not good, it hurts.' They have the responsibility of wearing them. (15-year-old girl; Public School)

Men don't want the responsibility. (15-year-old girl; Public School)

Girls were absolutely opposed to abortion, while boys saw it as a simple solution to an undesired pregnancy:

I think that women should have abortions when they can't support their children after they are born. (14-year-old adolescent; Public School)

> *There are lots of ways to avoid having children. The health center gives us birth control pills.* (14-year-old adolescent; Public School)

Marginalisation based on Social Class and Race

Prejudice was often mentioned in the focus groups but more so in public schools. One of the most frequently addressed issues, both in public and private schools, was prejudice against lower social classes. Public school students narrated examples of daily occurrences that they attributed to their social condition. The municipal government, for example, offered free urban transportation for public school students. However, this depended on the good will of the bus driver – the driver would not always stop at the bus stop and when he did, he often limited the number of children that could get on the bus. The government had also recently adopted a card system that registered students and gave them the right to free urban transportation by bus to school. However, a time restriction was placed on use of the card so that those students needing to take more than one bus to reach their destination had to wait 30 minutes between their first bus and the next one before the card could be used again. Those students depending on two buses to get to school therefore had to leave home much earlier to take account of the 30 minutes waiting time between buses:

> *I'm tired of this bus card. You can only use it every half hour. I take the bus from my house to somewhere nearby, ten minutes away. After I get there, I have to wait another 30 minutes before I can get another bus. Then they tell you to get off the bus.* (14-year-old boy; Public School)

Others complained about benefits offered by the municipal government such as the school uniform. The T-shirt adopted by state schools was orange with the municipal government symbol. According to the students, this was a cause for embarrassment since the uniform was similar to the city cleaning crew uniform. Some adolescents described situations in which they were called '*garbage man*' by private school students.

Adolescents also reported that they were discriminated against based on their appearance. Students who lived in low-income communities and studied in public schools in the southern zone of the city were, for the most part, from poor families where parents relied on education as a hope for a better life for their children. Most of these children and adolescents had only one pair of pants that they wore all week long. Most could not buy fashion accessories, such as backpacks and tennis shoes, which are common among better-off young people. Many poorer students described embarrassing daily situations. These included people grabbing onto their belongings for fear of being robbed or even speeding up or running away with distrustful looks when others came close:

> *Some people are prejudiced ... like on the street, if we go to a mall, we have a way of dressing and people notice your sneakers and say 'Look, they're from the favela.'* (Group of street children and adolescents)

To walk into the mall wearing the uniform is like you're naked. They look at you as if you've just got out of jail. (Mixed group of 14 and 15-year-old adolescents; Public School)

There's some prejudice. They think you don't have rights just because you live in a less privileged place. It's too much inequality. (Mixed group of 14 and 15-year-old adolescents; Public School)

However, the children and adolescents who experienced discrimination actually behaved in the same way as these other children by making condescending comments towards people with 'bad hair', those in a worse financial situation than themselves, or children who lived in the streets. The references to 'bad hair' illustrated the complicated linkages between discrimination based on class and race, since the references to hair type are associated with race. 'Bad hair' is that attributed to people of African descent, which is hard to comb, or even frizzed or curly hair or thicker hair. 'Good hair', as it is popularly classified, is that which is either straight or wavy and easy to comb. 'Good hair' is much more desirable and can increase the person's self-esteem.

In the private schools, some participants felt that those people who do not work, have a home or earn an income cannot be considered citizens. When we asked what the difference was between themselves and street children (since they mentioned that the difference existed), they promptly answered:

We study and they beg on the streets. (8-year-old boy; Private school)

We have family and they don't. (7-year-old boy; Private school)

They may have families but ... (8-year-old boy; Private school)

We have good manners and the street kids don't. Our parents pass onto us what they learn in church, in classes and from their parents. This is passed down through generations. They don't do that. (8-year-old boy; Private school)

When asked the reason for this difference, they also had a ready answer:

Well, because we live in a house and our parents work, when we want something and ask them for it, they buy it. These people don't even have a house and live on the streets. We have everything they don't have. (8-year-old boy; Private school)

The group of adolescents from the Landless Movement also told of the discrimination and prejudice they suffer away from their camp sites. They said that because they did not have a house, they were constantly teased by their classmates at their schools or on the streets. They thought that most people do not believe that claiming land is a right and that those members of the Landless Movement take advantage of that situation:

You are only in the movement to eat and sleep. (Group of adolescent boys from the Landless Movement).

You don't have a home, you have nothing. (Group of adolescent boys from the Landless Movement)

Rural/Urban

There were also some interesting differences in how the urban children understood the word 'community'. Some children and adolescents associated the word 'neighbourhood' with physical proximity and people living close by who can do some favour or lend something:

It is a large street where people live together. (8-year-old girl; Private School)

However, most children were unable to differentiate between community and neighbourhood. Many associate community with *favelas*:

I know. It's a favela. *Like Rocinha. A certain gangster rules Rocinha. He's the owner of the community. He owns Rocinha.* (9-year-old boy; Private School)

The favelas *are where there is drug dealing.* (Adolescent; Public School)

In the city of Rio de Janeiro, the idea of community took on meanings that were coloured by class identity. A Public School adolescent who lived in Rocinha said:

I'm not ashamed of saying where I live, but I'm also not proud. I prefer to believe that one day I'll get out of there.

The manner in which the media portrayed the *favelas* also came up with Public School adolescents:

Nobody sees that in the favelas *there are people trying to help, by doing social projects. Everyone only sees the negative side: robbery, death, kidnapping. That's what gives the* favela *that image of a place where children grow up to be gangsters. That's because the newspaper only shows these things and doesn't show places that help children, the social center. All you see is robbery and death. If you look at the front page of the newspaper, you'll only see the negative side of the* favelas.

In a very different way, the description of 'community' by a group of adolescents from the Landless Movement also had to do with identity:

Community is a gathering of many people, united in the struggle for one common goal. Such as the Landless Movement.

Conclusion

The idea of basic human rights and freedoms does not rest on the (innate or acquired) abilities of an individual – adult or child. Nor does the entitlement to human rights and freedoms presuppose any particular knowledge or sense of oneself as a right-holding being. Universal human rights are based on respect for the innate dignity and worth of each person, both in his or her own right and as a member of communities, groups and society as a whole. The notion of universal rights means precisely that there are no preconditions attached to the fulfilment of basic rights. However, governmental obligations corresponding to economic and social rights are defined in terms of progressive realisations that the ability of states to meet their obligations depends on their particular stage of development, particularly financial constraints. Accordingly, universal human rights are few and the corresponding governmental obligations are set at the minimum level feasible in all corners of the world (Tomasevski, 2003). In this concluding section of our chapter, we provide some specific and general implications for researchers, policy makers, child activists and children's activists.

The UNCRC emphasises that children must both be seen as well as heard. From our research, a multi-dimensional picture emerges of how Brazilian school children think of themselves as right-holding beings. To recap briefly, the participants had some sense of both individual and collective human rights. They were aware of the different forms of rights – social, economic and political – and were able to provide multiple instances of violations of these rights through their personal experiences of hunger, poverty, and discrimination. The powerful and poignant discussion around how our participants would create imaginary countries underlines the degree to which children are aware of, and troubled by, inequality, injustice and violence in their homes and communities. They held the state directly responsible for the violation of many of these rights. It was more difficult for our participants to articulate the linkages between rights and responsibilities as well as the linkages between the ideas of community, collective rights and citizenship.

Adult society was repeatedly held up as the frame of reference through which our participants articulated their understandings of rights. For instance, the older participants in our study expressed a desire to be recognised as beings with rights who were entitled to be given more freedom and responsibility for making their own choices. Unfortunately, our participants who experienced class- and race-based discrimination also experienced adults as the primary violators of their rights. Adults are the primary source of information and learning about rights and it was interesting to see that our participants were able to list their responsibilities and duties much more easily than their rights.

The ideal and the implementation of children's rights, and particularly the right to participation, are contested and complex. This complexity poses some challenges for critical researchers and advocates for children's rights. There is clearly a need for more research that foregrounds the perceptions and voices of children – the intended beneficiaries of progressive legislation such as the *Statute on the Child and Adolescent* 1990. When the children speak and we listen, it becomes clear that change has been slow to happen. There is a yawning gap between well-intended laws and policies and substantive opportunities for children and adolescents to express themselves and participate actively in day-to-day community life. We have learnt that children feel unheard and unacknowledged as holders of rights in both their families and schools. We also heard a great deal of confusion and misinformation about what is meant by the notion of children's rights and participation.

What then should be the role and responsibility of the researcher? First and foremost, children and adolescents need to be actively involved in the research project. Otherwise the research becomes yet another activity in which children's participation is circumscribed and exploited by the agenda of researchers. We chose to collect data through dialogue- and discussion-based activities in which the children and adolescents were able to share their own ideas and listen to the ideas of their peers. In this sense, there was an active component of participation by the children in our research. A limitation of our study was that we did not take any of their possible agendas into consideration when planning the project or analysing and presenting the data. We believe that the children's knowledge about their rights and abilities expanded through their participation in these discussions, but a great deal of work remains to be done in rights education.

Seconds, along with creating opportunities for individual growth and transformation, the research project must contribute to the creation and expansion of cultures of rights in all the spheres of children's daily lives. As advocates of children's rights, we must continually work to find research methods that actively contribute to the process of individual and institutional transformation. Whilst outside the scope of our preliminary research project, another essential component of a transformational research project would ideally be dialogue with the young participants and the participation of teachers and families.

Finally, a culture of rights cannot exist in a culture of inequality. To do research on children's rights, therefore, requires close attention to the dynamics of race, class, gender and sexual orientation throughout the research process. In our study, these dynamics influenced the forms of participation that we facilitated through our research, as well as the meanings of rights and responsibilities that emerged from the children and adolescents.

Brazilian activists and researchers have been central players in the global movement to place children's rights at the centre of social policy. Indeed, we have enough examples of activism in schools and communities from all around the world to demonstrate that adolescents and children are eager and willing to be full and active members of society. It is our hope that the findings of our preliminary research will contribute to more nuanced theorising and policy-making about the rights and abilities of children and youth.

5
New Zealand

Nicola Taylor, Anne B. Smith and Megan Gollop[1]
Children's Issues Centre, University of Otago, New Zealand

Introduction

This chapter explores how New Zealand children and young people understand the concept of citizenship. If children are to become full members and citizens in a democratic society, as is advocated by many (James & Prout, 1997; Mayall, 2002; Pufall & Unsworth, 2004), their participation needs to be framed by an understanding of the meaning of citizenship. Whether they feel they belong in society is likely to influence whether they are confident and motivated enough to believe that they can bring about change. A previous international survey (Torney-Purta, Lehmann, Oswald & Schultz, 2001) suggests that 14-year-olds in most countries have an understanding of fundamental democratic institutions and values, but frequently this understanding is superficial. Little is known about how New Zealand children understand citizenship, so this study explores their perspectives in order to help inform future efforts to enhance their citizenship. While our research is part of a wider international project on children's perspectives on citizenship (Smith, 2005), this chapter focuses on the New Zealand data.

Children and Citizenship

Children's understanding of, and participation in, civil society benefits them directly, and has long-term significance for society because it encourages the development of knowledge, skills, values, and attitudes that are fundamental in sustaining a democracy. If children develop a belief in themselves as social actors who have some control over their own lives, then they are less likely to depend on others for coping with problems (Flekkoy & Kaufman, 1997; Kaufman & Rizzini, 2002; Limber & Kaufman, 2002; Melton, 1998, 2002; Smith, Nairn, Sligo, Gaffney & McCormack, 2003; Rizzini & Thapliyal, 2005). Encouraging children to express their opinions and feelings about citizenship (and other issues) also signals respect for children as human beings (Grover, 2004; Morrow, 1999; Weithorn, 1998). Through participation as citizens, children learn ideas and values that are not easily understood if they are merely passive learners. Active participation can give children valuable experience in making difficult decisions, promote a sense of mastery and control, support a developing sense of altruism, and set in motion a lifetime pattern of engagement in civic activity (Alderson, 2000; Flekkoy & Kaufman, 1997; Fletcher, Elder & Mekos, 2000; Nairn, 2000; Smith et al., 2003; Youniss, McLellan & Yates, 1997). Participation by children and youth in school and community activities is also predictive of positive academic attitudes and outcomes (Eccles & Barber, 1999; Lamborn, Brown, Mounts & Steinberg, 1992).

Although citizenship has sometimes been criticised as an individualistic concept, this has been challenged on the grounds that citizenship is learned and practised in the contexts of family, school and community social participation. Without the opportunity for meaningful participation in their everyday lives, children are unlikely to have a good understanding of citizenship concepts. Joseph's (2005) study of Lebanese children showed that they learned about rights and responsibilities through webs of community and family relationships. 'To have rights, the children knew that they had to know who had the resources, skills, and services to offer them rights' (Joseph, 2005, p. 11). Joseph found that children's rights and responsibilities were 'delicately negotiated possibilities which had to be constantly worked through known relationships' (Joseph, 2005, p. 2). It is likely to be through social relationships and processes in society that children come to understand citizenship:

> *A social model of citizenship emphasizes the ways in which people are connected to each other, rather than being viewed as acting as individualized, autonomous, rational beings separate from each other. The idea that citizenship is conferred upon people according to a system of 'rights' and 'obligations' should by its very nature assume that people are connected to others in profound ways.* (Cockburn, 1998, p. 100)

Having children experience responsive social relationships and interactions is for promoting their understanding of citizenship (Smith, 2002). Joint involvement with others in challenging activities, feeling comfortable, accepted and tuned in to the other participants in a group (and group members being sensitive to you) are factors likely to contribute to effective participation. Adult support can capture the young person's interest, help focus him/her on the goal, draw attention to critical features of the task, and reduce the complexity of the task. But there has to be social engagement before children can learn and gradually take on more responsibility. As children gain experience and their skills and competence grow, they become more able to initiate and share responsibility.

Cultural and Historical Context

Māori people migrated to New Zealand, a small South Pacific nation, several hundred years ago, but it was the British colonisation of New Zealand in the 1800s that diversified the population and dramatically changed the political, economic and social landscape. The Treaty of Waitangi, signed between Māori and Queen Victoria in 1840, ceded the right to govern New Zealand to the

British, but was intended also to protect Māori values and treasures (including land, fisheries and collective family values). Subsequent diseases, wars and land confiscations, together with urbanisation and the imposition of mainstream education and English-language requirements, eroded the economic and social well-being of Māori family life (Cram & Pitama, 1998). However, a recent renaissance in Māoridom, and respect for the Treaty as the nation's founding document, has revived the language and enabled significant financial settlements to be paid to tribes for the past grievances they suffered as a result of their colonisation experience.

New Zealand has a total population of 4.25 million people, of whom a quarter are children under the age of 15 years. The majority of the population is of European ethnicity (80 per cent), followed by our indigenous people, Māori (14.7 per cent), Asian people (6.6 per cent), Pacific peoples from Tonga, Samoa, Fiji, Niue, Cook Islands (6.5 per cent), and other (0.7 per cent) (Ministry of Social Development, 2004). Children are more ethnically diverse than adults, with 18 per cent of children identifying with more than one ethnic group, compared with 6 per cent of adults (Statistics NZ, 2001).

New Zealand's most common family type is a couple with children (42 per cent), compared with couple-only families (39 per cent) and one-parent with children families (19 per cent) (Statistics NZ, 2002). Of those households with children, there is an average of 1.9 children per household (Ministry of Social Development, 2004). Sole parents, Māori and Pacific families have been particularly adversely affected by the neo-liberal economic reforms of the 1980s and the 1991 budget cuts (Blaiklock, Kiro, Belgrave, Low, Davenport & Hassall, 2002; Child Poverty Action Group, 2003; UNICEF, 2005). While the proportion of families living in poverty has recently decreased, it is low-income and beneficiary (especially sole-parent) families with children who remain concentrated below the poverty threshold and who have poorer health and education outcomes (Ministry of Social Development, 2004). Income inequality has increased dramatically in New Zealand, with the gap between high- and low-income (80th to 20th percentile) households widening by 17 per cent between 1982 and 1998 (Law Commission, 2002). It is households with children that are skewed towards the lower echelons of income distribution (Ministry of Social Development, 2004), with around 29 per cent of our children currently living in poverty (UNICEF, 2005).

New Zealand takes children's rights seriously and is committed to improving the well-being of its young citizens. A Children's Commissioner was appointed in 1989 and the New Zealand Government ratified the UNCRC in 1993. The *Agenda for Children* (Ministry of Social Development, 2002) and the Youth Development Strategy (Ministry of Youth Affairs, 2002) both drive policy development and service delivery for children and young people, and emphasise their right to participate and have a say in family, institutional and community settings where they will be affected by the decisions made. The Children's Issues Centre, established in 1995, has played a significant role in research, education and advocacy, and been part of an active network of child advocates within New Zealand.

Research Methodology

Our qualitative research study involved the use of focus groups to explore children's understanding of rights, responsibilities and citizenship. Focus groups were chosen as an effective means of accessing the subjective experience of children, giving them the opportunity to be valued as experts while working collaboratively with their peers and a facilitator to develop and articulate their thoughts (Gibbs, 1997).

Participants (Sample)

Children: Participants were recruited through primary and secondary schools known to our research centre or our networks. All schools barring two readily agreed to participate when invited, but one later withdrew citing insufficient interest by its male students. The schools that did participate identified students who fitted our criteria and sent home an envelope containing a parent information sheet, parent consent form, and parent questionnaire. Each school took responsibility for collecting the signed parent consent forms and arranging a convenient time for the researchers to meet with the children.

Sixty-six children and young people from eight schools participated in the focus group discussions (see Table One). Thirty-two were aged 8/9 years (12 girls and 20 boys), and 34 were aged 14/15 years (23 girls and 11 boys). Thirty-four children were from low socio-economic (SES) schools, and 32 from high SES schools. Twenty-seven children were located in rural/provincial areas in the North and South Islands of New Zealand, and 39 in the cities of Auckland (New Zealand's largest city), Hamilton and Dunedin.

Table One: New Zealand child participants in the citizenship study focus groups

SCHOOL 8/9 Years	Boys	Girls	Total
Primary School A: Low SES, urban, North Island	4	8	12
Primary School B: Low SES, urban, South Island	7	-	7
Primary School C: High SES, rural, North Island	9	-	9
Primary School D: High SES, rural, South Island	-	4	4
14/15 Years			
High School E: Low SES, urban, North Island	-	12	12
High School F: Low SES, rural, South Island	3	-	3
High School G: High SES, urban, North Island	8	-	8
High School H: High SES, rural, South Island	-	11	11
TOTAL	**31 boys**	**35 girls**	**66 students**

Teachers/Parents: Questionnaires were distributed to ten teachers in each school, and to one parent of each child in the study. These were returned direct to the Children's Issues Centre via stamped self-addressed envelopes which we provided. Completed questionnaires were received from 31 teachers and 40 parents/caregivers.

Procedure

The focus groups were held in schools between September and November 2004 and generally were of one hour's duration, although some were around 45 minutes long. While we asked for ten children to be available for each focus group, this was not always achieved due to absences, small class sizes, or lack of sufficient numbers of willing students.

Each focus group began with an explanation about the study, completion of the student consent forms, and a warm-up exercise asking each child to give their name and to say where they were born. This then led into a discussion about citizenship, as some children (or their parents) were born overseas. Discussion on issues such as what it means to be a citizen of New Zealand, how someone becomes a citizen, and how other people can tell if a person is a citizen, developed easily out of this warm-up exercise.

The students were then split into groups of three to four students initially to discuss the current state of their rights and responsibilities, and then undertake an imaginary country exercise. We adapted an interview schedule that had been drawn up by the Childwatch International Citizenship Research Network; this covered the topics in an interactive format to retain the children's interest and fit within the time that each school had made available for the focus group. Each small group was given two large sheets of paper with pre-printed grids – one asking about their perceptions of the current situation in New Zealand, and the other asking them to think about what their life could be like in an imaginary country. Prompts in the various headings on each sheet helped the students to conceptualise what was meant by 'citizenship', 'rights' and 'responsibilities'. The researchers also engaged in verbal prompting and discussion with the small groups as they worked on completing the sheets. Each focus group was conducted by two researchers who shared the facilitation and note-taking roles. As the data was recorded on the sheets by the children, we did not need to audiotape the sessions.

Key Findings

Rights

Children in the focus groups at both age levels did not have any difficulty in finding a meaning for the concept of 'rights'. The children's written responses were analysed according to whether they fell into one of the three groups of rights identified by Lansdown (1994) in the UNCRC – Participation rights, Provision rights, and Protection rights. Table Two gives examples of qualitative responses for each category of right.

Table Two: Examples of rights identified by children

PARTICIPATION RIGHTS	PROVISION RIGHTS	PROTECTION RIGHTS
Rights at Home		
• to have a say • to get to decide sometimes • the chance to be in charge • more independence • to do what you want with your own body – looks, hair, body piercing	<u>Physical</u> • somewhere to live • be clean and warm • own bedroom • clothes <u>Recreational</u> • to watch television • to have a social life <u>Economic</u> • access to money • an allowance for chores • to earn own money <u>Care</u> • love you • are nice to you • kind babysitters	• to feel safe at home • not to be abused • not to be hit
Rights at School		
• to be respected by others • to participate in decision-making • to express our opinion, share our ideas • to have our say via the school council, house leaders or the Board of Trustees • choice of subjects	<u>Education</u> • to learn • to go to school • good teachers <u>Health</u> • more choices at the canteen to be able to eat healthily • hygienic facilities <u>Recreational</u> • to play • to have fun • to go on a school camp • to play sport	• feeling safe • not being bullied or teased • to have bullies taken seriously
Rights in the Community		
• to have a say in the decisions made • speaking up • to be an individual • to be treated with respect in shops • the right to move around freely • to go places by yourself • to have your own time	<u>Recreational</u> • a safe place to hang out • some place to go and enjoy ourselves • access to sports grounds <u>Economic</u> • to have money for our activities • access to a job <u>Health</u> • to receive medical treatment/ care	• to feel safe to walk down the street • to feel protected • to have bullies taken seriously • non-discrimination • not having bad neighbours • to stop people drinking and smoking

Participation rights at home, school and community focused on such issues as being listened to, respected, having choices, being able to express opinions, being involved in decisions, and being treated fairly. Only one child expressed the wish for participation through formal representation in the school context – '*to have our say via the school council, house leaders or [school] Board of Trustees*'. Being allowed to choose subjects and being acknowledged by teachers was also mentioned at school, but other participation rights identified were similar to those in the community and home. Unrestricted movement, free time, access to local space, and respect from people in shops, were rights mentioned specifically in relation to participation in the community.

Children identified a variety of *provision rights* in their different contexts (see Table Two). At home the most common of these was physical provisions associated with family life (a home, a bedroom, personal space, clothes, a bathroom). Many children also wanted economic resources – for example, in the form of pocket money – recreational resources such as access to friends, and a few children mentioned someone to love them and be kind to them.

Protection rights were much less frequently mentioned, but children did say they wanted to feel safe at home, at school and in the community. They did not want to be abused or hit, and they wanted bullying to be taken seriously as an issue.

Figure One gives an overview of the numbers of responses in each category of rights, for each context. In every context, participation rights were more likely than provision or protection rights to be given as examples in focus group discussions. The total number of responses for participation rights was highest in the school context, closely followed by the home context. Provision rights were the second most important at home and school. Interestingly, protection rights were rarely recorded in all three contexts, though in the community context protection rights were mentioned very slightly more often than provision rights.

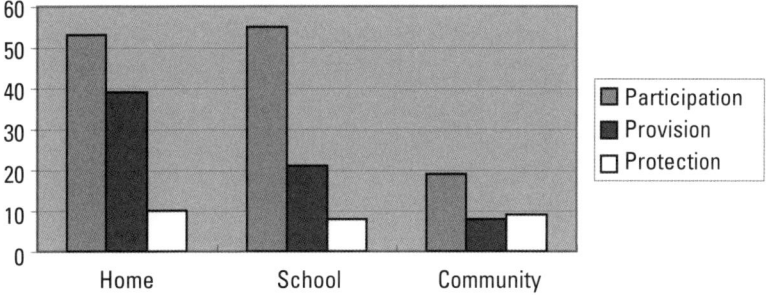

Figure One: Number of children's responses relating to participation, provision and protection rights in each context

Responsibilities

Table Three gives examples of four categories of responsibilities identified by the children:

Table Three: Examples of responsibilities identified by children

OBEY THE RULES	LOOK AFTER ENVIRONMENT	HELP/CARE FOR OTHERS	PARTICIPATION
Responsibilities at Home			
• tell the truth when you've done wrong • treat others fairly and with respect • not be naughty • don't be mean to pets	• doing chores • jobs around the house • sweeping the floor	• care for others and be nice • help others when hurt • if a new person comes to stay, make them welcome	• participating in family activities like birthday parties
Responsibilities at School			
• listen to teachers • don't be mean and push in line • follow the right process to change things • obey fair rules	• emptying the rubbish bin • respecting school property • keeping the school tidy • not littering	• be polite • get along with others • respecting other people, especially teachers and classmates	• having a say • to learn • to do my schoolwork • participate in school activities
Responsibilities in the Community			
• don't smoke • stay away from construction sites • don't take pills off strangers cos they might be drugs • don't damage public property or other people's things	• keep the community clean and tidy • don't litter • pick up rubbish • recycle	• help the blind • give to the poor • collect for charities • contribute to school fair • help elderly people across the road	• take part in the 40 hour famine [fundraising for World Vision] • do community service • support community projects and fundraising

Obeying the rules by behaving well and <u>not</u> doing things you are not allowed to do, and doing things you <u>should</u> do, was one category of responsibilities identified by the children. At home this was mostly about truthfulness, fairness, and not treating others unkindly. At school it included not pushing in line or bullying others. In the community, obeying the rules included avoiding harmful substances (cigarettes, alcohol), being honest (paying when you buy things), and not damaging property.

The second category related to *looking after the environment*. At home this usually involved domestic chores like cleaning, doing the dishes, or outdoor jobs (mowing the lawn or doing farm work). At school, looking after the environment involved keeping the school and its grounds clean and tidy. Similarly, in the community the second category was about not harming the environment (through graffiti or by dropping rubbish) and helping to clean up.

The third category of responsibilities was *helping/caring for others*, and involved relationships with, and support for, other people (who varied according to context). At home, the people included parents, siblings, other relatives and visitors; at school, they were peers and teachers; while in the community they tended to be other people at risk of harm or who were vulnerable (the elderly, the blind, the poor).

The fourth category we have identified as *participation*. This involves children's participation in family activities at home, learning and recreational activities at school, and community service in the local community.

Figure Two shows the number of responses in different categories for each context. At home it was *helping/caring for others* which was the most frequently mentioned responsibility, followed by *participation*, which included being involved in family activities. In the community, *helping/caring for others* and *participation* were also important, but it was *looking after the environment* that was the most commonly mentioned responsibility. *Obeying rules* was the least mentioned at home, and the second least mentioned at school and in the community. *Looking after the environment* was infrequently mentioned in the school context.

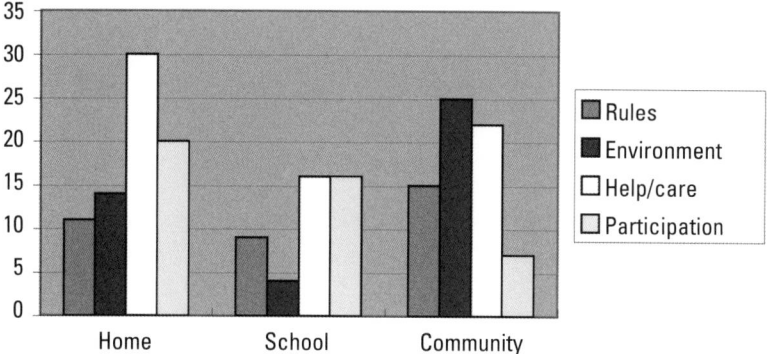

Figure Two: Number of children's responses relating to types of responsibilities in each context

Table Four: Children's meanings of citizenship

RESIDENCE	FAMILY Birth/Marriage/Parents	ACTIVITIES Working/Voting
• living in a certain place • to be a citizen by being there for a very long time, around 40 years • you would have to live there for about 25 years before you can be a citizen • had been in the country a while	• marry someone • you can become a citizen of another country if you were born there • where you were born (a legal citizen) • if your parents are citizens	• getting a job, especially in a trade or profession that the country needs or wants • had a job • were working somewhere • you are a citizen if you can vote • someone who has something to say or cares about where you live

Citizenship

The understandings that children had about what defined citizenship were quite varied, with length of residence, family bonds of birth, marriage or parenthood, and participation in the privileges of citizenship such as working and voting being among the most common meanings identified. Examples are to be found in Table Four.

Several children mentioned that a person could be a New Zealand citizen yet still retain links with other nationalities. Reflecting New Zealand's colonial heritage and multiculturalism, the children most commonly related to Pacific (Samoa, Tonga, Cook Islands, Fiji, India) and European nations (England, Ireland, Scotland, Wales). Several children showed their awareness that they were descended from people who had been citizens of other nations.

A common response when asked how one could tell if someone was a New Zealand citizen was by physical characteristics such as accent, skin colour, '*blood*', or appearance ('*looks which are different in different countries*'). However, some older girls specifically said that '*ethnicity and looks can't be used to tell if someone is a citizen*' because while you might sometimes be able to distinguish a tourist '*you can't tell if someone who is Japanese or Chinese in New Zealand is a citizen or a tourist, although if they are a citizen they should be able to talk English fluently*'.

A few young people defined citizenship as associated with actions and affiliations: '*by how they act*', '*kiwi ingenuity*', '*if they like farming*', '*if they like Watties [tomato] sauce*', '*if they support the All Blacks, Vodaphone Warriors and the Highlanders* [national sports teams]' and '*their beliefs*'. Two girls' focus groups commented that '*you can't tell if someone is a citizen or not*' or '*it can be hard to tell*'. Sometimes you had to wait for the person '*to tell us*'.

Only one group of older girls began to get close to a more abstract and less pragmatic and legalistic meaning of citizenship. One girl said that citizenship gave people legal rights such as being permitted to engage in paid employment, and provided as an example that Asian international students at her school were not allowed to get a job. Others in the group felt that everyone should have the same citizenship rights (which they identified as human rights), involving more than just legal citizenship. This group also reflected on citizenship at home. Some girls thought citizenship did not apply to membership of a family at home, but others thought that home contexts involved a different kind of citizenship and that you did have rights at home. This group talked about citizenship as being connected to acting responsibly, being independent and being able to be trusted.

Who helps children to become good citizens?

Unsurprisingly, the majority of people whom children thought could help them become good citizens in home settings were parents (n=25) and other family (siblings, uncles, aunts, grandparents, cousins) (n=20), with friends being mentioned only twice. One focus group thought: *'People who are nice must have good parents.'* In contrast, at school, friends or other children were the most frequently mentioned (n=17), followed by teachers (n=16), though several children said that teachers could also be a barrier to their citizenship. A much wider array of people were mentioned as helping children to be good citizens in community settings. Interestingly, the most frequently mentioned were government officials (national and local) (n=10) followed by the police (n=9), and neighbours (n=6). One focus group thought that *'the government helps through providing money for people and social assistance'* and another group thought they provided *'help with jobs and money'*. Other people such as nurses, doctors, firemen, teachers and youth workers were mentioned by a small number of children.

Distinctions between contemporary and imaginary countries

The second part of each focus group in all eight schools explored children and young people's perceptions of the rights they could enjoy and the responsibilities they could incur as citizens of an imaginary country. They all enjoyed the experience of thinking about a completely new country and had no difficulty expressing their views and comparing these with their current lives in New Zealand.

Only one group gave consideration to how the new country should be organised through laws, decision-making processes, economy and land ownership:

> *The amount of land should be divided up equally. Everyone would have their own piece of land and there would be something like a draw to decide which bits of land people got. They would need some way to decide that, that was fair, like who got to live by the sea. ... People wouldn't work for money, but would work from need – could have a different economy where people traded and used a barter system ... We could invite other races in. Could sell off land. ... All crime should be forgiven within 24 hours, as forgiveness*

would lead to no wars. ... Need some kind of democracy and communication between old and young people. ... You would need laws, but one law for all people – you wouldn't have different laws for different people. ... The new country should have systems in place which allowed for conflict and debate, as healthy debate allowed some things to move forward. (14/15-year-old girls' Focus Group)

Citizenship rights: The children and young people identified several key rights they thought they should be entitled to in the imaginary country:

Respect and participation was raised by just under half of the students. The 14/15-year-olds emphasised the right to '*have a say*', '*to be given opportunities to discuss issues*', '*to be respected like an adult*', '*to be listened to*', '*to have a youth representative on the local council*', '*to be independent when you want and support yourself*' and to have the right '*to make your own decisions without parental help*'. One group of 14/15-year-old girls particularly wanted young people '*to be involved and consulted about strategic planning*' as plans made now affect them in the future. The 8/9-year-olds also wanted '*to have a say*' and '*a way to get their ideas to the government*'. They suggested '*having children in charge for one day a month*' and having '*children rule adults*'. The right to vote at an earlier age was raised by nine students, only one of whom was in the younger 8/9-year-old age group – '*each house should get a voting paper and children get to vote*', '*high school students especially should vote*'.

Safety/protection was also commonly identified (by about one in four students) as a key right, such as the need for the citizens in the new country '*to feel safer*', have '*no violence*', '*no hitting of kids*', '*no bullying anywhere especially by parents*', '*no picking on kids*', and '*no-one being mean*'. They wanted the right to protection and '*security*', '*not to be killed*', '*friends who don't hurt you or other people's feelings*', '*people to be nice to you*', and '*to feel safe in public places*'. One group of 8/9-year-old boys suggested '*destroying all modern weapons*'. Laws and Police were also needed '*so you can't just go out and use weapons*'.

Adopting a healthy lifestyle in the imaginary country was thought to be important by both older and younger students: '*keep healthy*', '*eat low fat food*' and '*have food and drink available when you need it*'. Some wanted the right to '*free pizza*', '*to eat our own food/diets*', and to '*choose what we eat and when we eat*'. The 8/9-year-olds wanted there to be '*no smoking/drinking*', but the 14/15-year-old girls thought the legal age for these, and the driving age and the age of consent for sex, should be lowered. Some suggested '*banning drugs*', while others wanted to '*legalise marijuana for medical reasons*'. Some of the younger children wanted to get rid of '*headlice and bugs*' and to '*not have to pay for dental appointments*'. Having a '*nice home*' or '*good house*' and a '*garden*' were thought important by the boys.

Access to leisure/recreation/sports were rights desired in the imaginary country. The younger children wanted the right to play. This included sports, games, their Playstation, and to play whatever they wanted to play. They did not want to be excluded by people. The 14/15-year-olds focused more on their entertainment needs – '*have more parties*', '*more things to do*', '*free entertainment for young people*', '*fun activities in the community*' and '*more public parks.*' They also emphasised the right to get involved in sports and to set up their own teams and tournaments.

Access to education was a right most children wanted in their imaginary country – although some 8/9-year-old boys suggested '*no schools ever again!*' Several other children thought that they should be able to go to school everyday and emphasised their right '*to learn*'. School '*should be an enjoyable place so learning can become an easier activity.*' The 14/15-year-olds raised school issues a lot and were particularly concerned about their right to exercise more choice about uniforms, subjects and the length of time they had to remain at school – '*loosen the school rules on hair and clothing*', '*allow a choice of clothes to wear to school*', '*no school uniforms*', '*allow a choice of subjects especially when you know what you want to do for a career*', '*the right to decide the length of years we have to spend at school*'. The older students also emphasised having '*the right to decide what the school does or how it is run*', wanted to have younger teachers and to have a say about which teachers were employed. Some also wanted their school canteens to sell healthier food.

Access to economic resources was important for many children in the imaginary country. The 8/9-year-old children were keen to receive free or discounted goods, more pocket money and the right to spend this as they chose – '*a free $100 voucher to go to any shopping store*', '*low prices on everything*', '*get more pocket money*', '*be able to spend your money on things you like*', and '*kids can go out and buy stuff*'. The 14/15-year-olds suggested being able to work at a younger age (e.g. 14 years). One group of 14/15-year-old girls wanted to get '*a weekly allowance from the government*', and a group of the older boys thought they should be able to '*earn money at school*'.

Other rights mentioned including the right '*to have privacy*', to '*stay up late*', '*to live forever*', '*to live longer*', '*to have kids days off*', '*to have a special day – everything for free!*', '*let me rule the world*' and '*do operations to make kids good.*' Some children wanted '*to have as many pets as we want*' and to '*have a curfew so kids don't watch adult-only programmes*'.

Citizenship responsibilities: The children and young people identified a range of personal, familial and societal attributes they considered they could contribute to make the imaginary country a good place to live.

Personal attributes were the most frequently mentioned responsibility by all age-groups. Focus group participants thought citizens in the imaginary country should '*be responsible*', '*set a good example*', '*do their job properly*', '*think about the consequences of their actions*' and '*respect others*' in the community, especially the elderly. Other personal attributes included being '*considerate*' and '*getting along with people*', '*laughing with people not at them*', being a '*good sport*', '*sharing*', being '*nice and friendly*', '*helpful*', '*good*', '*tidy*', and '*happy with what you've got*'. The 14/15-year-olds also talked about being a '*role model for younger citizens*' and '*listening to younger children because they may have important ideas too.*' A group of 8/9-year-old boys wanted '*adults to have joy and love so they don't get grouchy with you*'.

Environmental awareness in the imaginary country was a real concern for all age-groups. They considered that they had the following responsibilities – '*no tagging*', '*don't graffiti things*', '*don't litter*', '*pick up rubbish*', '*help the ozone layer*', '*no spray cans*', and '*more recyclable materials*'. They wanted to '*keep the country green*' and have '*lots of plants*' and '*clean streets*'.

Societal norms/laws and adhering to them was mentioned as an important responsibility, for example, '*don't speed when you are driving*' and '*don't drink and drive*'. Five students (from four schools) said there should be '*no swearing*' and others wanted '*no robbers*', '*no burglars*', and '*no baddies that sell drugs.*' Health and safety norms were also raised – '*no smacking*', '*no spanks*', '*no alcohol*', '*no smoking*', '*don't get drugs*', '*no violence*' and '*no bullying anywhere*'.

Altruism and '*community service*' were considered virtues in the imaginary country, with the students mentioning the need to '*give money to charity, Jesus/ God, and the church*', '*build things for the community*', '*help anyone who needs help, especially old people*', and '*look after new or younger members of society*'.

Immigration and the access of people from other countries to the imaginary country were considered responsibilities for some students, although some discrimination was evident. Three groups thought '*it should be harder for immigrants to get citizenship*' and expressed such ideas as '*get rid of all Somalians*', '*don't let Asians flood in*' and '*don't let in any refugees from Asia or Africa*'. But other students felt that it was important to have people from other countries who could say '*why don't you do something this way?*' or to let Asians in '*because they bring lots of money*'.

Should young citizens have more rights in the imaginary country than they do in their own country? All the children who responded to this question, except one group of 8/9-year-old girls, thought that young citizens in the imaginary country should have more rights than they currently enjoy in New Zealand now. They also envisaged the new country as being safer, nicer, healthier and happier to live in: '*We should have heaps more rights than we do at the moment. We want the power*' (14/15-year-old girls); '*yes, because the imaginary country is healthy, doesn't have many consequences, you could do whatever you wanted, no jobs, there's no rubbish, you'd always be safe and protected, everyone has a house to live in and lives happily*' (8/9-year-old girls); '*Some people in New Zealand are violent and mean, but in the imaginary country they aren't*' (8/9-year-old boys).

The group of 8/9-year-old girls who thought young citizens in the imaginary country should not have more rights said this was '*because they are just the same practically in every country and you can't have everything you want.*'

The influence of age and gender on children's responses

Age: The 14/15-year-olds provided more comprehensive and detailed discussions about citizenship, rights and responsibilities. The older girls, in particular, were more likely to consider the questions/topics under discussion from more angles and to extend their responses with additions and qualifications. While it could be said that the 14/15-year-olds expressed a more sophisticated understanding than the 8/9-year-olds, the younger children certainly contributed fully to the discussions and had little difficulty with the concepts of rights and responsibilities. One group of 8/9-year-olds had studied a component of the human rights curriculum earlier in the year at school and their ability to draw on this knowledge base was clearly evident in their focus group. The only real age difference to emerge in the data was in the type of examples students used to illustrate their rights and responsibilities. The 14/15-year-olds expressed typical youth-related issues and concerns about autonomy, participation, sport, leisure and recreation, entertainment, choices at school, sexuality, alcohol, driving motor vehicles, leaving home and voting. The younger children emphasised issues and concerns pertinent to middle-childhood, such as babysitting, playing, being nice and not being naughty. They also provided an extensive list of the type of chores they help out with at home.

Gender: We experienced the greatest difficulty attracting 14/15-year-old boys into the research as high school boys seemed the least interested in the citizenship topic. Those older boys who did participate were also less expressive than the girls, but nevertheless contributed willingly to the focus groups. There were no gender differences evident in terms of the rights and responsibilities raised by the male and female students. The 14/15-year-old girls, because of the depth of their discussions did, however, give more examples of rights in the school and community settings than male students.

Parent and Teacher Questionnaires

Forty parents/caregivers (including two grandparents caring for their grandchildren) completed the questionnaire, 32 of whom were female and 8 were male. The majority (67.5 per cent) were European, 15 per cent Māori, 10 per cent Pacific, 5 per cent Asian, and 2.5 per cent of other ethnicity.

Thirty-one teaching staff returned completed questionnaires, 25 (80.6 per cent) of whom were female and six (19.4 per cent) were male. Nineteen worked in a primary school, eleven in a high school, and one worked as a resource teacher for learning and behaviour in both primary and high schools. The majority (93.5 per cent) were of European ethnicity.

Overall, the parents and teachers were highly supportive of children having rights in all three contexts of home, school and community/neighbourhood. All the rights listed in the questionnaires scored agreement ratings of over 90 per cent, except for the children's right to have places to go to hang out in the community, which received agreement from only 66.7 per cent of parents (but 90 per cent from teachers).

There was much greater variation amongst the adults concerning children's responsibilities in the home, school and community, although parents and teachers consistently selected the same responsibilities as the ones they felt less comfortable about. Even so, agreement remained high (over 90 per cent) for all the responsibilities listed in the questionnaire except the following: that children had a responsibility to help decide on rules at home (84.2 per cent parental and 80 per cent teacher agreement); to help care for siblings (71.8 per cent parental and 80.6 per cent teacher agreement); to protest if there was an injustice at school (80 per cent parental and 83.9 per cent teacher agreement); to try and change the school rules if needed (59 per cent parental and 76.7 per cent teacher agreement); and to participate in local community activities (72.5 per cent parental agreement).

Parents and teachers generally agreed that, if a child's rights were not being respected at school, they would take action. No respondent said they would ignore this. Actions which involved the child were the most favoured by the parents (such as helping the child to develop strategies, telling the child to tell the teacher, or talking to the teacher with the child), and some said they would approach the school principal. All the teachers said they would talk to another teacher, and strategies involving the child (helping the child to develop strategies and talking with the child) were also popular. Talking to the principal and school counsellor or health nurse was also suggested by the teachers. Most parents and teachers said they would not want to take the matter further with the Board of Trustees or an external organisation (like the Ministry of Education or Education Review Office), although some felt this would depend on the nature of the issue.

The majority of the parents (57.5 per cent) had not heard of the UNCRC and 15 per cent were unsure. Of the 27.5 per cent who had heard of the Convention, 54.5 per cent said they did support it and the rest were unsure mainly because they did not know enough about it.

Nearly all the parents (95 per cent) and teachers (90.3 per cent) thought of children and young people as citizens, with 71 per cent of parents and 58 per cent of teachers believing children became citizens at birth. Thirteen percent of parents and 29 per cent of teachers opted for children becoming citizens from the age of 10 years and over.

Discussion and Conclusion

Our findings confirm the view that children and young people are able to contribute meaningfully to discussions about their rights and responsibilities, to understand how people become citizens, and to participate positively in their homes, schools and communities. Almost all the focus groups were able to discuss these concepts with insight and understanding. Even children as young as 8 or 9 years are able to make a meaningful contribution to dialogue about rights, responsibilities and citizenship.

Participation rights were a salient issue for children of all ages and in the three contexts of their lives discussed – home, school and community. The freedom to take an active part and have a formative role in society was also a desired feature of the imaginary country. Young people wanted to participate more fully in family, school and community decision-making processes. Having a say and being listened to featured strongly in their discussions. These findings show that New Zealand children see themselves as active agents in society, rather than just being acted upon by society, a finding reflected in previous research with young people who were older than the participants in this study (Taylor, Smith & Nairn, 2001). Although being a citizen did involve provision and protection rights as well, protection rights featured less prominently in children's understandings. This contrasts with the image of young people as victims of various ills in society, a dominant adult construction of childhood (Piper, 2000; Smart & Neale, 2000).

The imaginary country exercise proved a useful way of asking the students to reflect on the reality of their current lives in comparison with their anticipated role in a new land. The fact that all the students conceived of this new country as a more secure, safer, happier and healthier place, with greater freedoms and respect than they currently enjoyed, says something rather significant about their lives in New Zealand today. They all perceived the imaginary country as an opportunity for an improvement in their current situation. Their concern for the environment, and for undertaking acts of altruism and charity, are optimistic signs that children are thinking about the values important to a democratic society.

Previous international research (Torney-Purta et al., 2001) showing that 14-year-olds' understandings of fundamental democratic institutions and values are present but superficial is not reflected throughout this study. Older children were understandably (because of their greater experience in wider contexts) more able to provide detailed, abstract and rich reflections of citizenship concepts than younger children, but the younger children also had enlightening and relevant ideas. It was useful that the methodology for this study used children's everyday lives and experiences as a context for evoking an understanding of citizenship. The study seems to support the view that children see themselves as part of society, and that this understanding is forged through social relationships, shared activities, and responsible roles in the various contexts of their social lives. Some of the older girls showed a relatively high level of abstract thinking and understanding of infrastructure, democracy, law and economy in society, at a level that would probably not be achieved by some adults.

There was little sign of any great alienation from their country by these children, although a few were critical of the constraints that adults and teachers put on their citizenship. While the child participants in this study came from a variety of socio-economic and geographical backgrounds, our sample did not specifically include children who had been marginalised by poverty, loss of land or removal from their family. It is not surprising therefore that our international colleagues in countries such as Brazil (Rizzini, Pereira, Princeswal, de Jesús & Botafogo, 2005) and Palestine (Shaheen, Abu Baker, Bany Odeh, Dkedek &

Abu Ghosh, 2005) have reported stronger feelings of exclusion and alienation amongst marginalised children than was present in this sample of ordinary New Zealand children. Interestingly, the New Zealand parents and teachers who completed the questionnaire were generally very supportive of children having rights in all three contexts of home, school and community/neighbourhood and said they would take action to ensure these rights were respected. Just over half these adults were, however, unaware of the UNCRC.

Being optimistic about New Zealand society, we could attribute New Zealand children's understanding of citizenship and desire to be citizens, at least partly, to a serious effort by the government to pay attention to the participation rights of children and young people. These have been expressed in our government's national plan for children, *Agenda for Children* (Ministry of Social Development, 2002), and through the prominence given to child advocacy issues in the media by NGOs and other groups. Children in New Zealand have, in the last few years, been given more visibility and voice. Nevertheless, there has also been a high level of attention accorded recently to widespread violation of rights and lack of implementation of the UNCRC, especially with regard to physical violence against children (Action for Children and Youth Aotearoa, 2003; UNICEF, 2003).

This study provides a starting point for further investigation of children's citizenship, and for the development of processes and practices within homes, schools and communities to enhance children's understanding. The study has many limitations, including sample composition and size, and the data having been collected from one-off focus group discussions. A more sustained interaction with the children might have allowed researchers to facilitate a deeper level of discussion. The research provides a snapshot of New Zealand children's constructions of citizenship, which tend to be framed within their personal lives rather than from any abstract understanding of democracy and society. The challenge for researchers now is to work with community leaders, teachers, parents and children to develop methods of enriching our understanding of citizenship. In sociocultural terms, adults working with young people need to scaffold children's developing understanding and challenge their existing ideas so as to extend their repertoire of skills (Vygotsky, 1978). This can be best achieved when there is clarity about the values and goals underpinning the meaning of citizenship in each cultural context. Yet this excerpt from a Brazilian paper implies that adults are unclear about the concept of citizenship, and this will have significant implications for citizenship education:

> We think that the concept of 'citizenship' is not talked about, explained, discussed, disseminated and demanded enough, and therefore, its meaning, as well as the rights and duties that go along with it, is unclear. On the other hand, it may be used too much, as a word that is politically correct, and as such it becomes meaningless. (Rizzini et al., 2005, p. 8)

Our study has, however, clearly shown that children themselves can make a valuable contribution to national and international discussions about citizenship, and we would argue that their perspectives should not be ignored.

6

Norway

**Anne Trine Kjørholt, Håvard Bjerke, Gjertrud Stordal,
Line Hellem & Pernille Skotte**[1]
Norwegian Centre for Child Research, NTNU,
Trondheim, Norway

Introduction

As part of the implementation of the UNCRC, there has been an increasing concern about the need to inform children and young people about their rights. Like other countries, Norway has been criticised by the United Nations Committee on the Rights of the Child for paying insufficient attention to informing children about their rights, which argued that an awareness of rights is a precondition to claiming these entitlements in everyday life. Knowledge is lacking about how Norwegian children understand their rights and responsibilities in society. Results from the International Civic Education Study suggest that most 14-year-old pupils in Norway and the 27 other participating countries do have an understanding about what a good citizen is and what they should do to be one (Mikkelsen, Buk-Berge, Ellingsen, Fjeldstad & Sund, 2001; Torney-Purta, Lehmann, Oswald & Schultz, 2001). However, little is known about how children understand themselves as citizens with rights and responsibilities at home, at school and in the community. In general, the citizenship literature includes remarkably few empirical studies (Lister, Smith, Middleton & Cox, 2003).

The aim of this chapter is to shed light on what children in Norway consider to be their rights and responsibilities in society, as well as if, and how, they consider themselves to be citizens. Through our study we had the opportunity to hear from children themselves about what they understood to be important issues concerning their status as citizens within the Norwegian context. However, as discussed in Chapter One, the concept of citizenship is contested in the sense that there are different theories about what it means, how the status of citizenship is achieved, and what this status implies with respect to rights and responsibilities. Theoretical perspectives and discussion in relation to the findings in the empirical study are therefore included in this chapter. Children's notion of participation is given particular attention because this is a central dimension of citizenship. Furthermore, as we shall see, children express conflicting views on their status as social participants in society. This underlines the importance of interpreting children's perspectives in the light of critical thinking about methodology and theory. Children's voices are always expressions made within a particular social, cultural and political context. In order to interpret and understand children's perspectives, we therefore need to understand this context. Our presentation of the children's perspectives therefore follows a brief discussion of the Norwegian cultural and political context, with specific emphasis on children's rights to participation.

Children as Citizens: The Norwegian Context

Located in the northern part of Europe, Norway has approximately 4.6 million inhabitants, of which 24 per cent are below the age of 18 years and 7.7 per cent of the child population are defined as immigrant children (Norway Statistics, 2005). The birth rate has remained around 1.8 for the last 15 years, which is quite high in comparison to other European countries. The child mortality rate is amongst the lowest in the world. Over time, the welfare policy of the Nordic countries has developed an extensive relationship between children and the state, emphasising children as individual rights holders, regardless of their family backgrounds (Satka & Eydal, 2004). Norway, like other Nordic countries, is well-known as a forerunner in the field of children's rights. A comparative study of child policy and children's rights in five European countries revealed that Norway tends to be the leading country when it comes to regarding the child as an active agent in his or her own right (Bartley, 1998; Therborn, 1993). In a variety of different contexts, Norwegian children and young people are seen as competent social actors, invoking their rights to influence their everyday lives as well as society in general. Researchers, political activists, NGOs and child experts share a positive attitude towards implementing children's rights to participation in their local environment, urban planning, politics, decision-making processes in families, and in influencing everyday life and curricula in schools (Kjørholt, 2001, 2002).

However, the extent of empowered participation is often limited and the position of children as political actors can be unclear (Kjørholt & Lidén, 2004). How children's rights to participation in different contexts are implemented varies. This reflects ambiguities, as well as uncertainties, about what it means to be a child-citizen, and to what degree children and young people are attributed rights as autonomous citizens with power and responsibilities on a par with adult citizens (Kjørholt & Lidén, 2004).

Norway took an active part in the drafting of the UNCRC, and was one of the first countries to ratify the Convention in 1991. In 2003 the Norwegian Parliament incorporated the UNCRC into the Human Rights Act. National laws affecting children must now be read according to the UNCRC. Western Europe, Germany, Great Britain, Italy and the Nordic countries have received much attention for their efforts to realise the concept of children and youth as citizens (Kjørholt & Qvortrup, 2000). This means that children and youth are given a voice, to a certain extent, in various matters that affect their lives. Norway was the first country to establish the Children's Ombudsman (in 1981). Other examples of institutions set up to secure children's rights in Norway include the Children's Municipal Officer, regulated by amendments made in 1989 to the Planning and Building Act. The Municipal Officer safeguards the interests of children and young people and voices concerns regarding the consequences of decisions taken by public authorities on them.

Participation rights also include recognition of children as political participants. Youth Councils have been created in recent years in Norway to enhance children's political participation. Organised by the municipalities, these allow the voice of children below voting age to be heard. The number of Youth Councils has increased during the last few years, with nearly three out of every four municipalities in Norway having established these democratic spaces for young people (Lidén, 2003).

Many participatory activities initiated by national and local authorities since the early 1990s can be characterised as ad hoc and short-term. They suffer from their lack of integration into permanent and legal structures. Older children and youth are first and foremost regarded as social participants in Norwegian society, even though the UNCRC participation rights, in principle, concern every child below the age of 18 years (Kjørholt, 2002). A survey of participatory activities in Norway confirmed the widespread nature of children's participation in this country (Kjørholt, 2002). During the period 1985–95, four out of ten municipalities reported that they had developed participatory projects. About one-third of the projects were aimed at including children as participants in democratic and political decision-making processes, mostly at a local political level. When participatory projects were initiated, it appeared easier to engage older children and young people in the activities. More than 60 per cent of the activities were actually aimed at young people aged 14 years or older (Kjørholt, 2002). This directing of participatory projects in favour of youth and 'older' children reveals how age remains a category for exclusion from rights to various kinds of participation by some (mainly younger) children (Kjørholt, 2002; Moss, Clark & Kjørholt, 2005).

In Norway, children start school at the age of six years. Primary (6–13 years) and secondary (13–16 years) schooling is mandatory and free. The public education system is strongly positioned in Norway, with only 2 per cent of primary school aged children attending private schools in 2005 (Norway Statistics, 2005). Education for democracy and civic participation is an important part of the curriculum for Norwegian public education. Student councils are mandatory in all schools from the fifth grade (from around the age of 10 years), and the members represent the students on the school board. It is also common to have student councils for children younger than eleven years of age.

Nevertheless, it has been argued that notions of participation and 'interests' still need further clarification (Kjørholt, 2001, 2004). Conclusions from two research projects in Norway, based on interviews focusing on children's perspectives as participants, support this view. In an evaluation of how a project entitled '*The Meeting Place*' was implemented, Sletterød and Gustavsen (1995) found a difference between adults' and children's experiences concerning the notion of participation. While adults characterised the process as child-centred – because in their view children were the main leaders – the children themselves viewed the process as exclusively adult-directed. Another study, conducted by an anthropologist, found that many children in projects aimed at realising children's rights of participation felt that they were merely symbolic participants with no real influence (Haugen, 1995).

The symbolic importance of children as participants is increasing in modern societies (Kjørholt, 2004). Vestel, Ødegård and Øia (2003) argue that projects that have received a great deal of positive attention by adults are not having the intended effects according to the children themselves. In other words, even though children are seen as competent social actors and individual rights holders by the adult population in Norway, and even though several institutions exist which are intended to secure children's rights to participation, the question remains of how children themselves experience their right to participate in society. This issue will be further explored in this chapter, but we first elaborate on some of the theoretical perspectives of relevance for our project.

Theoretical Approach

Recently there has been a growing number of studies examining the meaning of citizenship for children and young people (see Chapter One). According to traditional liberal theories of citizenship (Marshall, 1964), children are seen as 'not-yet-citizens' and are excluded from citizenship because they do not have political rights such as the right to vote. Cockburn (1998) points out that traditional notions of citizenship will have to change if they are to accommodate children. He argues for a social model of citizenship that emphasises the ways in which people are connected to each other. This challenges traditional liberal theories of citizenship related to the concept of human beings as autonomous and rational subjects. Others have argued that children will be constructed as 'second-class citizens' within an adultist view of participation as a normative stance when only certain types of activity are considered to constitute citizenship (Moosa-Mitha, 2005). Moosa-Mitha argues that we should define children's citizenship rights by taking their citizenship status seriously, without taking adults as the standard by which their citizenship is measured. One way of achieving this is to broaden the concept of participation 'as the expression of one's agency in multiple relationships within which citizens are present in society' in order to recognise different ways of participating (Moosa-Mitha, 2005, p. 375). An important question, following this line of argument, is what kinds of activity are considered to constitute citizenship for children?

Rights to participation are seen as a fundamental part of citizenship (Hart, 1992). Jans (2004) regards citizenship as a form of participation and involvement – indeed the only area in which children can actually have the status of citizens. However, this is then a 'children-sized citizenship', a dynamic and continuous learning process. Ben-Arieh and Boyer (2005) also emphasise citizenship as an acquired skill that requires learning and experiencing, and not something a child is just born with. They state that 'child participation *is* child citizenship' (Ben-Arieh & Boyer, 2005, p. 51) because participation is the only way that a child can learn and experience citizenship. Kjørholt (2004, p. 258) also argues that children are 'doing citizenship' by means of discourses on themselves as social participants in society: for example, by actively 'working on' relationships with others, engaging in mutual social processes of autonomy, and belonging to different social and cultural communities.

Giving children citizenship rights raises fundamental questions connected to notions of citizenship, childhood, and social and democratic participation. What does it mean to be a citizen? What is social and democratic participation? And what does it mean to be a child? (Kjørholt, 2002, 2004). Until recently, discussion of these topics has mainly been conducted within the fields of philosophy and law. Giving children rights as citizens challenges traditional theories of citizenship, which are based on liberal notions of democratic participation and the ideal of the rational autonomous individual (Kjørholt, 2001, 2004).

As an empirical and analytical concept, citizenship has at least three main dimensions (Delanty, 2000): a) *rights and duties* in a legal framework; b) *participation*, which says something about a practice within a social system; and c) *identities*, which can be understood in a psychological framework as a sense of citizenship (Conover, 1995). An important challenge is to gain insight into children and young people's own perspectives on citizenship. With this in mind, the aim of our study was to explore the following questions in focus-group interviews with children:

- How do children understand their rights and responsibilities in general, and their participation rights in particular, at home, at school and in the community?
- How are different notions of participation and citizenship reflected in children's views?
- What ideas about children as citizens are reflected in their own discussions of participation more specifically?

In the following section, we present the methodology and results regarding how Norwegian children understand their rights and responsibilities in different contexts. We then explore how children understand the concepts of citizenship and participation in general, before turning to the different views expressed on the issue of participation. We emphasise that the reflections outlined in this chapter are ideas for further exploration rather than final and conclusive statements.

Research Methodology

Studies of children's understanding of their rights have been dominated by psychological and legal perspectives (Schmidt & Reppucci, 2002). Vignettes presenting situations in which a child might assert a right have been used as a method in a number of studies in different parts of the world (e.g. Cherney & Perry, 1996; Limber, Kask, Heidmets, Kaufman & Melton, 2000; Melton, 1980; Ruck, Keating, Abramovitch & Koegl, 1998; Saporiti et al., 2005). However, such research has been criticised for being too conflict-laden, and as seeking to elicit abstract reasoning about hypothetical dilemmas, instead of applying a more open-ended format (Helwig, 1995).

There are few empirical studies of how different people understand themselves as citizens, and previous research has tended to focus on political literacy and attitude surveys. In the UK there have been a growing number of studies giving young people the opportunity to talk about citizenship in more detail (e.g. Hine, 2004; Lister et al., 2003). This research has involved children at different ages and used repeat interviews and focus-group methodology. In our international comparative study, it was decided to use qualitative research methods that involved the use of focus groups to explore children's understanding of rights, responsibilities and citizenship. Focus groups were chosen as an effective means of accessing the subjective experience of children, giving them the opportunity to be valued as experts while working collaboratively with their peers and a facilitator to develop and articulate their thoughts (Gibbs, 1997).

There were a total of 53 participants in our study, recruited from four different schools in a medium-size Norwegian town. The schools were strategically selected, based on social welfare statistics for the school districts in the municipality,[2] including rates of unemployment, the educational and income levels of the adult population, and the percentage of non-western immigrants within each school district. A summary of the participants' age, gender and socio-economic characteristics in each focus group are presented in Table One.

Of the 53 children who agreed to participate, 28 were 8/9 years old and 25 were 14/15 years old. Among the 8/9-year-olds, there were 18 girls and 10 boys. Among the 14/15-year-olds, there were 15 girls and 10 boys.

Seven focus-group interviews were conducted. These groups are our unit of analysis, and each individual child's response should be understood within this group context. Our intention was to have gender-based focus groups comprising approximately eight participants each. However, for practical reasons, and because of the understanding we reached with the school administration and teachers, the focus groups were made up of single-sex male and female groups in Primary School B, and mixed-sex groups within each age category in the other three schools. The number of participants varied from six to eleven in a group. In almost all the groups some of the participants spoke more frequently than others. We also saw a tendency in those groups with more than one boy for the boys to dominate and speak more frequently than the girls in the group.

Table One: Norwegian participants in the citizenship study focus groups

SCHOOL 8/9 Years	Boys	Girls	Total
Primary School A: Low SES, group 1	1	6	7
Primary School A: Low SES, group 2	3	6	9
Primary School B: High SES, group 3	6	-	6
Primary School B: High SES, group 4	-	6	6
14/15 Years			
Secondary School C: Low SES, group 5	1	5	6
Secondary School D: Low SES, group 6	3	5	8
Secondary School D: High SES, group 7	6	5	11
TOTAL	**20 boys**	**33 girls**	**53 students**

The focus-group protocol, drawn up for the entire international project, was translated and adapted to fit the Norwegian context. In all the groups, children were asked to reflect on the meaning of concepts that they were not very familiar with, especially the concept of citizenship. This emphasises abstract reasoning, instead of more open-ended reflections based upon activities in their everyday lives. However, we noted that the children followed up and reflected on the answers given by the other children in their group in a positive and stimulating way, linking the discussion to their own experiences. Two research assistants attended each interview: one to conduct the interview and the other to act as a facilitator. Each group session was recorded and transcribed by the two research assistants. The focus groups lasted for about one to two hours.

Due to our limited sample and the chosen methodology, we have not been able to draw any statistically valid conclusions on variations based on socio-economic status, gender or age. Nevertheless, in analysing the data we have identified some differences between the groups of 8/9-year-olds and the groups of 14/15-year-olds that we consider relevant. We have therefore included the age variable in the tables and the analysis of the results.

Key Findings

Rights

In each focus group our opening question about rights was: *What is a right?* The most common first answer in both age groups defined rights in relation to what they can do – for example, '*that all children have the right to do the same'*, and *'that you are allowed to do certain things'*. Some of the 8/9-year-old children tended to think of rights as a definition of what the right solution is in a certain situation, such as *'It is right to put thieves in prison'*, or as one girl explained it: *'There are many things that are right, and to have rights, that is right.'* Other children were aware of different rights and mentioned the rights to water, clothes, food, life, a house, money, leisure time, to have a Mum and a Dad, to go to school, participate in sport and activities, and to have help from a doctor. One focus group in particular mentioned many of these rights, and their teacher told us that they just had discussed rights in their class.

Generally, we saw that at the age of 8/9 years children had an understanding of what a right was, but confused it with other concepts that were similar for them. Their responses varied from very concrete wishes like *'All have the right to go to Tivoli'*, to more abstract issues of injustice such as *'All children have equal value'*; from individual claims like *'You can do what you want to'*, to more collectivist claims like *'People in other countries are not going to starve to death.'* In this way the children showed an understanding of the complexity of the question of rights. In all three focus groups with young people aged 14/15 years, they mentioned that there were some limits on what one has a right to do – for example, *'You cannot do something that will have a negative effect on others.'* This older age-group also seemed to have a more complex and diverse understanding of the concepts under discussion.

We have analysed the responses in the different focus groups according to age and whether they fall within one of the three groups of rights identified by Lansdown (1994) in the UNCRC: *Participation rights*, *Provision rights*, and *Protection rights* (see Table Two).

Participation Rights

We see both differences and similarities in the way children in the two age-groups responded to the question of rights at home, at school and in the community. *Participation rights* were mentioned by both age groups at home and at school, but were not identified by the 8/9-year-old children in the community. The right to participate in decision-making was most clearly stated in relation to home, although the children's comments meant that differences were visible between families. In the groups of 8/9-year-olds, the children discussed their right to decide which leisure activity to take part in, to choose and visit friends, when to go to bed, what to have for dinner, or for how long they could play on the computer or watch television. We noted that the 14/15-year-olds were not so concerned about these issues anymore. This could be explained by the fact that they were older and therefore allowed to decide these issues themselves in most families: it was no longer of great importance for them. Instead, they were more concerned about issues affecting their lives, like having the right to participate in deciding where to live after their parents' divorce, choose their own religion, and to obtain some help and assistance from their parents if they could not manage on their own. It appeared that, to a larger extent, they lived an independent life, while the younger children still had a strong relationship with their parents at home, with more negotiations over decision-making in concrete situations.

Both at school and in the community, the young people aged 14/15 were concerned that their rights to express their opinions and be heard were limited. They told us about pupils at school who had raised their voice in a protest and been punished for this later on when they received their grades. In their opinion this was unfair and limited their freedom of speech. In the community context, young people mentioned situations in which they were not being heard by the decision-makers about different constructions and activities in their neighbourhood (new playgrounds, roads, houses, youth clubs etc.).

Provision Rights

Children aged 8/9 were more concerned about their *provision rights* at home than were the older children (see Table Two). In all contexts, they were very much concerned about their opportunities to be with friends. This might be said to reflect notions of a 'good childhood' in Norway. Interestingly, though, this is not a right mentioned in the UNCRC, or in much of the debate about what the rights of children should be. In the context of rights at school, there was a difference regarding what was of special concern to the children between the different age groups. Both groups mentioned the right to have school breaks, to get support, to eat and to rest. However, while the younger children were concerned about their right to play, the older pupils were more focused on their right to an education, including proper school materials and good teachers, and being given tasks according to ability.

Protection Rights

Protection rights were less frequently mentioned in both age groups. Only in one of the groups of 14/15-year-olds was explicit mention made of their right to protection, in the context of a discussion about the responsibilities of their parents. Children aged 8/9 years talked about their need to be protected at home, at school and in the community. At home, protection rights were mainly related to what they identified as the parents' responsibilities to decide, but they also thought about the right to protection of children who do not have responsible parents, or even a bed to sleep in. At school and in the community, they mentioned their right not to be bullied and stressed the need to take this issue seriously.

All the children acknowledged that, just like adults, they have rights. As the examples above indicate, the children mainly defined a right as something a person is entitled to. Little reference was made in the focus-group interviews to rights as regulating what children should not be exposed to. The issue of protection was also seldom referred to by the children.

Responsibilities

Responsibility appeared to feature in both the language and lives of the children. We constructed three different categories from the answers they gave to open-

Table Two: Examples of rights identified by children at different age groups.

PARTICIPATION RIGHTS	PROVISION RIGHTS	PROTECTION RIGHTS
	Rights at Home	
	8/9 YEARS	
• To decide which leisure activity to take part in • To be allowed to decide a little by yourself • To be allowed to go to the toilet whenever one wants • To be allowed to visit friends in their homes	• To food • To have a room • To have a bed to lay in • To play • To have some friends • To have a mum and dad	• Not play on the computer every day • Not be allowed to stay up all night • All children do not have to work • Children are not going to sleep on the streets alone
	14/15 YEARS	
• To have and express your own opinions • To say what you want • To participate in deciding where to live if your parents are divorced • To withdraw your membership of the state church and choose your own religion	• To get food that you want to have • Love and care	• To be protected and taken care of by your parents
	Rights at School	
	8/9 YEARS	
• To be allowed to do what you want in the breaks • To get angry • To be sad • To play football during breaks	• To raise your hand and get help • To get food/be allowed to eat • To have school breaks, and some time outside • To have friends and someone to play with • Time to do their homework	• Not being teased for being different • Not to be bullied
	14/15 YEARS	
• To express your opinion • To protest/demonstrate without being punished (i.e. national tests) • To decide in matters that concern ourselves (i.e. homework).	• To get free education • To school breaks, to eat and rest • To receive help • To be given tasks according to ability • Proper school materials, like books • Good teachers • To medication given at school.	

Table Two: Continued.

	Rights in the Community	
	8/9 YEARS	
• To be outside playing (but not in the evening, not in the neighbour's flowers, and not with everything) • To play with others (friends) • To do sport • To be with friends at each other's homes • To have a picnic on the grass or something like that, if they want	• To have fresh water	• Not allowed to dress up and rob other people • To get help if you get hurt • Not to be bullied
	14/15 YEARS	
• Right to express our opinion, but are not heard. • To move around, except on private property • To protest and demonstrate, as when youth clubs are being closed down. • To be a member of an organisation		

ended questions about children's responsibilities at home, at school and in the community (see Table Three). The first category includes responsibilities identified in relation to children's personal lives and their belongings; the second category relates to responsibilities identified in relation to other people and expected rules of conduct; and the third category includes responsibilities identified in relation to activities that need to be done at home, at school, and for the environment in the community.

Table Three shows that children in both age groups have identified a variety of responsibilities within the different categories of home, school and community. Personal responsibility is highlighted in relation to their own room and personal belongings, and their participation at school. Young people aged 14/15 years also identified responsibilities in relation to decision-making (where to live, to work hard, not to use drugs), for their own learning at school, and for their own actions in the community.

It is arguable that most of the social and collective responsibilities they identified were tasks delegated by adults to children, or activities that were in accordance with given rules, rather than responsibilities in which children had a personal investment. With regard to home, there were differences between how

Table Three: Examples of responsibilities identified by children.

PERSONAL/INDIVIDUAL RESPONSIBILITY	SOCIAL RULES OF CONDUCT	COLLECTIVE RESPONSIBILITY
	Responsibilities at Home	
	8/9 YEARS	
• To tidy your own room • To flush the toilet • To wash my hands • To close the door • To go to school by myself • To remember when to leave home for school • To go to bed myself • To do my homework • To look after important things we have (wallet, x-box playstation, other belongings) • Look after and care for pets, if you've got one	• All children must be nice and helpful.	• Look after and help with siblings • Help empty the dish-washer • Maybe help make dinner • Help the parents at home if they are sick • Clear the table • Pick up the mail
	14/15 YEARS	
• To finish a task or do some work on your own • To keep your room tidy • To clean up after yourself, e.g. if you spill a glass of milk • To take part in the decision on where to live • To look after the house if you are home alone • To make the right choices (like doing your homework, going to school, not becoming a drug addict) • Stand up for your decisions and take the consequences for your actions		• Set the table • Look after and do babysitting for siblings • Walk the dog every day • Work at home (some get paid with a weekly allowance) • Help clean and tidy at home
	Responsibilities at School	
	8/9 YEARS	
• Work at school • Learn things by ourselves • Do our homework • Look after ourselves • Not touch other people's things • Listen to the teacher • Make up for things we have done wrong	• To be good and not silly • Not to run and stuff • Not say anything that will make others upset • Let other children play with them • To look after those in lower classes (helpmates)	• To clean the desk and put up the seat • When we have finished playing with something, to put it back in its place • To keep the school tidy

Table Three: Continued.

• Look after your books, pencil box and other belongings	• Make sure that all children feel they are worth the same • Must not be rude to each other • Must be nice to each other	
	14/15 YEARS	
• To be at school on time • To do your homework • For our own learning • For our own actions, e.g. if we destroy something we have to replace it or make sure it is replaced • Responsible for the books we get	• Do to others what you want them to do towards you • To follow the rules in the classroom (no bullying, raise your arm, be quiet in class). • Be quiet while other people work • To interrupt in case of bullying (some discussion) • To make sure no one is bullied • To take care of the well-being of others	• Help clean and keep order (prefects)
	Responsibilities in the Community	
	8/9 YEARS	
• Responsibility for one's possessions	• Not run in the corridors of our building • Not do things that we aren't allowed to do in the street • Not be unkind to other people • Make sure that your dog doesn't scare others • If they have children, they should not play loud music • If you borrow something, you have responsibility for returning it	• Clean outside to make it nice and tidy • Help make it a nice place to live • Take care of nature • Don't throw away garbage • Not throw away things with toxic substances in natural areas
	14/15 YEARS	
• Look after yourself • When you are 15, you are responsible for your criminal actions and will be punished. • To buy and make sure you have a ticket on the bus • Make sure not to get drunk and start hitting people	• To calm down at night and not make noise disturbing the neighbours (e.g. loud music). • Not to spread false rumours • If you see someone being knocked down or killed, then you have a responsibility to notify • Take care of each other	• Not make a mess, and throw garbage in the bin • Not to destroy and pollute the environment

the children related to the normal expectations in their family. Some children expected to receive a weekly allowance for the work they did at home, while others just undertook various activities routinely and did not expect to receive any money as a reward or salary. In relation to school, they identified rules about how to behave, but attributed some responsibilities to students for looking after and following up other students – for example, like a prefect or a class monitor with responsibility for keeping the classroom tidy or ensuring that all pupils are in the school yard and not the classroom during a break. In relation to the community, the focus-group participants also related responsibilities to rules and things that they are not supposed to do, which were all decided by adults. However, it was evident from the discussion about responsibilities at home, at school and in the community that most children perceived their actions as something that went beyond a unidirectional delegation of tasks from adult to child. They accepted that it was 'fair' and 'normal' to have some social and collective responsibilities.

Citizenship

Generally, the concept of citizenship is difficult for children to grasp. Many of the children we interviewed had never heard the word or did not know what it meant. In the Norwegian language there is a separate word, *statsborgerskap*, for the formal relationship between the individual and the state. This represents a narrow definition of the concept of citizenship, referring to legal membership of the nation state. In political science in Norway, however, another word is used to include notions of participation and identity, namely *medborgerskap*. This represents a broader definition of the concept of citizenship that is more of a normative ideal. Both the formal and more substantial parts of the relationship between the individual and the idea of the state are included in the concept of citizenship. In Norwegian, an analytical concept to describe this relationship is *samfunnsborgerskap* (Brochmann, 2002), which unites two concepts: society and citizenship (*samfunn* and *borgerskap*). The concept of *borgerskap* in Norwegian might in itself be negatively identified with the bourgeoisie. In our interviews with children, we therefore chose to use the word *samfunnsborgerskap*, since we considered it to be the one most similar to the general meaning of citizenship in the other participating countries. This word was also used by Norwegian researchers in the Civic Education Study (Mikkelsen et al., 2001).

None of the children aged 8/9 years had heard the word before. One said she had heard the two words separately – that is, *samfunn* (society) and *borger* (citizen). Another said he knew what it meant to be a citizen (*borger*): '*It is those who live in this country*'. To facilitate discussion with the youngest children, the interviewers defined the concept of citizenship as being a citizen in society and as taking part in decision-making at different places. This limited the discussions to how children participate and take part in decision-making at home, at school and in the community. When asked directly if children could be citizens, some of them said:

Yes, in certain ways. For example, if we have something at home, then we also have to be allowed to decide about it.

You have to be allowed to decide some rules that we are going to follow, and things that are good for us.

I think we should have a right to decide a bit, because it is not only adults that are important. If we didn't take part, it would be unfair. For us, maybe.

They expressed a common view that children are participants in society in their own right. Talking about what it means to be 'a good citizen', the children identified collectivist values:

To decide things that are right for other people as well, not just things that are right for yourself.

To decide fairly, and in a way that other people are fine, not just you.

That they are good, like being kind and do things for others to help them.

The children thought that they could be a 'good citizen' if they '*Plant some flowers, so it will look nice*', and '*Be kind to each other, and let everybody join in playing.*'

When talking about participation, the children mentioned different activities they have taken part in, and issues they were allowed to decide about. At *home* they have different experiences of decision-making, such as deciding what to have for dinner, what kind of television programme to watch and when to go to bed. They did not agree on the limits of their decision-making. For most of the children it seemed that the decisions were taken by their parents, though more or less in understanding with their children. Some disagreed with this, while others thought this was fine. At one of the *schools* the group of girls mentioned something they called a '*children's meeting*' at which they were '*allowed to decide pretty much*' such things as what they were going to eat at a special event, and what movie they would watch during a special hour. They compared it to an adults' meeting at work: '*It is almost like that, only it is a children's meeting at school.*' Another girl mentioned that they had a working plan where they were '*allowed to decide the order of what we are going to do.*' She thought this was nice because then '*it is more up to us to decide what task to do first and last.*' Children in the focus group at another school said they sometimes decided what classes they were going to have, what they might do in gymnastics, or what songs they would sing. They also took part in decisions to decide what they would do if they were going to a museum or something similar. In the school break they were allowed to do what they wanted – '*except to hit someone else*'. In relation to the *community*, they did not identify many examples of their participation. One girl mentioned that she and her brother walked around and picked up garbage, even dog excrement. In another focus group, a boy said that children in his neighbourhood were sometimes allowed to take part in decisions on rules and regulations by putting their suggestions in a box.

Most of the young people aged 14/15 years had heard the word citizenship (*samfunnsborgerskap*) before, but were not sure what it meant. The most frequent definition they gave was that it means being a *citizen* in a *society*. Their examples of such explanations of citizenship included:

You are in a way a member, or what I am going to call it, in a society.

To be a man or a woman in a society.

Being part of a society. A citizen. Being a member of a city or a country. Maybe.

This understanding granted citizenship to members of a society regardless of their age. The definition was used to argue that children, like adults, are citizens because '*we live here as well*', and '*are part of the society as well*'. Some saw it as something that is equal for everybody and said that:

Every person is a citizen in a society. [...] You cannot have the right to be it or not. [...] You are in a way born as a citizen. At least in the society you are born and grow up in. [...] You don't choose if you are [a citizen] or not. You just are.

A few of the participants identified broader understandings of the concept. For example:

That you are part of the society and then you have to take a responsibility, for the society and your own actions, and to those who belong to the society.

You are not automatically a citizen if you live in a country. You have to do something for your country.

In one of the focus groups, the young people discussed in more detail what was required in order to be a citizen. They said: '*it depends on how long you live there*' and '*it depends on if you feel like a citizen.*' They seemed to agree that, if one felt like a citizen and was looked upon as a citizen, then one was a citizen. However, they were not sure how a person became one – by birth, by application or if '*you just are*'. Interestingly, no one related it to the age of majority before discussing how they themselves participated in decision-making (we include examples of this later in the chapter).

Three perspectives could be identified in terms of what the young people said it meant to be 'a good citizen' and what they could do to be 'a good citizen'. The first was linked to moral values like:

You do not only think about yourself, you think about others as well.

That you take care of the place you live in and the society around you. To take care of means not throwing garbage, cleaning up, and not creating hostility in the society.

Keep the environment clean.

When someone like robs a shop and things, it affects everyone.

Another perspective was linked to following your duties, rules and the law:

Follow your duties.

Follow the rules and have good behaviour.

Behave properly in a way. You are a good citizen if you do not violate the law and do what you are supposed to. A bad citizen if you are in jail.

Listen to what adults have to say.

Be invisible. Do not distinguish oneself in a negative way. If you are being loud and making a fuss, then people will look at you in a negative way and then you are not a good citizen. But if you do the work they give you and you have never done anything wrong, then they cannot say you are a bad citizen because then you are a good citizen.

A third perspective was linked to being an active member in the community:

I am a good citizen. That means that I serve the society, by doing something active in the society. For example, help out in my neighbourhood (dugnad).

Do voluntary work. That is more common in the USA, like being a fireman.

To be a good citizen, you could join an organisation.

To help, for example, old people crossing the street, or tourists if they are looking for the right direction in town. Not just walk straight past them.

The young people emphasised taking care of the environment, caring about other people in society, obeying rules and laws, and taking an active role in the society as important to being a good citizen. None of them questioned their own opportunities to be a good citizen.

In the groups of 14/15-year-olds, the concept of citizenship was also connected to participation rights as part of their status as citizens. When asked directly what it meant to participate, some of them said:

Taking a responsibility.

Taking part in voluntary activities (dugnad) in the community.

If something is going to happen..., and you disagree, instead of just sitting down and saying you can do nothing about it, you can try to do something about it.

Politically you can be active in an organisation.

The groups of 8/9-year-old children mentioned different activities they took part in, and issues they were allowed to decide in different settings to describe how they participated.

The 14/15-year-olds questioned their participation and were, to a larger extent, critical about the situation as it is today. Talking about participation at *home*, they shared experiences that were very different. Many of them thought that the family was not together very often because '*Young people are with friends, at training and so on – and parents are working.*' They regarded this as a reason for not participating very much in family life: '*We participated more when we were younger, but then we were more with our parents. Now we are only together when we eat.*' Increasing independence has, they thought, affected their participation at home and the time they spend with their parents. Some of them felt that this should be related to decision-making. One boy said:

I think young people who help out and stay more at home should be more involved in decision-making at home than those who never help with the cleaning or babysitting and so on. It should depend on how much responsibility they take.

Compared to the younger children, we can see that the older age-group discussed decision-making at *home* by relating it to issues about their own behaviour in different situations and contexts. This was even more dominant with regard to *school*, where the rules were stricter and threats of punishment were in force. The pupils had different opinions about the fairness of these rules and whether they should be allowed to decide more or not. In some schools they were also doing a service, like being a prefect in the school halls and the playground, making sure that other students followed the rules, and cleaning and picking up rubbish. '*That is really the cleaners' work*', as one boy said! They did not agree whether this was an appropriate role for them or not. Some saw the benefit of their service, while others thought it was just silly.

Another dominant view expressed about their participation was that they do have some influence at school since: '*We are the school in a way. [...] Teachers would have nothing to do without us – they should thank us!*' As the pupils said '*it is actually fairly democratic at school*', they do have something to say and have been given the opportunity to influence decisions through their own class hour (*klassens time*) and the student council. However, many of them were frustrated because '*anyway it is the teachers and the headmaster that in a way decide.*' Even so, most of them thought it was good to have a student council where issues are discussed. Usually they obtained a positive result, even if '*it is not sure that we will get it the way we want it.*'

The students did not mention many examples of their participation in the *community* and were even more critical of their modest opportunities to influence decisions. Some argued that '*I don't think we actually care much about our neighbourhood, and what's going on there*'. Others were concerned that '*We have no influence*', while some mentioned a few examples of how they could influence members in housing cooperatives (*borettslag*), youth clubs, or in other activities they took part in. Most of them agreed that '*They listen more to adults.*'

We now turn to examine how the students explained the differences between children and adults. Examples of dialogues concerning the issue of participation are given, and conflicting views on children as participants in society are confronted.

Children as Participants: Different Voices

When defining and talking about the concepts in general, the focus-group participants expressed a common view that children are participants in society in their own right. The children granted themselves the status of citizenship, and they saw participation rights as an important aspect of their citizen status. To be a citizen implied both rights and responsibilities, and there were active and passive ways of being one. As we shall see, however, when discussing concrete examples related to their participation rights in different contexts, conflicting views on children as participants were expressed. This conflict was more apparent among the older children.

Equality – Difference

As a follow-up question to the discussion of rights and responsibilities at home, at school and in the community, we asked the children if they had the same kind of rights and responsibilities as adults and, if not, how they were different? Kjørholt and Lidén (2004) have argued that the construction of children and young people as citizens in contemporary societies has been characterised by ambivalence and a lack of clarity related to whether such constructions express *difference* or *equality* in relation to adults. How did the children and young people in our study define the borders between adults and children with respect to rights and responsibilities?

The children in both age groups all saw a difference between children's and adults' rights and responsibilities. Some of the basic rights, like the right to food, a house and to express your opinion were, however, regarded as equal. These few examples were the exception, as the children only saw differences elsewhere. They all mentioned that adults could decide over children, and that adults were allowed to do more things than children, such as drive a car, vote and drink alcohol. Through an examination of the reasons they gave for these differences, along with their comments on issues like work and age limits for what they can and cannot do, we can identify a spectrum of ambivalence and vagueness related to constructions of the categories 'children' and 'adults.' Unsurprisingly, the different views were most clearly expressed in the focus groups of 14/15-year-olds, but they were also present in the younger children's reflections.

We now explore each argument more thoroughly and focus on the different positions reflected in these understandings of participation. As will be seen, how these relate to the concept of children as participants with rights and responsibilities reflects different, and perhaps contrasting, views of what childhood is and should be about.

A. Childhood as a separate life world, free from 'adult responsibilities'
The main argument within this perspective is that children should not have to participate and should be spared the burden of participating in society. This seemed 'natural' for the younger children and was something they did not question. Some of the children aged 8/9 years talked about the advantages they experienced because adults had more challenging responsibilities (like going to work, buying food and looking after their children) that children had the right to be protected from. The only thing children needed to do was go to school: '*Adults have to work, but children do not – they only work at school*', as one of the girls said. Another girl followed this up by commenting that:

Children also have the right not to work until they are old enough to manage to work on their own. You should rather use your childhood to go to school and learn things there.

Thus, the younger children explained the differences between them and adults by referring to responsibilities and ideas about what children should do in their childhood. Several of the groups with 8/9-year-old children related the differences to work, while some of them talked about school as their work. However, there was a difference: '*Adults have to work to give their children what they need, but children do not need to work to give adults what they need*' as one of the girls said.

In their view, adults have the responsibility to look after children, give them food and comfort them if they get hurt. When asked why there are differences between adults' and children's responsibilities, two girls commented:

Adults have more responsibilities because they are bigger than us, and we do not like understand everything. They understand a lot more than we do, and that is why they have a responsibility to make sure we are fine.

Besides, adults have lived longer than children, so they have been able to have a bit longer life. Therefore it is very important that they look after the children. Children are very important, and it is worse if we die than if they die.

Some of the children aged 14/15 years also explained the differences between adults' and children's rights by referring to different responsibilities. All agreed that adults have more responsibilities. Adults have to take care of children, get a job, pay taxes and pay the bills, while the children need to '*do their homework and get a future*', as one boy explained it. The difference between adults and children was also related to the way they thought about issues. This was expressed in such ways as: '*Adults worry too much*', '*We understand things differently than adults*', and '*Adults do things so complicated, in a way.*' This difference was also used to explain why children were not included in decision-making:

> *They [children] think about other things. We kids can be a bit more ... like selfish and only think about ourselves and what we are going to do and so on. We don't care so much about other things, and I think it is supposed to be like that ... when you are young, I mean.*

Children were described as being more occupied with other things related to their own interests, like school, friends and how to spend their spare time. Childhood was seen as a separate life world or time where people should be free to play and enjoy life. Adults, on the other hand, were considered more experienced and responsible, and able to consider issues beyond their own limited self-interest.

In this view, the notion of participation was associated with responsibility. Participating in society was equivalent to being responsible – a characteristic mainly associated with adulthood. The group of 14/15-year-olds were concerned about the interconnectedness between rights and responsibilities, at the same time as they questioned the reasoning for the limits on their responsibilities. During a discussion about the right to vote, some were concerned that they then had to take responsibility as well, because '*young people should not have too much responsibility when they have school and other things to think about.*' They also questioned their own responsibility in relation to criminal offences and moral conflicts, for example, whether children had the same responsibility as adults to help a person who had been hurt in the street, or to ensure no one was bullied.

Some of the young people saw the question of responsibility as a conflict between a desire to protect children and the demand of parents and others that they should take responsibility and be active participants in society:

Interviewer: *Do you think it should be a right not to worry?*

A: *Yes. And if adults say that we are not grown up enough, but still say that we should pay attention to what is going on in society, why should we do it actually if they think that we are not adult enough to vote? It is like they have two opinions – that we should pay more attention, and that we are only kids who are not allowed to do very much. [...] That is why I think young people should not need to take responsibility for what is going on in the world and so on. The only thing I read in the newspapers is the cartoons, and I am satisfied with that.*

Interviewer: *Do you agree with her?*

B: *Yes. They say that we are going to be like adults, but if we behave like adults then they get scared, and then they want us back like kids again.*

C: *I am going to be a kid as long as I want too!*

Thus, this group of young people criticised adults for having two opinions, but at the same time they seemed to be ambivalent and unclear in relation to the question of their own participation. At one point they emphasised that children, like adults, have both the knowledge and the capacity for participation, but, on the other hand, some of them wanted to be spared the burden of being a responsible person and to remain a child for as long as they could.

B. Children as citizens-to-be

While the previous theme was about how children should be spared responsibility, this one explores the argument that children are not able to participate. The children and young people in our study both supported and raised questions about this argument. Even if they agreed that adults should have greater responsibilities than children, they did not necessarily think that children should be spared having any responsibility at all. '*We do manage to take care of ourselves a bit, and we also need to learn to take care of ourselves until we are adults*', said one of the 8/9-year-old girls.

Some of the 14/15-year-olds went further and questioned the idea that they did not have any responsibilities. They linked this to choices they had had to make in their own lives and by challenging adults' construction of them as not being able or having the knowledge needed to 'manage' in society. This is evident in the dialogue below:

A: *I think young people have more difficult choices to make than adults ... like, it is when you are young that you have to work hard and decide what to be in life. If I do not get good grades now, it is not certain that I will get a job when I get older.*

B: *[...] We have other choices to make. Generally adults are finished thinking 'am I going to try that', 'am I going to make it really good', and so on. They have already taken that decision.*

A: *They do not understand that we also have to make some choices. They don't think we manage anything.*

C: *They underestimate us. (others agree)*

B: *They have forgotten their own youth.*

D: *And at the same time, I think it was easier when they were young. There was not that much bullying and group pressure like there is today.*

From their perspective, young people have to make a range of difficult decisions in their daily lives and are faced with many challenges that are demanding and put pressure on their ability to cope and handle different situations. In real life they had to manage themselves, even if adults did not think they were capable of doing so.

Since the young people expressed ambivalent opinions, it was unclear what they would really have preferred. This was apparent in a discussion about the kind of responsibilities children should have in an imaginary country:

> A: *[...] If you think about it, it would not be good if we were allowed to decide.*
>
> B: *Oh yes, it would have...*
>
> A: *We do not have a strong enough will to say like 'no, we have to take responsibility'. It is even hard for us to get up in the morning!*
>
> B: [interrupting]: *But it's fun to have responsibility too, because then you can decide a bit.*
>
> C: *Yes, but you will get more responsibility when you are an adult.*
>
> B: *Yes, but then it is just only boring responsibility, then it's bills and so on. When you are a kid you have, like, fun responsibility.*

Several supported the argument that, in some situations, children were unable to manage in the same way as adults, and that there were some limits. This was illustrated in their discussion about the age of voting. Some argued that the right to vote should start at the age of 16 years, '*because when you are 16 you are really quite an adult*'. Drawing on the 'maturity' argument, some girls thought it should be 16 years for girls and 18 years for boys, '*because boys are less mature in their minds than girls.*' Another argument for the age limit being 18 years was the way that children behaved, '*being foolish and playing around*' and '*not being serious enough.*' The right to vote was also related to an interest in, and knowledge about, politics. Those who argued for the age of 16 years thought this should be a right that would give those who were interested and wanted to vote the opportunity to do so. Others thought it was fine to wait until they were 18 years old. In one focus group, the participants were concerned that adults could take advantage of children's vulnerable position and use it to further their own best interests:

> A: *[But] there is a difference between adults and children. They have more experience and insight [about things].*
>
> B: *They understand more. And it could be like ... if children had the right to vote... then parents could use their kids, and ask them to vote for what they want.*

C: *They could have, like, given them ice cream if they did what they were told. (laughter)*

A: *And, like, 'I will tidy your room every week if you vote for this and this.'*

C: *I would have no idea what to vote for if I was going to vote now.*

Childhood, in this perspective, is seen as related to children being immature, vulnerable, less knowledgeable and uninterested in politics, in contrast to the understanding of adults as being wise, having more life experience and knowledge. Participation was described as something one had to qualify for. It was argued that people had to be able to consider the social consequences of their actions beyond their limited self-interest. Children were not considered able to participate because they lacked the knowledge and social capacity required for participation on these terms.

The children in our study did not agree on how they should participate, but instead presented arguments for and against this in relation to the question of ability. Several of the focus groups with young people aged 14/15 years discussed the age of majority. They linked this to when they would be able to take care of themselves, the age at which they thought their parents were, or should be, responsible for them, and the age at which they should have the right to vote. There was no agreement in any of the focus groups about a particular age limit. Some thought the age of majority should be lowered to 15 or 16 years; others argued that the minimum age of voting should be 18 years in national elections and a bit lower at the community level; and some thought it was fine the way it already was; while others said they '*really don't care.*'

C. Children as marginalised: The lack of political power

The third perspective was represented by the argument that children were actors with a right to participate in social as well as political matters. However, a sense of frustration could be identified as the powerless situation of children was pointed out. The children argued that children's views were not taken into account in important decisions, and that some of the institutions established to secure children's right to participate were of merely symbolic importance. It was only the young people aged 14-15 years in the study who presented these arguments and expressed their frustration at not being taken seriously, especially at school and in the community. To illustrate children's lack of political power we now present a case-study focusing on children's participation in a school reform process.

Case study: School reform

Dominating both of the focus groups at Secondary School D was the frustration of not being listened to in a recent class reform process at their school. According to the young people (aged 14/15 years), there had been a controversial and highly debated change in their school structure that had divided the pupils, most of the teachers and the headmaster. They said a new structure had been introduced that took the existing classes (with about 25 students each) and divided them into larger groups (of around 40 students), who were then divided into smaller groups again during some school hours. The pupils now had eight different groups to adjust to, and they were required to change groups all the time. The students had not been involved in the decision-making and, one boy said, '*We are like animals used for research purposes.*'

When the new structure was introduced to the students, many of them disagreed with it, but the decision had been made anyway. They said that only one pupil in their class had agreed with it, but that the teachers had said it was fine. One girl even claimed that the teacher had lied to the headmaster, telling him that the pupils wanted the change. She was supported by one of the boys in the focus group, who said that the teacher had changed their message and had claimed that they were positive. The students felt bad about being treated like this, and one boy said:

I think it should have been a majority decision, or like a democratic system. We could have had an election. It is we who are going to learn something, not the teachers!

One of the focus groups mentioned that their class had prepared a petition on which those who were against the proposal wrote their names. However, it seemed as if the teachers and the headmaster did not care: '*they just threw it away and did not consider the majority's opinion.*' The pupils also wanted to protest through a boycott or strike, but a teacher persuaded them to let the matter rest, otherwise, if they stayed out of school in protest, they would drop one grade. All of the students found this very unfair:

I think it is very stupid that they don't care about our opinion.

We were threatened to accept their decision.

They give us a choice, but what a choice! (ironic)

They say we can do what we want, but then it will have consequences for our grades.

The students said that the student council had not been allowed to discuss the issue either because the decision had already been made by the politicians. They thought this was stupid and hoped that the politicians would visit their school to see the consequences. However, they did not think this would help. As one frustrated boy said: '*They will probably just say, "Well, do you want to change it again to the way it used to be?" But now it is too late. We have got new friends.*'

The pupils also thought the change was unfair because it did not affect the other grades (8 and 10) of children in the secondary school in the same way. The 10th grade was not included because it was their last year at school and they had to focus on their final exams. The pupils in the 8th grade were new to the school, with new classes anyway, so they were not affected as much. But the pupils in our focus groups had, in their one year at the school, got to know the people in their class, found some friends, and then had been split up. In their view:

They should have waited for new generations to come. We should have been allowed to finish our school with the classes we had.

They could have started with the new classes that were coming to the school that had not been part of the old system. We had just got used to our class and found friends. And then we were split up.

I lost many friends through that. All my best friends are in the other class.

Like one person I used to hang out with almost every day, I never get to talk to now.

The effects the change had on friendship patterns were very important for the pupils. Later in the interview, when they discussed how the situation could be improved at their school to uphold children's rights, one of the focus groups again mentioned the school structure as an example:

A: *For example, in the case of the school structure, they decided, before we got the opportunity to say anything at all, whether it was going to happen. They were not open to discussing what we had to say at all.*

B: *They did say that they would listen to us and that we should have the final word and all that, but they didn't care about it for a second. And that is bad. It would have been one thing if they said that they would decide, but when they say that we can participate in deciding and then did nothing about it, that's what's bad. The way they do it, in a way ...*

C: *And we had to take the consequences.*

The students thought the decision was idiotic and described the outcome as chaos. First, they complained that they had lost contact with many of their friends. They had been given the opportunity to prioritise who they would like to be together with, but many did not get their first choice. Second, they said that the change had affected their grades. One of the boys said that the average in his class had dropped quite a lot because of all the confusion and noise. He could not concentrate properly and did not work as well as before. '*You feel insecure,*' one of the girls said. A third very important issue was the pupils' feeling that they had been neglected. They had the right to give their opinion, but were not heard, '*so it didn't help much,*' commented one boy. A girl followed up on his comment and said: '*It was not good to be neglected. [...] They don't think about the best interests of the students.*' Also, when the decision was taken, the pupils did not receive any information about what was going to happen. The headmaster provided some information, but they had had to sort much of it out by themselves and had found that difficult.

The young people were also frustrated that they were not taken seriously in the community. For example, one focus group said that there had been a petition involving many young people protesting against a plan to build apartment blocks on a football field they were using. They were frustrated that they were not listened to because, as one boy said, '*Had it been adults, then they would have taken it [the petition] more seriously.*'

On the other hand, the pupils understood why this occurred, and their dialogue gave some support to the argument that children should not be given political power:

Interviewer: *If, for instance, a road is being planned, do children have any right to participate in decisions about where it should go?*

A: *They say so, but they don't listen. Nobody listens to kids. Unless they are over 18, that is.*

Interviewer: *So you can express your opinion, but you are not heard? [Several children express agreement]*

B: *[...] Not when it comes to deciding for the society and so on. [...] There is a reason why there are elections only for people above 18 years.*

A: *They say that kids don't understand what they're voting on.*

B: *Kids have other priorities than to vote on who is going to be the next prime minister, or ...*

Interviewer: *So you think that children are not really interested in issues like who is going to decide?*

A: *Some are interested.*

B: *Yes, probably some are. But, like, most of the time, young people have other things to think about, like school and friends and ...*

A: *But they also say that kids are not smart enough to understand what they vote for.*

B: *That's wrong.*

Interviewer: *So you don't think that it should be like this?*

A: *It is in a way ... Kids are smart enough to understand what is happening in the world and things. We are. It's just that we don't always want to understand. Like me, I don't want to understand anything about war and all that. I only get sad about things like that.*

The different arguments about children as participants in society are evident in this transcription. The first is represented by Person A (a girl), who asserted that in principle children do have the right to participate in decisions, but that in reality they are restricted from doing so. Another perspective was presented by Person B, who stated that children in general have no interest in participating because they have other interests and that in any case they should be spared the burden of participating in difficult decisions. The third argument was referred to indirectly by Person A when she commented that some people thought that children were not smart enough to influence decisions. From this dialogue, it is evident that the various arguments are inter-related and combined to explain why children are being marginalised and lack political power.

Discussion

Since the ground-breaking study by Gary Melton (1980) in the USA, there has been consensus that children are concerned about their rights, and that their logic about such matters appears to be shaped more by age than socio-economic and cultural factors (Cherney & Perry, 1996; Limber et al., 1999; Melton, 1980; Melton & Limber, 1992; Ruck et al., 1998). In a recent study which compared Spain and Italy, it was found that factors such as age, gender and culture, as well as social context and living conditions, make little difference to children's views of their rights (Casas et al., 2006; Saporiti et al., 2005).

In our study we have identified differences that can be related to age. Comparing the data with the five other countries participating in the research project might provide some understanding of cultural differences between children's attitudes towards their rights and what they define as important in the concept of rights, especially in relation to the different views on participation and protection rights. Melton and Limber (1992) found that American children had particular concerns about self-determination and freedom of expression, while Norwegian children had particular concerns about nurturance rights, special entitlements and the protection of children. In our study, the Norwegian children were definitely concerned about participation rights, but they were concerned about provision rights too, and the younger children (8/9 years) also mentioned protection rights.

Our findings are consistent with observations from other studies that children's undertaking of different tasks at home is a vital, but often overlooked, aspect of the division of labour in the household, and that children's experiences of responsibility challenge the notion that childhood is a time 'free' from responsibility (Such & Walker, 2004, 2005). The focus-group participants said that exercising responsibility at home, at school and in the community was not generally a negative experience, and was often actively accepted by children as part of their childhood. However, as we have seen, they also recognised that adults have a special responsibility for them which is different from their own responsibilities. In a way, they saw themselves as *both* independent enough to be responsible and productive, *and* dependent upon their parents for some guidance and help. These findings are similar to those presented by Virginia Morrow (1999) from her group discussions with 12/14-year-olds in England.

Citizenship was a new concept for most of the children in our study. Nevertheless, they still managed to reflect on the meaning of the concept and share different opinions about what constituted a good citizen. Both the 8/9-year-olds and the 14/15-year-olds mentioned caring about other people and the environment as important. This echoes some of the findings in the Civic Education Study, in which 14-year-olds were asked to rate the importance of a range of statements about what it is to be a good adult citizen (Mikkelsen et al., 2001). To obey the law was regarded as important by the greatest number of students. Also ranked of high importance was the responsibility to do something to protect the environment, to work in the best interests of people in the neighbourhood, and to follow political debate in the newspapers and on the radio or television. Only a minority of the students ranked taking part in political debates regularly and being a member of a political party as important (Mikkelsen et al., 2001, p. 116). A significant difference between the studies was that we also asked the focus groups what children could do to be good citizens. We found that none of the pupils questioned their opportunity to be good citizens and that they included themselves as citizens. This contrasted with findings from a UK study with an older group of young people aged 16–22 years, who saw themselves as excluded from being good citizens since they were not in 'waged employment, paying taxes, with their own house, family and car' (Smith et al., 2005, p. 433).

Norway is considered an initiator in terms of taking children's rights seriously. Several institutions have been established with the intention of securing children's participation rights, in relation to both their everyday lives and society in general. However, the extent of their empowered participation is often limited, and children's position as political actors is unclear (Kjørholt & Lidén, 2004).

In our study, we found that the focus-group participants expressed ambivalence towards the idea of children as participants in society. On the one hand, the children considered themselves citizens with rights and responsibilities in society. On the other hand, conflicting views about the notion of children as participants – reflecting different ideas about childhood – could be interpreted as ambivalence towards seeing themselves as political actors. With this ambivalence in mind, we might pose the following questions for further investigation:

- Can the children's ambiguities towards being participants in society be seen as mirroring the ambiguity in society in general over granting children the status of citizenship?
- What importance does this ambiguity among children have when it comes to establishing institutions for implementing and improving the right of children to be participants in society?

The conclusion of this first part of our study echoes Virgina Morrow's (1999) finding that the main concern of children is to be accorded some dignity and respect 'as people' and to have a say in the decision-making process: to be heard, but not necessarily to make decisions on their own or to have ultimate control over the process (pp. 165–6). Like the children quoted in Morrow's paper, our Norwegian children also seemed to be reflecting what has been termed a 'social' model of citizenship. As Cockburn (1999, p. 100) argues, this implies 'the ways in which people are connected to each other, rather than being viewed as acting as individualised, autonomous, rational beings separate from each other'. Furthermore, some of the responses indicate an interrelatedness of rights, in the sense that different forms of participation are connected to protection and provision in dynamic ways. However, in order to obtain greater insight into this, more extensive and complex data related to different forms of participation in children's everyday lives is needed.

7

Palestine

Mohammed Shaheen
Center for Development in Primary Health Care
Al-Quds University Child Research Unit, Palestine

Introduction

Childwatch International supported the initiation of a research group from six countries to study children's views on the concepts of citizenship, rights and responsibilities in their local contexts. This chapter reports on the views of Palestinian children and young people on these issues.

Socio-cultural Context

Palestinian life has been transformed since the start of the Second Palestinian Uprising (*Intifada*) in September 2000 and the large-scale Israeli re-invasion of Palestinian towns and villages in 2002. Unemployment is now estimated at 34.3 per cent, with many families facing financial difficulty due to rising unemployment and access to work in Israel being denied. Around 80 per cent of the population has an income below the poverty level. Regular curfews, and the network of almost 700 checkpoints, roadblocks and other fixtures, severely restrict movement and limit people's ability to reach their work places and schools, seek health services, engage in community activities or pursue other semblances of normal life (CAP, 2004). Women and children are amongst the most affected population groups as a result of the continuous and unstable political and economic conditions in the West Bank and Gaza Strip. For example, a total of 971 children have been killed in the Israeli-Palestinian conflict violence, representing 18 per cent of the total number of conflict deaths (OCHA, 2007).

Israeli military operations, clashes and arrests occur almost daily. There is a strong Israeli military presence at checkpoints and throughout the districts of the West Bank. Movement and access to local services and facilities in West Bank cities, which serve the villages of the districts, are dependent upon permission from Israeli soldiers at checkpoints. Villages have been virtually cut off from the facilities of the West Bank cities. The rapid construction of the Separation Wall has detrimentally impacted on the north and north-western areas of the West Bank. Teachers, health workers, farmers, land-owners and other workers and family members experience significant daily access problems.

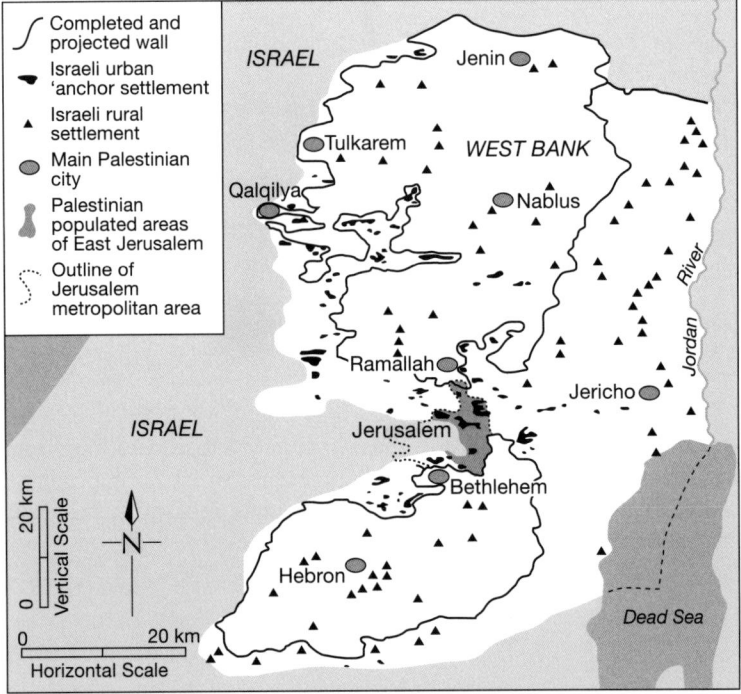

Israel's Separation Wall in the West Bank, May 2003. Adapted from maps by PASSIA, the PLO Negotiations Affairs Department and NAD-NSU.

Israel became a State Party to the UNCRC in 1991. In 2002, upon its initial review of Israel's compliance with the Convention, the UN Committee on the Rights of the Child underlined the applicability of the Convention in the Occupied Palestinian Territory (OPT) and Israel's responsibility to implement its provisions therein (Defense for Children International, 2007). Despite this clear and well-defined legal obligation to respect and ensure Palestinian children's rights, Israel denies the applicability of human rights treaties in the OPT and continues to violate the UNCRC and its obligation to implement it. The concept of rights among Palestinians, including children, is therefore not very well received since they see that their rights are not enforced in the Palestinian Territories by all parties – including Israel, the International organisations and the Palestinian Authority.

Palestinian children under the age of 18 years of age constitute more than 56 per cent of the Palestinian population. They are active political agents in national liberation and political recognition efforts, but do not have an organised voice to influence political, civil and social policies. Although children are active politically, they lack formal political recognition in the UN charter since Palestine is not recognised as a full member of the United Nations. Ironically, child protection as per the UN Charter lies under the responsibility of the Israeli Government as an occupying force. Yet the Israeli military occupation violates various Palestinian children's rights on a daily basis – for example, children are punished for exercising their right to participate in resisting Israeli occupation. Children also have no organised means of influencing local policies despite the fact that they represent more than half of the Palestinian population.

Palestinian children are subject to continuous trauma resulting from the political and security instability and military and political-related violence. A significant number unfortunately suffer from stress, including Post-Traumatic Stress Disorder (PTSD), as a result of the political violence and military occupation. In a survey of 2100 Palestinian high school students, it was found that approximately 34 per cent suffered from the signs and symptoms of PTSD (Shaheen & Abdeen, 2004).

On a more positive note, children's education receives significant support and recognition from the Palestinian Authority and society. Educating children is regarded as part of the Palestinian struggle for liberation, recognition and hope for a better future (Alpha International, 2004). However, the school curricula lack a focus on issues related to civil rights, responsibilities and citizenship (Hine, 2004). In the absence of laws to protect them, and effective implementation of existing laws, children continue to be subject to violence by educators, parents, adults, Israeli soldiers and often their peers. Children have a sense of being abandoned and this causes feelings of frustration and bitterness among them.

Aim of the Research

The main aim of this research was to explore the perspectives of Palestinian school children, aged 8/9 years and 14/15 years, on the various aspects of children's rights, responsibilities and citizenship within their own reality. The study was conducted as part of an international initiative to explore how children from different cultures regarded these key concepts and how they related to them.

The key concepts were defined as a general reference for the researchers as follows:

A right – something which people are entitled to – for example, children have a right to go to school in most countries.

A responsibility – an obligation or something which people are expected to do – for example, children are expected to comply with school rules.

A Citizen – a member of a society or local community. In democratic countries this is usually marked by rights (e.g. the right to participate) and responsibilities (e.g. to obey the law).

Research Methodology

The research team followed the approach recommended by the principal researchers who developed the tools for conducting the focus groups. We undertook a sensitive cultural translation of the protocols and questions to ensure their suitability for use in the Palestinian context.

Research Context and Sample

In-depth focus groups were conducted with Palestinian children in several schools in the West Bank. The selection of these groups was based on the criteria outlined in the international study protocol. The students were selected for the focus groups according to the following criteria:

1. Age (8/9 years, 14/15 years);
2. Gender balance (girls and boys);
3. Different socio-economic status (by including students in both public and private schools);
4. Different regions within the West Bank (including cities and the Jenin camp);
5. Willingness to participate.

A letter was written to school principals so the field researchers could gain official entry to each school. The school administrations then put forward our request for student volunteers in the relevant age groups. Schools were also asked to obtain permission from parents for their child's participation in the focus group discussion.

Table One depicts the locations of the twenty focus groups that were formed in coordination with the school principals and parents. The final selection was based on convenience sampling while taking into consideration the specific age and gender of the target students.

The research was conducted in three West Bank areas: Jenin and its Camp, Jerusalem and Ramallah. Twelve of the children's groups belonged to a low socio-economic level (Jenin camp, and the district of Ramallah), while the other eight groups belonged to medium and high socio-economic levels (Jerusalem and Ramallah city). The selection of schools was based on the need to represent different socio-economic levels and types of schooling. Private and government schools were selected in three regions of the West Bank:

- **Ramallah district:** This district is considered relatively better off economically and socially from most regions in the West Bank. It is the region where the political leadership, intellectuals and professional organisations are located, but there are also refugee camps and villages where people from lower socio-economic populations live. Two schools were chosen: a private school in Ramallah, which enrols students from relatively high socio-economic conditions, and a school in the Betonia

Table One: Focus groups conducted in Palestine

Age Group	8/9 years		14/15 years		Total
Socio-economic level	**Girls**	**Boys**	**Girls**	**Boys**	
Medium/high	1 Jerusalem - -	1 Jerusalem 1 Jenin -	1 Jerusalem 1 Ramallah -	1 Ramallah 1 Jerusalem 1 Jenin	8
Low	1 Jerusalem 1 Betonia 1 Jenin Camp	1 Jerusalem 1 Betonia 1 Jenin Camp	1 Jerusalem 1 Betonia 1 Jenin Camp	1 Jerusalem 1 Betonia 1 Jenin Camp	12
Total No. Focus Groups	4	5	5	6	20

village in the suburbs of Ramallah which enrols students who are generally from the middle and lower socio-economic levels.

- **Jenin District:** Jenin camp, city and villages are considered among the poorest areas in the West Bank and the hardest hit by Israeli incursions, attacks, closures and curfews.

- **Jerusalem:** East Jerusalem is part of the West Bank that was annexed by the Israeli Government after the occupation in 1967. The Palestinian Arab population is diminishing proportionally as a result of the Israeli policy to transform Jerusalem from having an Arab Palestinian majority to a Jewish majority. The Palestinian population in Jerusalem enjoys relatively better services and living conditions than in other cities and localities in the West Bank as they are entitled to benefits under the Israeli social welfare system.

Table Two depicts the number of Palestinian children and young people who participated in the focus groups. There were 181 students in total – 83 of whom were aged 8/9 years and 98 of whom were aged 14/15 years.

Of the 20 focus groups, four were conducted with girls aged 8/9 years (39 students), five with boys aged 8/9 years (44 students), five with girls aged 14/15 years (43 students), and six with boys aged 14/15 years (55 students). The focus group sessions were planned for two hours, but their implementation went much longer than expected (three hours). Each session was conducted by one researcher and an assistant who shared the roles of facilitation and note-taking.

Table Two: Palestinian child participants in the citizenship study focus groups

Age	Boys	Girls	Total
8/9 Years	44	39	83
14/15 Years	55	43	98
TOTAL	**99 boys**	**82 girls**	**181 students**

Fieldwork

The field work started in March 2004 and ended in July 2004. Four junior researchers conducted the 20 focus group discussions with the children and young people. Each had a university education, a background in health or social sciences, and experience in conducting focus groups and qualitative research. The field researchers were assigned from the selected study regions as follows:

- Maisaa Abubaker: Major in psychology – Jenin
- Sahar Dkeidek: Major in Health Sciences – Jerusalem
- Kifah Bany Odeh: Major in Health Sciences – Ramallah
- Wafa' Dabbas: Major in social studies – Ramallah

Three days' training and orientation was undertaken with the researchers on the purpose of the study and its methodology. This also covered qualitative research features and their relevance to the aims of the project, and interviewing skills, including how to ask and probe the children's responses to the key questions, document children's responses, analyse the data and report the findings for each focus group. Two field researchers were assigned to conduct each focus group discussion: one asked the questions and led the discussion, while the other researcher observed the process and documented the children's responses. The field researchers were encouraged to record the responses in the language and words used by the children during the discussion around each of the key research questions. The topics were not perceived as threatening, neither to schools nor to parents, and many children enjoyed being away from their regular classroom education.

The focus group discussions followed the same guidelines stated in the original study protocol in order to make the data collection process as comparable as possible with that used in the other five countries. There was, however, a need to frame the questions in a more culturally applicable and sensitive manner, while maintaining the purpose and intention of the research. On average, eight children attended each of the focus groups and their discussions lasted two and a half to three hours.

Key Findings

Rights

This concept was the easiest for the children to understand, but they were sceptical of its application in the Palestinian context. The main focus of the children's perceptions of children's rights was on their basic needs, including being free and able to live in peace and security. Some of the students from the higher socio-economic class referred to the concept of rights as '*to be able to live the good life, such as having a car, a house, a job and status*', while some children from lower socio-economic levels focused on the need '*to live securely and in peace*', but also possess basic things in life.

In a conflict situation, children's rights can be violated given that many casualties during the *Intifada* involved children. The principles and provisions to protect children in armed conflict are laid out in the Geneva Convention (1949) and their Additional Protocols (1977), the UNCRC (1989) and its Optional Protocol on the involvement of children in armed conflict (2000), and the Rome Statute (1998) of the International Criminal Court (UNICEF, 2006). Children's perceptions of their rights were influenced by the violence and unstable political reality affecting Palestinian children under occupation. Some of the children were explicit about their rights – for example, '*to move freely*' and '*achieving national independence*'. One of the children said: '*Rights mean that children like us live securely, safely and peacefully and achieve our independence and freedom.*'

Ahmad, a male child aged 14, from Jenin camp stated that:

Part of our right is to walk in wide streets with lights, not to have to fear being hurt by soldiers and not to be checked at military checkpoints.

A female student, (Muna) from Ramallah, aged 16, said:

Are not we children like other children in the world? We deserve to have a homeland and independent country so we can play and go to school without fear.

Young people aged 14/15 focused on other related meanings such as:

- To live in dignity. As one student stated: '*We the children suffer from humiliation almost every day, either from Israeli occupation or from our teachers, parents. We have the right to live a dignified life free of oppression and fear.*'
- To move freely without restriction or barriers so we can enjoy playing, travelling and meeting peers from different localities. Palestinian children are very aware of the checkpoints and military barriers in their everyday lives since they all commute to their schools, visit their relatives or see these barriers when they play.
- To be free from harm. This is again related to the fear and traumatic

experiences that children are exposed to as a result of the political violence and military actions in the different areas within the West Bank.
- To achieve our national independence.
- To participate in national elections and decide on issues that affect them. This issue was mainly raised by students enrolled in private schools and was less evident in the focus groups held in public schools.

Younger children (8/9 yrs) focused on basic needs, expressed as:

- Possessing things;
- Rights to food, shelter and play;
- Something you need and is necessary for children to live in good conditions;
- Things that we like to achieve.

When considering children's **rights within homes**, the children expressed their desire to have more freedom at home, and be as valued as adults in making decisions. They wanted recognition of their ability to express themselves, and to be able to select their friends without interference from their parents. The control of Palestinian parents over their children's freedom is motivated by the adults' desire to minimise their children's exposure to violence outside their home and avoid the likelihood of harm occurring through confrontations with Israeli soldiers. Other children expressed various basic rights such as:

- To be asked their opinion on family matters;
- To possess private rooms;
- To watch television freely without control;
- To select their friends without interference from their parents;
- To select and eat the food that they like;
- To be given the chance to participate in recreational events.

The majority of the study participants agreed that children should have the following **rights within the school environment:**

- To be treated well by teachers;
- To receive a good education;
- To be treated equally in respect of gender, age and social class;
- To have a safe and adequate place to play;
- To express their opinions without being penalised;
- To have computers and good teachers, healthy toilets and laboratories;
- To participate in extracurricular activities;
- To reduce the school load to suit their age.

When considering children's **rights outside home and school,** the children focused on their right to play, have a good education and be heard by their teachers. Many of them expressed the following rights:

- To walk without being hurt by others;
- To be free from obligations, such as schooling;
- To treatment with respect;
- To children's clubs;
- To move around without being stopped by Israeli checkpoints;
- To recreational places and activities;
- To be heard by others, especially through the media.

The children thought that their rights should be more valued than adults, while adults should have more responsibilities in the community. Some of them stated '*our rights and needs are bigger than responsibilities*', '*we are different from adults because we have different roles*', and '*we have more rights than adults should have because we are children.*'

Students from the Jenin camp were clearly influenced by their political and social reality. For example, one student said:

After the Israeli soldiers demolished our home at Jenin camp, the United Nations helped rebuild the old houses, but they will never bring back my father who was killed by the Israeli soldiers.

Responsibilities

Children focused on addressing their responsibilities towards their families and community, such as obeying their parents and teachers and keeping the environment clean. The young people aged 14/15 years viewed 'responsibility' as more like an obligation towards their families, environment and community at large. The younger children focused on their responsibility to be good students and to obey their parents.

Some of the older children aspired to liberate their land from occupation and ensure the safety of their parents and relatives. One student said: '*We as children can't watch our land being taken from us without defending it.*' Another stated: '*We have to make sure that my parents and my brothers and sisters are not harmed by others, especially the Israeli soldiers.*'

Others believed that responsibility was the ability to bear difficulties and face challenges, but felt that parents did not give them clear responsibility. This notion may also be influenced by the paternalistic nature of Palestinian society, whereby children are considered minors and incapable of taking full responsibility. One child said that '*responsibility is mainly for adults and not children and it is more for boys than girls.*' Such responses may also be influenced by the idea that Palestinian children regard adults as citizens – especially since adults carry passports, can vote, go to work and make decisions at home and in the community. However, children view themselves as 'incomplete citizens' insofar as they cannot do what adults are allowed and capable of doing. Children consider men as being more capable citizens than women, a view which is influenced by the status of women within Palestinian society.

Other children expressed their responsibility towards the environment – '*We need to keep our home and neighbourhood clean and make it green all the time.*' Others emphasised the need to help their parents financially through finding work that brought them some income. One of the children in Jenin camp stated: '*My father is ill and can't work and my mother can't work because we are six children. I am the oldest child and should help my family in this difficult situation.*' The economic conditions and rising financial hardship have contributed to the increase in child labour in Palestinian society. Children's work has become part of the family coping mechanism.

Children's responses to their **responsibilities at home** included:

- To help my parents;
- To clean my room;
- To care for younger brothers and sisters;
- To respect and obey parents;
- To help in home related tasks such as purchases of necessary goods for the house;
- To work to help my parents earn income.

Children's **responsibilities towards their community and in the surrounding environment** included the following:

- To protect local gardens and environment;
- To help poor children and neighbours;
- To follow moral and ethical codes to guide people's behaviours;
- To respect others' rights to do things they like;
- To respect public property;
- To respect the religion and customs of our neighbours;
- To help older people;
- To participate in cultural activities;
- To defend our people against danger and occupation;
- To participate in voluntary work to clean the environment.

Children's understanding of the environment was influenced by the increasingly poor conditions in almost all areas of the West Bank: the deteriorating environment, infrastructure, checkpoints, separation wall, garbage pile-ups and open sewage system, especially in the refugee camps. They indicated that responsibilities for the environment meant '*that people have more trees*', '*can rebuild destroyed houses*', '*have clean water*', '*have new buildings*', '*pave damaged streets*' and '*have nice views*'.

Their main **responsibilities towards the environment** included:

- To protect trees and plant new trees;
- To protect the water and keep it clean;

- To ration the use of water;
- To make the environment clean.

Citizenship

The children had more difficulty understanding the meaning of **citizenship**. In some focus groups the interviewers needed to clarify this concept by providing examples. Many children questioned the interviewers on what was meant by citizenship. A few older children responded to the question by saying that citizens:

- Have rights and responsibilities;
- Hold an identity;
- Obey laws of the state;
- Follow religious instructions;
- Have rights and obligations;
- Are individuals who live in the country.

The Imaginary Land Versus the Contemporary Land

The imaginary country exercise attracted the children's attention much more than the earlier concepts – perhaps reflecting the political reality of their daily lives and their aspirations and hopes for a better future. The students were asked to build a new imaginary country different from the one they live in currently. In groups, they drew and named the new land, and also discussed their perception of the rights and responsibilities of a 'good citizen' that they would like to see in the new imaginary country. Responses were reported by each group, while some individual responses and quotations were also encouraged and documented.

Children enjoyed the exercise of drawing the imaginary land since they were dreaming of freedom, respect, happier lives and a more stable environment. Some children wanted to create a land for children only, without adults, where they could create their own rules and regulations. The children in private schools focused on names for their lands that reflected better and more enjoyable lives than those they had currently. They named their imaginary country the '*Land of Beauty*' and the '*Land of Paradise*'. Some thought it too difficult to have a land of their dreams, while another group called their imaginary land '*The Land of Sweet Dreams*'. The children from less advantaged schools and poorer areas, such as Jenin camp, called the new land '*The Land of Heroes*', '*A Land of Freedom*' and the '*Impossible Land*'. Others called their land '*the broken chain*', symbolising their dream of becoming free from restrictions, barriers and occupation. A group of girls of lower social status called their land '*the new Palestine*'. They wanted to keep the present Palestine, but to make changes that provided a better fit for children. One of the girls said: '*In new Palestine we will create new law, new borders that allow us to move freely and guarantee that all children do things that they like and enjoy better living conditions.*'

Perceived Rights in the New Land
The children expressed different views on their rights in the new country as they perceived it. Some demanded that a new constitution be put in place which secured children's rights to free expression of their thoughts, free movement, a prohibition on violence and killings, and equal shares of things including money. This perception may have been influenced by the fact that children, especially those from the lower socio-economic class, strive to have the right to possess things like other children who enjoy better living conditions.

Some other children thought that they should have rights like adults in the new land. They did not want to be told what to do, nor be punished by adults for doing things that they, as children, liked. The students felt that, in their current land, adults did not allow them to express themselves freely and would punish them if they did things that adults did not like at school or home.

The girls again expressed the need for more freedom to go out, have friends and not be controlled by adults at home or at school. They also wanted to have separate rooms at home and engage in activities without adult interference. They hoped that the new land would not have any discrimination between adults and children and between boys and girls. As one child said: *'In the new land no child has less than others and we want to have equal rights and responsibilities.'*

Perceived Responsibilities in the New Land
Children expressed their desire to have fewer responsibilities and more rights in the new land, since they had taken on so many responsibilities in their current land. They were determined to protect their new land since it was their own creation and responsibility. Others types of responsibilities included:

- Having rights and responsibilities;
- Having an independent state;
- Free expression of opinion;
- Co-operating with people;
- Helping poor children and providing them with all they need.

In other words, children generally wanted more freedom from the paternalistic and controlling ways of adults, to be free from occupation, lack of security, extreme poverty and serious inequity, and to maintain good relationships with each other. One of the children said:

> *If we have a new land or country we would like to assume responsibility for preventing adults from controlling our lives and we will create schools that will allow children to play and have fun and not to study only.*

Meaning of a 'Good Citizen'

Since the children had difficulty understanding the concept of citizenship, it was hard to obtain relevant answers to the question about what it means to be a 'good citizen'. The researchers were tempted to provide some examples to children, but this was discouraged in the training and general methodology. Some children said: *'being a citizen is to be old enough to work and earn money.'* Others said that good citizens are *'those individuals who are able to serve their country and their people'*. One child said that *'to be a good citizen is to carry an official identity card'*, while others said: *'Not to lie to my mother'*, or *'to be allowed to work and settle in my land without being forced to become a refugee'*. Other suggested that to be a 'good citizen' meant:

- Respecting others;
- Avoiding causing problems;
- Improving my nationhood;
- Obtaining a high level education;
- Helping the poor and needy;
- Defending my land.

The responsibilities and duties of a 'good citizen' included:

- Protecting our land;
- Listening to parents' advice;
- Keeping the law and order;
- Helping to solving others' problems;
- Serving his/her people and nation;
- Not betraying his/her own people;
- Developing and improving public services.

These responses indicate that the children had a high sense of responsibility towards their communities, families and country influenced by the fact that Palestinians are yearning to build their nationhood and achieve freedom from outside control and Israeli occupation. The concept of 'good citizenship' is very much influenced by Palestinians' lack of experience of nationhood, unlike other children, and Palestinian children continue to see themselves as different from others who have recognised countries where their human and political rights are respected.

The Meaning of Participation/Sharing

Many children felt that they did not play an active role in family and community matters and thought that they were treated as incapable of making decisions on issues related to their school, home and community. Children in the Ramallah district stated:

> *It is very difficult to convince our families to allow us to participate in how problems are solved at home or to become part of children's clubs that teach us how to become useful to people in our neighbourhood.*

Children expressed a great desire to be part of formal clubs that could organise them and teach them how to become effective members of their communities. One student said: '*We are treated as minors by adults although we can help them in many things such as in cleaning our neighbourhood and in helping the poor.*' Children expressed their dissatisfaction with how society treats them and how they are obliged to follow adults' ways of doing things at home, school and in the community at large.

In general, children's understanding of participation involved being part of activities designed by their parents and their communities. Younger children again faced difficulties in understanding the concept of participation, while the older children, especially those from private schools, indicated the need for children to participate in community and voluntary work and to help needy people, especially the elderly.

Participation within schools was mainly related to extra-curricular activities – as many students felt that the school system and curricular responsibilities denied them the opportunity to be involved in more enjoyable learning and voluntary activities such as:

- Helping to clean the school;
- Helping in school morning hours;
- Participating in sports activities;
- Participating in decisions at the school level;
- Participating in school committees;
- Participating in the organisation of school exhibitions.

Most students expressed a lack of satisfaction with the current school system and said that their main motivations for going to school were to talk to their friends and to make new friends.

With respect to participation outside of homes and schools, the children focused on activities that they enjoy or consider need to be done, such as:

- Designing the playground;
- Picking olives during the olive season;
- Religious and national activities;
- Participating in forcing the occupation army out;
- Peaceful demonstrations;
- Social and relief activities;
- Various political activities against occupation.

Palestinian children actively participated against occupation during the first and second uprising, yet felt marginalised in terms of their influence on the social and educational policies and programmes that best suit them. There were, however, differences between the students attending the private and public schools. Private school students were more relaxed about discussing the different issues raised by the research, including sensitive topics such as their view of their rights in their schools. They were able to grasp the meaning of key concepts and questions and participated in more elaborate discussion and feedback than the students enrolled in the public schools. The private school students had more exposure to the citizenship concepts and had received more education about children's rights. They held critical viewpoints, and were more rebellious and aware of the things they needed to change about their current reality.

Conclusion

This study is the first research project that has been conducted with Palestinian children, aged 8/9 years and 14/15 years, using this methodology to ask them directly about their perception of children's rights, responsibilities and citizenship. The study has proved to be very relevant to Palestinian children. Almost all the 181 children who participated in the focus groups expressed interest in participating in similar types of research in the future. It was evident that the children appreciated participating in an activity that allowed them to express themselves on issues that are of interest to them. While the topics addressed in these focus groups were difficult to deal with, the children managed to provide their perspectives within the framework of their unique Palestinian context.

The largest complaint by children related to the school environment, where children felt that they are not listened to by school teachers or administrators. Few said that they had any real say at school. Only a small number of schools had policies that encouraged children's participation in the school's decision-making processes. However, many of the students at these schools were sceptical about the efficacy of their participation and felt that their involvement was token. There is therefore a need to promote research that allows children to share their experiences and voice their concerns. They are desperate to be heard and deserve to have a voice on what they see as their essential right – the right to have a voice in all matters that affect their lives.

The following issues have been identified as a result of our experience in conducting the focus groups in Palestine:

1. The Research Methodology

Children enjoyed the exercise because it gave them a valid excuse to be out of their class, to be listened to and given adequate attention. However, more time was needed for the focus groups than was allowed by the participating schools (around two hours). The focus group protocol was perceived by some children as too long and insufficiently distinctive. The younger children (8/9 year olds) had difficulty in understanding the concepts of rights and responsibilities, and especially citizenship. However, they liked the imaginary country exercise and could articulate what they wanted to happen differently from their current reality. Engaging children through drawings and group activities can be very effective in soliciting more spontaneous and in-depth responses (e.g. the imaginary land).

The children managed to express their thinking freely, without influence from teachers or family members, which allowed the field researchers to obtain in-depth information from the focus group discussions. This has not always happened in other studies undertaken within schools, where it has been observed that children's responses have been influenced by the presence of teachers or school officials. A participatory research model allows children to express themselves once they have established a trusting relationship with the researchers. Allowing adequate time for trust and rapport building, before starting the discussion on the actual research questions, is therefore essential.

Some questions were considered too provocative and sensitive. Students sometimes failed to differentiate between responsibility and authority. Girls were more co-operative and responsive, while boys were less attentive. However, both girls and boys were active participants in the focus groups. The older children were more able to respond to these questions than the younger children, especially given the complexity of the issues discussed. Children in private schools were able to express themselves more freely and dynamically than children of lower socio-economic status. However, children in the camps were much more passionate and spontaneous about the issues affecting their lives, particularly once they had been given sufficient time to 'break the ice'.

2. The Political Situation
Closures, military incursions, checkpoints, Israeli occupation, economic hardship and the resulting psycho-social tension in the West Bank all had an effect on the children's responses, but this varied according to socio-economic status.

3. Rights and Responsibilities
The children, in general, could not differentiate between rights and responsibilities and they experienced some confusion in responding to the questions. Poorer children focused more on basic needs, such as their **rights** to food, security and private rooms. They also focused on the need to liberate their land, achieve national independence and move freely within the country. The older children in private schools focused on their right to express their opinion and to have equal opportunities/rights for male and female children. They also wanted to be allowed to participate in decisions at home and school and to participate in voluntary work within their communities. Some of the children, especially in private schools, indicated that they have more rights than adults and felt they needed to be free from parental control and able to decide on choosing their friends and clothes. Children also expressed their right to select their own teachers and to have a better quality education.

Palestinian children are not fully aware of their rights as spelled out in the UNCRC. They regard such rights as more like slogans, rather than being real. This is due to their experience of the gross violation of human rights under Israeli occupation and the economic and social hardship affecting most of the Palestinian population. Children are in need of more education, information and programmes to better inform them of their rights and responsibilities. They are eager to learn to become good citizens.

Almost all the children expressed their right to live in peace and security, to achieve an independent state, have freedom of movement, be respected by teachers and parents, have a clean environment, and liberate their land from Israeli occupation. In the new imaginary land they identified more freedom to move around, without checkpoints and barriers, and better safety with no crimes and violence. Children of lower socio-economic conditions also wanted jobs to be found for their parents.

The children in private schools were much more aware of their rights compared to children in other schools, and they seemed to be more exposed to children's rights as expressed by the UNCRC.

Girls, particularly those socio-economically better-off, focused on the need to be treated equally with their male peers – especially in the way they dress and in their ability to do things that boys are allowed to do.

The children in government schools who came from less advantaged communities were more reserved in their focus group discussions and what they thought about their own rights and citizenship. They were also more critical of their schools and families for not allowing them to express themselves and to be accepted as children.

With respect to **responsibilities**, the children thought that adults should have less rights and more responsibilities. Some children, especially those of lower socio-economic status, said that children have to obey the instructions of their parents and teachers. They also highlighted their responsibility to defend their land, protect their parents, help the elderly, protect all family members from harm, protect the environment and help the poor. The children also said that they are obliged to respect rules and regulations within schools, succeed in assignments, respect their teachers and parents, and maintain cleanliness.

While children realise that adults are responsible for providing their basic life requirements, they are not satisfied with adult society looking on them as minors incapable of actively participating in and serving their local communities. Girls, especially those in the private schools, were unhappy about having less rights than boys – particularly since they are required to undertake more responsibilities at home, in addition to the school, when compared with boys.

4. Citizenship

Children's views about the concept of citizenship were more problematic and confusing than those on rights and responsibilities. Most of their responses on the idea of citizenship were mixed with comments about their perception of rights and responsibilities. Therefore, limited responses were obtained. The older children did, however, provide some meanings of citizenship such as *'being part of the place or live in the country'*, *'obey God and follow religious instructions'*, *'holds an identity'*, *'owns land and building'* and *'obeys local laws.'* Palestinian children have been denied experience of the full meaning of citizenship as a result of the occupation, absence of a sovereign state, absence of the enforcement and execution of laws, and confused identity.

Children mainly associated the concept of citizenship with having an identity, a state, a place to live in and the right to protect one's children. This notion is highly politicised as a result of the unstable political conditions in Palestine.

5. The Imaginary Land

Children enjoyed the imaginary land/country exercise and expressed interest in living in a different country that had better living conditions, greater security, a cleaner environment, freedom, no soldiers to restrict their movement, or control by parents who prevented them from doing the things they liked to do. The older children, especially in private schools, had a more creative imagination and emphasised names such as the land of '*heroes*', '*freedom*', '*beauty*', '*new hopes*' and '*new Palestine*'. The poorer children focused on defending the land and their parents, and protecting the environment. Many of them realised that this was an impossible and unrealistic option and were somewhat sarcastic in their responses. However, this exercise was, in part, a therapeutic session which enabled them to free themselves temporarily from the current hardship, trauma and frustration that afflicts the total population in the OPT.

8
South Africa

Rose September & Hazel Roberts[1]
Child & Youth Research & Training Programme,
University of the Western Cape

Introduction

South Africa was ruled by the oppressive and inhumane apartheid regime prior to 1994. The impetus for its existence and power was legalised racial discrimination, large-scale segregation and exclusion. From the 1950s on there was ongoing resistance to apartheid, but this movement gained momentum after 1976, when schools became important sites of struggle and youth assumed a pivotal role in resistance efforts. The period between 1976 and 1987 was an especially turbulent one, characterised by violence, large-scale detention, even of children, and long periods of interrupted schooling. The release of Nelson Mandela from prison in 1990 marked the start of the transition to democracy for the country. A landmark for South Africa was the first democratic election in 1994 and the inauguration of Nelson Mandela as President. In 1996, a new constitution was developed, which guaranteed all citizens a range of rights and freedoms. Given the country's long history of resistance, there is a strong human rights focus in government policies, while discourses on rights are a growing part of daily existence in South Africa. Most significantly for children, section 28 of the Constitution (1996) provides for a range of children's rights pertaining to their survival, growth, protection and participation. The country has also signed and ratified the UNCRC (1989) and the African Charter on the Rights and Welfare of the Child.

The Constitution (1996), together with these international instruments, has impacted significantly on the development of legislation and policies aimed at the progressive realisation of children's rights in South Africa. However, much remains to be done. After just over one decade of democracy, many South Africans are still coming to terms with life under a constitutional democracy. The concepts of rights and citizenship are therefore still relatively new for both children and many adults. While the promotion of children's rights is a significant progression, many adults in South Africa are sceptical and suspicious about the notion of child rights. There is some recognition that rights are important, but responsibilities must be equally promoted. For example, the new South African Children's Act includes children's rights as well as their responsibilities to family, community and state.

Children and young people's participation in the political struggle during the apartheid years is generally revered. However, in post-apartheid South Africa, children's participation in matters affecting their lives, as espoused in the international instruments, seems to be lagging behind. The purpose of this study was to examine the perceptions of children themselves, parents and teachers about key concepts generally associated with democratic societies which pertain to children (i.e. rights, responsibilities and citizenship).

Children's Rights, Responsibilities and Citizenship

Children's rights are enshrined in the UNCRC, which recognises children as a group to whom human rights apply. In addition to provision (services relating to health, education and leisure) and protection (safety) rights, the Convention also recognises participation and citizenship rights. Traditionally viewed as the domain of adults, these rights allow for children to express their views on issues that affect them, be listened to, taken seriously and be involved in decisions that affect their lives (Casas, 1998; Osler & Starkey, 1996). The participation of children is an integral element of their development as responsible citizens in their own right. It has long been recognised that including children in decision-making builds their self-esteem and confidence, facilitates independent thinking and equips them to take their rightful place as citizens. However, it appears that adults find it difficult to enable children to exercise their participation rights. The right of children to make their own choices and express an opinion challenges conventional beliefs about parental authority (Casas, 1998; John, 2003; Osler & Starkey, 1996).

Verhellen (2000, p. 33) suggests that the social construction of childhood today implies that children are seen as not-yets: 'children are defined as not knowing, not yet competent and not yet being'. Childhood is viewed as being in preparation for adult life and, observed from this angle, implies that adults are not used to treating children from a human rights perspective. In terms of their social grouping, there is a huge divide between adults and children and, from this perspective, adults may raise questions about whether children should be given the same rights (Casas, 1998; John, 2003). Having the same rights could threaten the dominant position held by adults and upset the balance of power between adults and children. In order for children to apply their rights, they need to have a sense of personal power. One approach to achieving this is advocating for children's policies that promote freedom of expression and access to information and educational opportunities (John, 2003; Melton, 1999; Smith; 2000). If children understand society, they will be able to participate and have agency rather than being passive recipients (Osler & Starkey, 1996).

Osler and Starkey (2005) suggest that it is their entitlement to rights that bestows citizenship on children and young people. They describe citizenship as a status, a feeling and a practice. Status refers to the legal nature of citizenship of a particular state, in which the state protects citizens through laws and grants social and civil rights (access to justice, freedom of speech). In return, citizens contribute to the costs of the nation. Citizenship as a feeling refers to a feeling of community and/or freedom to exercise one's heritage. Citizenship as a practice refers to an awareness of, and access to, human rights. This translates into political participation where citizens have agency to make a difference and defend their rights.

In South Africa, the rights of citizenship were acquired by all when power was transferred from the apartheid order – where the majority of South Africa's population was deprived of full citizenship rights – to a new democratic state. Given that the entire population needed to adjust to democracy, citizenship education is imperative, not only for children and youth but also for adults in order to develop a new sense of citizenship and an understanding of its implications (Enslin, 2003).

The way that children were viewed also required a dramatic turnaround in the new democracy. Under the apartheid state, children were viewed as non-adults on the way to adulthood and requiring the assistance and support of someone who had already reached adulthood (Ashley, 1989). This view is evident in the ideology espoused in schools where moulding children into the image of adults, and acceptance and obedience to authority are emphasised. The perception of children was that they should not express an opinion unless approved by the adult or teacher. The teacher was regarded as embodying the ideal qualities of the adult community and children were expected to aspire to that (Ashley, 1989). Thus the concept of nation-building taught in schools under apartheid was unsuccessful as the majority of citizens wanted to break down rather than build up the nation.

Today, citizenship and human rights are important pillars of the democratic government's agenda and have been entrenched in the country's Constitution (1996) and policies. The Constitution (1996, section 3(1)) acknowledges that 'all citizens are equally entitled to the rights, privileges and benefits of citizenship and equally subject to the duties and responsibilities of citizenship.' The Bill of Rights (section 7) affirms the values of human dignity, equality and freedom. According to the Revised National Curriculum Statement (RNCS) (Department of National Education, 2002a), education has an important role in realising the aims of the Constitution (1996). For example, it must 'develop the potential of each learner as a citizen of a democratic South Africa' (Department of National Education, 2002b, p. 1). The RNCS policy (Life Orientation) for grades R-9 envisages the kind of learner who espouses the values of 'democracy, equality, human dignity, life and social justice ... with a respect for the environment and the ability to participate in a society as a critical and active citizen' (Department of National Education, 2002b, p. 3).

In addition to rights, having knowledge of responsibilities and citizenship is also promoted in the RNCS policy. In this regard an important learning outcome for social development is that the learner will be able to demonstrate an understanding of, and commitment to, constitutional rights and responsibilities (Department of National Education, 2002a).

Osler and Starkey (2005) note that, in discussions on citizenship education, much more emphasis is usually placed on the responsibilities of young people than on their rights. This may be due to the lack of an agreed definition of responsibilities in international instruments. This lack of clarity results in rhetoric suffused with many underlying interpretations and assumptions. Osler and Starkey (2005, pp. 155–162), drawing on various international instruments that have attempted to define responsibilities including the Universal Declaration of Human Rights (1948), African Charter (1981), Council of Europe (1999) and the Commission for Global Governance (1995), list the following universal responsibilities as a starting point for developing a common understanding of the concept:

- Individual and collective responsibilities to others – everyone should respect and promote the dignity and human rights of others;
- Contributions to communities at local, national and global levels – for example: respecting the rule of law, working for freedom, justice, democracy and peace; and
- Responsibilities to future generations – for example: practising sustainable ways of living, preserving and enhancing the environment and humanity's intellectual and cultural heritage.

The above conceptualisation of responsibility seems to focus less on the individual than on the communal and collective responsibility for the common good. This concern, and acceptance of responsibility for others, seem to be acceptable behaviours for adults. However, it appears that when children want to assert their rights, responsibilities and participation, they are often misunderstood or their competency is questioned. In particular, it has often been assumed that, if educated about their rights, children and young people will begin to insist on rights without acknowledging the accompanying responsibilities (Osler & Starkey, 2005; Spencer, 2000). It is also claimed that young people tend to view responsibilities as falling within the adult domain, rather than their own. However, such misunderstandings undermine children's ability to recognise and accept their responsibilities (Osler & Starkey, 2005).

It is crucial for the development of democracy in South Africa that children are educated about their rights and responsibilities. Despite the intentions of the government and civil society's advocacy efforts, the new democracy in South Africa continues to face challenges in realising citizenship education and children's participation rights. These challenges may have their roots in the way the issues were institutionalised in the past.

Since children and youth in South Africa participated actively in the struggle against apartheid, it could be expected that, in recognition of this crucial role, young people's participation would be centralised and foregrounded in post-apartheid South Africa. Instead, to a large extent there is significant adult ambivalence about children's participation. For example, Rooth (2005) indicates that the Life Orientation school curriculum outcomes, which focus on constitutional principles such as diversity, human rights and gender equity as stipulated in the Constitution of South Africa, are not being followed through and monitored in all instances. This is partly due to teachers not being ready to engage with the expectation that children have rights. In addition, a crucial barrier to the realisation of children's rights in South Africa is that the country is only starting to put mechanisms and programmes in place to deliver on its obligations.

Issues of democracy and citizenship clearly continue to be concepts with which adults grapple. When asked to define their national identities, young South Africans tend to define their identities primarily in terms of their culture, experiences of the past, and how others view them (Mail & Guardian, 2007). It is therefore apparent that the perceptions of children's rights and responsibilities through the lenses of teachers, parents and children cannot be divorced from their lived realities.

In the rest of this chapter, the methodology, findings and discussion of the study are presented.

Research Methodology

This research study was conceptualised and designed as part of an international research project conducted in collaboration with research partners in the Childwatch International Research Network. The research project aimed to address the following questions:

- *What are children's understandings of their rights, responsibilities, and citizenship?*
- *What are teachers' perspectives on children's rights, responsibilities, and citizenship?*
- *What are parents' perspectives on children's rights, responsibilities, and citizenship?*
- *How do teachers and parents understand children's perspectives on rights, responsibilities and citizenship?*

The South African study included the perceptions of children, parents and teachers. The sampling and research methods used for each of these respondent groups are discussed below.

The Research Context

The Cape Town study was conducted in the Western Cape Province of South Africa (SA). The participants included a mixed group representing the racial diversity in the province. These are, White, Coloured and African. Coloureds constitute 53.9 per cent of the total population in the Western Cape Province, of which Cape Town is the capital city. The participants were recruited from two neighbourhoods, Kuils River and Khayelitsha. Khayelitsha is largely an informal settlement with a total of 329,017 predominantly African residents. Only 20 per cent of persons over 25 years have completed high school and 35.7 per cent of inhabitants are unemployed. Those who are employed, work in low-skilled poorly paid jobs. Most people live in informal housing and while 82 per cent of households have access to electricity, only 23 per cent have running water. Kuils River has a total of 44,782 residents of which 61 per cent are coloured and 29 per cent White. Approximately 44 per cent of persons older than 19 years have completed high school. Of the population between 15 and 65 years, 67.4 per cent is employed. Most households have piped water (78 per cent), flushing toilets (95 per cent) and electricity (98 per cent). Therefore, participants represent a wide range of socio-economic status (SES).

Sampling and Research Methods

Participating children

Ninety-six children from four schools were recruited to participate in the research. Fifty-six participants were between the ages of 8 and 9 years and 56 between 14 and 15 years. Primary School A and High School A were exclusively attended by African students, whereas Primary School B and High School B were racially mixed schools. The participants from these schools were White and Coloured. The African participants in the study were from low socio-economic backgrounds, whereas the White and Coloured children were from middle socio-economic backgrounds. In each age group there was an additional group of eight participants from a residential care setting. Table One presents a summary of the age and gender characteristics of the total sample of 112 participants.

Focus group methodology was used to collect the data from the children. Separate focus groups were conducted for the two age groups. Within each age group, three focus groups were conducted: a boys-only group, a girls-only group, and a mixed gender group. Participants at each school were selected by the staff of the participating schools. The focus groups were approximately two hours in duration. In summary, the discussions centred on the following constructs: children's rights and responsibilities in the home, school and community contexts; and citizenship. The children were also asked to envisage an imaginary country and identify what they considered to be important rights and responsibilities for children.

Each session was conducted by two researchers who shared the roles of facilitation and note-taking. All group sessions were audio-taped and field notes were recorded. The session recordings were transcribed verbatim and verified by the pairs of researchers who conducted the groups. The groups for the younger Xhosa-speaking children were facilitated by first-language speakers of Xhosa. The older Xhosa-speaking children were comfortable using English during the groups. The recordings were translated into English by the facilitators.

Table One: Composition of focus groups

SCHOOL 8/9 Years	Boys	Girls	Mixed	Total
Primary School A	8	8	8	24
Primary School B	12	12	-	24
Children in care	-	-	8	8
14/15 Years				
High School A	8	8	8	24
High School B	12	12	-	24
Children in residential care	-	-	8	8
TOTAL				112

Participating adults

The views of parents and teachers on children's rights, responsibilities and citizenship were elicited through self-administered questionnaires which included questions on children's rights and responsibilities in the school, home and community contexts, and citizenship.

Seventy-three teachers from three different primary schools completed the questionnaires. All the respondents were teachers of Grades 1–12. One respondent was a principal. Fifty-six were female and 17 were male. The majority were Black African (47.9 per cent), followed by White (39.7 per cent) and Coloured (8.2 per cent). Some teachers did not respond to the question of ethnicity. Two teachers were aged between 21–25 years; four were aged between 26–30 years; 18 were aged between 31–35 years; 27 were aged between 36–40 years; 13 were aged between 41–45 years; eight were aged between 46–50 years; and six were aged 51 years or older. The majority of the teachers were between 36 and 40 years old.

Forty-three parents returned questionnaires which had been hand delivered to them. Of these, 17 were males and 26 females. Three parents were aged 26–30 years of age; five were 31–35 years; eight were 36–40 years; eleven were 41–45 years; eight were 46–50 years; and eight were 51 years or older. Most of the parents were between 41 and 45 years of age. The number of children per respondent ranged between one and five children, with the majority (70 per cent) having 1–2 children. The participating children and parents were not matched.

Key Findings

Children's Perceptions of Their Rights, Responsibilities and Citizenship

Children's views on their rights

All the children had difficulty providing a definition of rights, but they had no trouble giving examples of rights. The younger children in particular displayed misconceptions and confusion about what rights are. They offered definitions of rights such as: *'It means people must do the right thing'* (8/9 years) and *'It means like maybe one does something right or something wrong'* (8/9 years). The three rights most commonly identified by 8- to 9-year-olds were the right to attend school, the right to be fed, and the right to play and recreation. The right to shelter was regarded as important, as were the rights to electricity and running water: *'You have the right to a nice home with a bed and clean running water and electricity'* (8/9 years). There was also a strong awareness among participants of the right to *'say no to drugs'*, alcohol, unwanted sexual advances, and sexual abuse: *'No one has a right to touch my body'* (8/9 years). One boy stated: *'It means no one should rape you'* (8/9 years). The younger children also articulated their participation rights such as voting. The right to freedom of expression (*'The right to say what's on your mind'*), especially in school settings, and the right to express disapproval (*'You have the right to talk about what you don't like'*) were also identified (8/9 years). A related right expressed was *'the right to ask questions'* (8/9 years).

The 14- and 15-year-olds expressed the right to food, clothing and shelter. The *'right to education'* and the *'right to be taught'* were also given prominence (14/15 years). Not only was it considered important to be able to access education, it was also asserted that children have the right to *'a safe environment in which you can learn* [translation]*'*, as well as a *'decent'*, *'clean'* school building (14/15 years).

The right to freedom of expression was articulated across all groups and strongly emphasised. Children stressed *'the right to say something'*; *'the right to your own opinion'*, *'the right to say what you want'*, *'the right to speak your mind'* and *'the right to freedom of speech'* (14/15 years). Linked to freedom of expression, some children felt that they have a right to *'say "no" if a teacher does something wrong* (translation)*'* or to *'say "no" to peers when they are doing wrong things* (translation)*'* (14/15 years). There was also the opinion that children had a right to voice their disapproval and be given opportunities to resolve disagreements: *'I have a right to complain to my mother if I notice that at home there is something wrong. And she must also sit down and talk about it, then we find a solution* (translation)*'* (14/15 years).

Older children valued justice and fairness in discipline in both the classroom and the community. One learner shared the following concern: *'When something happened in class when the teacher isn't in the class and the teacher comes back, she must listen to both sides of the story. Like must not punish the whole class'* (14/15 years).

The rights to love, parental care and nurturing were frequently expressed, demonstrating that, despite the developmental need for independence and autonomy at this age, these adolescents still valued the love and nurturing of parents. Respect was another prominent concern identified by the children. They considered it important '*to be respected by the grown-ups*', especially teachers (14/15 years). Protection was viewed as a parental responsibility: '*I've got a right to be protected by parents*' (14/15 years). They identified that they needed protection from '*drugs*', '*alcohol*' and '*child abuse*' (14/15 years). Safety and protection concerns were clearly prominent for these participants. They mentioned the '*right to safety and security*' and being able '*to walk around in the streets*' (14/15 years). Linked to protection and safety was the right to '*say 'no'*' to sexual abuse or coercion to engage in criminal activities. Less commonly expressed rights were the right to an identity, the right to play, the right to privacy and the right to religious observance. For some children, the right to a name and the right to be called by that name were important. They complained that adults frequently addressed them as 'you' rather than calling them by name.

The perceptions of children's rights in the school context focused on the classroom setting and the interaction between teachers and learners. Examples of rights identified were the right to be taught by the teacher, to be disciplined fairly, and to a clean and safe classroom environment. The discussions did not include any issues pertaining to the wider school setting, for example, children's rights regarding the curriculum content and methods of instruction or children's involvement in school governance.

Children's views on their responsibilities

The younger children displayed considerable difficulty in distinguishing between rights and responsibilities. Very commonly they identified responsibilities when asked to give examples of rights. The children seemed to view obedience to authority as an important responsibility in home, school and community settings. They regarded it as important to obey school rules, state laws, and parents' instructions. Parental authority was regarded as supremely important and many participants stressed that children should '*not be cheeky*' and that they should '*willingly do*' whatever parents request (8/9 years). Keeping bedrooms tidy, doing '*household chores*', '*look[ing] after siblings*' and taking care of pets were common responsibilities mentioned (8/9 years). There was a strong emphasis on taking responsibility for personal neatness and cleanliness, especially in making sure that school uniforms were washed and ironed. Repeatedly it was stressed: '*You have the responsibility to do your homework*' (8/9 years). In the school setting, it was considered important '*to listen to your teacher*', '*not to back chat to the teacher*' and '*to obey and honour your teacher's instructions* [translation]' (8/9 years). The children also expressed the importance of '*keeping our school clean*' and keeping classrooms tidy. They emphasised that in their communities they had a responsibility to keep the environment clean, '*not to litter*', and not to waste resources such as water (8/9 years).

For the older children, the concept of 'responsibility' was related to owning and possessing something and taking responsibility for it and not doing wrong. They also acknowledged that responsibility was in a reciprocal relationship with rights – that is, if you have rights then you also have responsibilities. Responsibilities identified by the children fell into three main categories: responsibilities in relation to rights, responsibilities in relation to a task or something that belongs to you, and responsibility in relation to the law.

Responsibilities in response to rights included: a right to live in or to be taught in a clean environment, therefore there was a responsibility to keep it clean; a right to play but a responsibility to be home on time; and a right to education but a responsibility to learn, do homework, attend school regularly, and be obedient to teachers. Examples of responses include:

We have a right to play, but a responsibility to go back to class in time (translation). (14/15 years)

We say you have the right to live in a clean and safe home but your responsibility is to keep it clean (translation). (14/15 years)

Responsibilities in relation to a task or possession included: looking after your body; tidying the home and especially one's bedroom; acting on a decision you have made; not taking something that does not belong to you; taking care of siblings; not vandalising public property; and taking care of the environment. Responses included:

I take care of my body. That's my responsibility. (14/15 years)

You have a responsibility not to throw papers and stuff around. (14/15 years)

Not polluting the sea. (14/15 years)

The following responsibilities in relation to the law were mentioned: obeying the law; reporting crime; obeying school rules; not vandalising, damaging or stealing property and reporting such behaviour to authorities; not polluting or littering; not causing a disturbance in the community (e.g. playing loud music); and acting responsibly in terms of time and task. Participants emphasized that '*It is your responsibility not to do wrong* (translation) (14/15 years)' and '*You shouldn't vandalise other people's property*' (14/15 years). They also stressed: '*Don't remove anything from school premises that doesn't belong to you*' (14/15 years).

In addition, respect was regarded as a key responsibility. They considered it important to respect teachers, parents, grandparents, friends, their '*fellow man*' and people of other religions. Overall, the responsibilities articulated by the children seemed to embrace the following values: cleanliness, honesty, respect for self and others, obedience, school pride, and caring.

Children's views on their citizenship

Some younger participants thought a citizen is '*someone who attends community meetings* [translation]' (8/9 years), while others associated citizenship with home ownership: '*someone who has a house in this place* [translation]' (8/9 years). Citizens were viewed by others as persons who were born in a country, had voting privileges, and had the right to reside in a country. The importance of adherence to laws was emphasised as a responsibility of citizens. Furthermore, it was indicated that citizens are '*equal in the eyes of the law*' (8/9 years). A citizen was regarded as '*somebody that doesn't do things wrong and fights for your country*' (8/9 years). A good citizen was identified as someone who '*does not fight*' with others, works at resolving community conflicts and who helps and respects others, especially elders. It was stated that children can be good citizens by helping others, obeying laws, obeying their parents, doing chores at home, and keeping their environment clean. One child expressed the obligations of citizenship as follows: '*If you are a citizen of a country you have to obey the laws set in place to govern that country* [translation]' (8/9 years).

There was general agreement among the older children that one becomes a citizen of a country by birth: that is, you are a citizen of the country you were born in. The acquisition of citizenship was more difficult to grasp. In some instances citizenship related to the right to vote and coming-of-age at 18 or 21 years old – that is, the age when one can do what adults do. Others suggested: '*each person is a citizen if you like be in a country for more than five years*'.

There was also uncertainty about when and how foreigners acquire citizenship. Students' examples of what it means to be a good citizen included: respecting others, not discriminating, not '*hav*[ing] *xenophobia*' (14/15 years), fighting crime, being honest, being law-abiding, caring for the environment, and contributing to society.

The participants had a harder time trying to list what children can do to be good citizens, and responded poorly to this question. However, there were a few references to obeying domestic rules and the laws of the country, being respectful and not discriminating. Some examples included:

> *A good citizen is someone who is able to say no to the wrong things happening in the community. For example, if community members caught a thief and then they take the law into their own hands and they beat him up and stone him – a good citizen is someone who says no to that and calls the police because community members do not have a right to do that.* (14/15 years)

> *A good citizen is someone who does not discriminate against people because they are foreigners. Like if a foreigner offers you food, you must not say no I don't eat foreign food (translation).* (14/15 years)

A good citizen is '*proudly South African*'. 'Proudly South African' is the slogan of a campaign promoting patriotism and economic growth by encouraging people to purchase locally-produced goods. In this way, people can '*support their country*' by contributing to society.

Envisioning an Imaginary Country

The 8- to 9-year-olds had difficulty with the imaginary country task, which demanded abstract thinking. Essentially, in their discussion of the imaginary country, they reiterated the rights and responsibilities expressed in relation to their contemporary country. The younger children indicated that citizens had the right to adequate infrastructure such as basic facilities and services which are required for the functioning of their communities, as well as recreational facilities. Basic needs such as food were considered a right, as were family, parents, friends and love. The right to be protected was emphasised strongly. Frequently mentioned were the rights to play, to have fun and have toys. Going to church was also seen as an important right in the imaginary country. Voting, too, was a right in this country. In the imaginary country, citizens had the responsibility of showing respect for parents and teachers and obeying authority. Not wasting resources and keeping the school, community and environment clean were also mentioned as important responsibilities. Sharing and not hurting others were considered part of the responsibilities of citizens. Good citizens were identified as those who did not waste or litter, took care of nature, did not steal, and completed their homework.

The older participants engaged more easily in the abstract thinking required for the task. They relayed a need for more freedom and rights and fewer restrictions and responsibilities in the imaginary country. These were expressed as:

To go to sleep whenever you want.

You can clean your room whenever you want.

A right to go out. Anywhere, any place.

A right to play with anyone you want to.

They must be happy and parents should let them do what they want to do.

We can tell big people what we think of them.

In this country, children would be able to develop their full potential. Examples of children's statements to this effect included: '*they need to use their talent*'; '*it is your right to feel special*'; '*to play soccer*' and '*they have the right to go swim*'. Education was also seen as a way for children to develop their potential and they expressed the right to be educated in a safe and caring environment, provided that they were not forced to go to school, and that school should not take up most of the day. The right to play, have fun and have a good life were important rights for all the groups. School, it was asserted, should be restricted to the minimum hours per day: one group said two hours is enough and other groups felt that '*they have a choice if they don't want to go to school or participate in sport, they don't have to.*' Another group said: '*They should have the responsibility, because we can't force our children to go to school. But they should have the responsibility to go.*'

The imaginary country would be a safe and secure place. This right to safety and security was expressed in the following ways:

They have a right to feel safe in their country' or 'safe at school'.

We won't live in fear of being robbed or getting raped. Like you must walk freely in the community without worrying about your cell phone or jewellery.

We do not have to fight in our new country. We should protect each other and act like one big happy family.

Stop crime because it starts with one person so you must stop that one person before it spreads to the entire community.

There was also a sense that the imaginary country would be safer and more secure than their present contexts. The emphasis on safety and protection reflects the crime and violence that is rampant in South Africa. The children (14/15 years) contended:

The crime must be less.

There must be more security.

More cameras must be put in streets.

Abusers must be punished more severely. Because ... a man who went into jail because he raped a girl ... And so he came out the next day.

Values such as obedience and respect within the home and school contexts were expressed as both a right and a responsibility. Students stressed the importance of being respected by, and being respectful towards, adults, teachers, and their peers, and of self-respect and being respectful towards neighbours.

Responsibilities towards the imaginary country were expressed as good citizenship. Examples given of gestures of good citizenship included:

Give ideas to the president, to help him to successfully govern the country.

You need to work with government.

Work with the community to clean the country.

We as children should stop adults from discriminating against foreigners and coloured people.

To communicate with any other race. And to learn about their culture.

Have the responsibility to help the adults be self-sufficient so that one day when they are big they can carry on the tradition. And to learn to dive for oysters. (14/15 years)

Being a good citizen was expressed as follows: *'If children are good citizens they will listen to their parents and then there will be no violence.'*

Summary

No salient gender or socio-economic status differences were apparent in the data. However, some clear age differences emerged. Both age groups found it difficult to define rights, but they were able to provide appropriate examples. The younger children tended to confuse rights and responsibilities, whereas the older children displayed a keen awareness of the reciprocal relationship between rights and responsibilities. Whereas younger children emphasised the right to play and recreation, older children stressed the right to freedom of expression – especially in the home and school environment – justice and fairness. Both groups highlighted socio-economic issues like the right to food, running water, clothing, and shelter, while older children also focused on parental love and nurturing. There was a strong emphasis on safety and protection issues by both groups which was especially vivid in the imaginary country exercise. The right to education and respect, especially from teachers, was highlighted in the school environment.

The younger children had difficulty defining responsibilities, but provided examples. These centred on being obedient to the teacher and parents, domestic chores and personal cleanliness. In addition to the above examples, the older children also demonstrated their understanding of responsibility in terms of themselves as individuals, their siblings, respect for other children and adults, the school, the environment and the laws of the country. Similar responsibilities were also expressed in the imaginary country exercise.

Similarly to rights, the concept of citizenship also caused confusion, with both groups having difficulty defining the concept, though they did so by way of examples. The 8/9-year-olds were able to provide appropriate examples of citizenship, but many of these focused on obeying laws and being obedient. The 14/15-year-olds linked citizenship to having the vote, not discriminating, being respectful and also obeying laws. The issue of obeying laws and obedience was also emphasised in responses to envisioning an imaginary country.

Teachers' and Parents' Perspectives on Children's Rights, Responsibilities and Citizenship

Teachers' Perspectives

Rights and responsibilities in the school context
The majority of teachers strongly agreed that children at school should have the right to access good quality education and resources, not be subjected to racism or discrimination, enjoy a healthy environment and feel safe. A minority of teachers disagreed with the following rights: the right to access free education

(12.3 per cent of teachers), to access recreational facilities (2.8 per cent), and the right to have an input in decisions (4 per cent).

Regarding children's responsibilities, all teachers agreed that children should have the following responsibilities at school: to respect the school environment or property; to respect, support and be obedient to the teachers; and to work co-operatively with others. Responsibilities that teachers strongly disagreed on were the responsibilities of children to protest if there is an injustice and to try and change the rules if needed.

Teachers agreed (95.5 per cent) that they would take action if the learner's rights were not being respected at school. The most likely action they indicated would be to help the child develop strategies for ensuring his or her rights (95.8 per cent), followed by talking to the child (95.8 per cent), while talking to the teacher (95.7 per cent) was also a highly favoured option. Results showed that going to an external organisation such as the Western Cape Department of Education (64.5 per cent) or School Governing Body (49.2 per cent) was an unlikely action that teachers would take; however, they indicated that such action would depend on the situation.

Rights and responsibilities in the home context
All teachers agreed that children and young people should have the following rights at home: to have access to health care if sick, be loved and cared for, have free time for play or recreation, be safe from violence, be able to have friends, and have access to food and shelter. The most common strongly agreed-upon right is to be safe from violence (93.3 per cent), followed by the right to be loved and cared for (92 per cent). The majority of teachers agreed that children and young people should have the following responsibilities at home: help with family chores, work co-operatively, respect and love siblings, respect and love parents, obey rules and be obedient to parents. A minority of teachers disagreed with the following responsibilities: caring for siblings (9.6 per cent), helping to decide on rules (2.8 per cent) and to have an input into family decisions.

Rights and responsibilities in the community context
All the teachers agreed that children and young people should have rights in their communities. The most commonly strongly agreed-upon right was the right to be safe in the community (82.7 per cent). This was closely followed by the right to be in a healthy environment (81.3 per cent). Other rights that the majority of teachers agreed upon were: access to information and advice, affordable public transport, play and recreational opportunities, not being subjected to racism or discrimination and a feeling of belonging. Rights that a small minority of teachers disagreed with were the right to have places to go or hang out, have ideas listened to, and have input into decisions.

For the teacher data, there was more variation in responses concerning the rights and responsibilities at school compared with those in the home and in the community. Overall, teachers agreed that the learners should have all rights and responsibilities at home and in the community.

Citizenship
Teachers (94.6 per cent) agreed that children and young people should be considered to be citizens. However, the question of the age when children and young people become citizens indicated a divide in results, with 58.3 per cent saying it does depend on the age of children and young people and 41.7 per cent saying that citizenship did not vary with age.

Summary
The participating school staff generally agreed that children and young people should have rights at school, at home and in the community. The issue that teachers felt strongly about in all three contexts was the right of children to feel safe and free from abuse. Teachers also strongly supported the action of helping the child to develop strategies for ensuring his or her rights if these rights were not respected at school.

There was strong agreement on responsibilities relating to obedience, obeying laws, following rules in the home and school contexts. These were: respecting and supporting teachers, obeying school rules and following school policy, being obedient to the teacher, helping with family chores, respecting and loving parents, obeying rules and being obedient to parents.

The most noticeable disagreements centred around children's participation at home, at school and in the community. These were: the right to have input into decisions, to help decide on rules, to try and change rules, to have ideas listened to, to care for siblings and to have places to go or hang out.

Teachers agreed that children and young people should be considered as citizens. However, just over half the teachers agreed that this is dependent on the age of the child or young person.

Parents' Perspectives

Rights and responsibilities in the school context
Regarding children's rights at school, two of the rights listed elicited 100 per cent agreement. These were the rights to access recreational opportunities and feel safe (free from bullying and abuse). Some disagreement by minorities was reflected in the other rights listed, with access to free education generating the most differences. 85.7 per cent of parents agreed that learners should have access to free education, while 11.9 per cent disagreed and 2.4 per cent were unsure.

Parents agreed (83.3 per cent) that they would take action if their children's rights were not respected at school, but differed in what action they would take. Actions such as helping the child develop strategies for ensuring his/her rights (94.1 per cent), talking to the teacher alone (69.4 per cent), talking to the principal (66.7 per cent), or talking to the teacher with the child (65.8 per cent), were favoured more than going to the School Governing Body (37.9 per cent), Western Cape Department of Education (24.1 per cent), or National Department of Education (28.6 per cent). Parents were divided on taking the matter further, with responses more or less equally split between agreeing, disagreeing and those who felt it depended on the situation. The most likely action taken would be to help the child develop strategies for ensuring his/her rights.

Regarding the responsibilities that parents thought children should have at school, all agreed that children should work co-operatively with others. Other agreed-upon responsibilities included: to be obedient to the teacher (90.2 per cent), to obey the rules and follow school policy (95.2 per cent), to respect and support teachers (92.5 per cent), to respect and support other children (97.6 per cent), and to respect school environment/property (95.2 per cent). There was less support for the following children's responsibilities: to work hard (87.8 per cent), to protest if there is an injustice (76.3 per cent) and to try and change the rules (70.3 per cent).

Rights and responsibilities in the home context
The majority of parents agreed that children should have rights at home. All agreed that children should have access to food and shelter, health care if sick, and free time for play and recreation, feel safe (free from abuse and violence), and have their ideas listened to. Although the majority of the parents also agreed with the other rights listed, there was some disagreement expressed by a minority of parents that children should be loved and cared for (2.3 per cent), be able to have friends (2.3 per cent), be subject to fair rules and discipline (2.3 per cent), have access to information and advice (2.3 per cent), and have input into decisions (4.7 per cent).

Regarding responsibilities at home, all parents agreed that children should help with family chores, respect and love parents, and respect and love siblings. The majority agreed that children should work co-operatively with family members (95.1 per cent), be obedient to parents (97.6 per cent), obey the rules (97.6 per cent), and have input into family decisions (95.2 per cent). Three parents (7.7 per cent) disagreed that children should help to decide on the rules at home, with 2.6 per cent being unsure whether this should be the responsibility of the children.

Rights and responsibilities in the community context
Compared with 100 per cent and 90.2 per cent of parents who respectively thought children should have rights at home and at school, 92.7 per cent thought that children should have rights in their communities and neighbourhoods. All parents agreed that children should have a right to affordable public transport, and play and recreational opportunities, to be safe (free from abuse and violence), not to be subjected to racism/ discrimination, to have a healthy environment (smoke and drug free) and have their ideas listened to. Parents further agreed that children should have access to information and advice (97.7 per cent), a feeling of belonging (95.3 per cent), and have input into decisions (90.5 per cent). Opinions of parents varied on the right to have places to go/hang out, with 78.6 per cent agreeing to this right and 16.7 per cent disagreeing. The highest disagreements by parents were 16.7 per cent and 7.1 per cent respectively for places to hang out and the right to have input into decisions.

The majority of parents agreed that children should have the responsibility in the community to care for the environment and property (97.6 per cent), respect neighbours and other members of the community (97.6 per cent), and obey the law and regulations (95.2 per cent). Fewer parents agreed that children should have the responsibility to participate in local community activities (85.7 per cent). Disagreement was highest (7.1 per cent) for parents' beliefs that children should participate in local community activities, a further 7.1 per cent were unsure.

Citizenship
The majority of parents had heard about the UNCRC, with 84 per cent (of the 67.4 per cent who had heard of UNCRC) indicating that they supported the Convention. Nearly all the parents (92 per cent) thought of children and young people as citizens. While 42.1 per cent indicated that citizenship did vary depending on age, 47.4 per cent indicated that it did not, 10.5 per cent were unsure, and 47.2 per cent believed that children became citizens at birth.

Summary
The parents generally agreed that children should have rights at school, home and in the community. Fewer parents agreed with children having the right to free education at school, places to go/hang out in the community, and input into decisions in all three contexts. In addition, fewer parents agreed that children should have input into decisions at school and in the community than at home. The number of parents disagreeing with these rights was small (ranging from 4.7 per cent to 16.7 per cent) in each case. However, all parents agreed that children should have their ideas listened to in the home context, while a minority disagreed with children having this right in the school context. Parents all agreed that children should have the right to feel safe and free from abuse in all three contexts. The least agreed-upon right was having places to go or hang out in the community. Parents also strongly supported the idea of helping children to develop strategies for defending their rights at school.

While the majority of parents agreed with children having responsibilities at school, home and in the community, there were some responsibilities that had less support. These responsibilities included changing the rules at school, working hard at school, participating in decisions about rules at home and at school, helping to care for siblings, protesting if there is an injustice and participating in local and community activities. The responsibilities that the majority of parents mostly agreed with were: working co-operatively with others; being obedient to parents and teachers; obeying rules, laws and regulations; respecting and supporting other children, teachers, parents and siblings.

The parents indicated that they had heard about the UNCRC and thought of children and young people as citizens. There was however some disagreement on when exactly children became citizens, with only 47.2 per cent of parents saying that children become citizens at birth. The balance of parents' responses regarding when children became citizens was spread between ages one to eighteen and beyond.

Discussion

The overall picture presented by the findings of this study suggests that there is a remarkable awareness as well as knowledge about children's rights, responsibilities and citizenship among children, parents and teachers. Children, although in some cases struggling to define these concepts, reflected their understanding by providing examples. In this study, the reciprocal relationship between rights and responsibilities emerged quite strongly in the older children's responses. In addition, it was evident that all the children had difficulties in defining citizenship.

While the children in this study indicated that they have considerable understanding of both their rights as individuals and their responsibilities towards other people, the parents and teachers wavered when it came to committing themselves fully to certain rights and responsibilities of children. As Osler and Starkey (2005) point out, children have often been undermined in terms of their ability to demonstrate their understanding and practices of this reciprocal responsibility. This ambivalence expressed by the adults participating in the study has crucial implications for how children participate in society. Including children in decision-making impacts directly on their ability to access opportunities, develop their capacities and on the quality of their lives.

The reluctance on the part of teachers and parents to enable children to participate actively in decision-making is reflected in their responses as well as those of the children. While the older children emphasised their rights to freedom of expression in the school and home environments, parents and teachers expressed some uncertainty about these rights. Specifically, the parents expressed ambivalence about children participating in decision-making regarding making rules, trying to change rules, or protesting if there is a perceived sense of injustice. Reluctance on the part of parents and teachers may be associated with the old saying that 'children should be seen and not heard'. This prevailing notion among adults may also be the result of the apartheid education to which many parents and teachers were mainly exposed. The Apartheid Government's Christian National Education ideology espoused the idea that children are adults in waiting, 'becoming' and ready to be moulded, thus negating their right to have a voice or an opinion in the present (Ashley, 1989). To some extent it appears that there is still a degree of suppression rather than empowerment present in some schools. For example, school is still very much viewed as a place to learn and not to challenge. The children in the study placed high emphasis on the importance of education. While they seemed less concerned about the content of the education, they were much more explicit about the quality of the relationships that they experienced and the physical environment in which they were educated. They were especially concerned about the importance of mutual respect and being included in decision-making. The lack of mutual respect also extended to their relationships with their peers. In this regard, there is growing alarm about the increasing instances of violent crimes committed by children in schools (Medved, 2007).

Respecting others, being obedient and obeying laws were highlighted as important responsibilities by all three groups in the study. The children and the adults placed strong emphasis on the importance of children obeying and respecting adults, authority and public institutions. From the children's responses, it is suggested that this responsibility placed on them to obey and respect adults is taken for granted by adults and is not to be questioned or challenged by children. Furthermore, the strong agreement by parents and teachers about the responsibility to obey affirms the expectations regarding children's behaviour at home and at school. These expectations seem to culminate in patterns of behaviour that reinforce children's exclusion.

Children are often told that they have a responsibility not to do wrong. However, this could mean that their capacity to develop through trial and error is often restricted (September, 2005). Teachers and parents agreed on the importance of assisting children to develop strategies to ensure that their rights were respected at school. They felt especially strongly about children speaking up in this regard. It is interesting to note that, in this instance, there was less stress on obedience while assertiveness was promoted. It therefore appears that adults are more supportive of children being assertive in the public domain (school) than in the private domain (home).

With regard to children taking responsibility for the care of siblings, both parents and teachers seemed to be ambivalent. Although they agreed that it may sometimes be necessary for children to do this, they were also concerned that children should not take up the responsibilities of adults but rather enjoy their childhoods. Participating actively in the care of siblings and adults is however not uncommon in South Africa. The phenomenon of extended families and the expression of '*ubuntu*' which accepts joint responsibility for such care is a strong feature of black communities especially. The increasing urbanisation has however impacted on these traditions and how families are constructed. In addition, the realities of poverty, unemployment, HIV/AIDS and child-headed households often compel children to take responsibility for their siblings and sick parents (Brooks, Shisana & Richter, 2004).

The South African Government has identified poverty as one of the biggest challenges facing the country and the children's responses reflect this concern. The children's emphasis on the quality of their socio-economic environments indicates that they too were not only aware of these realities but wanted to make a meaningful contribution. They especially referred to the high rates of poverty, the plight of homeless children, discrimination and prejudice against foreigners. The children were in agreement with parents and teachers regarding concerns about safety and protection issues. While the parents were mostly concerned about their children's safety at places where they hang out, for the children it was about the restriction being placed on their mobility because of the safety issues as well as the restriction placed upon them by their parents. From the children's perspectives, there seemed to be a point where they needed their parents to allow them more flexibility regarding these decisions. Adults, on the other hand, had difficulty in deciding at which point they could do so, especially in view of the many safety concerns. Children, however, also thought parents were not only over-protective but over-controlling. Could the latter be indicative of a gap in parents' knowledge about children's developmental capacities or perceptions of citizenship?

In this regard it was also interesting to note that more children than adults in the study thought that children acquired citizenship at birth. Adults in the study were split as to when children acquired full citizenship. Issues of citizenship and participation were not a familiar concept for children in the study. For the adults in the study who mostly grew up in South Africa during the apartheid years, the concept of citizenship may also have been viewed with scepticism insofar as in the past it was a word restricted to the white minority (Enslin, 2003). Whilst South African adults may still be becoming 'at ease' with their own liberties and citizenship in the new democracy, their children need more tangible experiences and modelling of these very difficult concepts. The reality is that if adults do not deal with these ambivalences about the status of children, they will continue to be 'conceived and treated as persons progressing towards autonomy' (Hart, Zeidner & Pavlovic, 1996, p. 46). These perceptions have important implications for how children are included and consulted in decision-making, and how their agency is accepted as a normal part of their development.

Overall, those rights and responsibilities of children agreed upon by parents and teachers left children with very little authentic participation. As Osler and Starkey (1998) point out, consultation with children and young people about their needs is rare and they are often not recognised as partners who need to be consulted. The perceptions of parents and teachers in this study paint a picture of children who are less participatory, subservient, submissive, and dependent on the approval of adults. The possible long-term implication of this for children is that they may become passive and insecure about their capacities to contribute meaningfully. In this study, children seemed to be consistently held in check and their mobility restricted by the power dynamics at play between themselves and adults. Because adults are the 'first comers', primary caregivers and the holders of resources it is easy for them to impose authority, dominance, and power over children. As asserted by Casas (1998) and John (2003), adults may be hesitant about promoting and facilitating children's participation rights as this could undermine or usurp this authority.

Conclusion

The children's responses in this study highlighted their lack of authentic participation in the school, home and community. Despite the progressive intentions of the country's constitution, ratified international treaties and government policies, it is evident that the perceptions and attitudes of adults regarding children's rights and citizenship are ambiguous and in constant conflict with their own values and beliefs pertaining to the rights of adults. While the majority of adults indicated that children must have rights, they found it difficult to affirm certain rights for children – especially those rights that may impact on their own as parents and adults. As a result, in these instances adults required children to be 'obedient'. Many children have internalised this as a desirable 'virtue'.

However, unquestioning 'obedience', subservience and passivity in children are disturbing signs that do not bode well for the development of democracy, equality and social justice. Moreover, when children's agency is not recognised, embraced and supported by adults, their citizenship and contribution to society is denied.

Clearly, children's participation is crucial for the development of a national democratic society. The children in this study were not only aware of their rights, responsibilities and citizenship but could relate these insights to what the government must do for them now in order to secure a prosperous democratic South Africa in the future.

9

Children's Perspectives on Citizenship: Conclusions and Future Directions

Udi Mandel Butler, Håvard Bjerke, Anne B. Smith, Brad Shipway, Robyn Fitzgerald, Anne Graham & Nicola Taylor

Drawing Together the Threads

This cross-cultural study has explored children's understanding of their citizenship, rights and responsibilities through the lens of their experience, and as applied to their own countries and in an imagined country. The project involved children and young people from six different countries (Australia, Brazil, New Zealand, Norway, Palestine and South Africa) in various stages of democratic development, each facing a variety of economic, social and political challenges. In this final chapter we explore the similarities and differences in the findings from the six countries in light of citizenship theory and previous research. We also consider the links between these findings and the current literature on citizenship described in Chapter One. Finally, we discuss some of the implications of the findings for theory, policy and practice, in the hope that this research might contribute to a better understanding of how democratic societies can promote meaningful citizenship for children and young people. First, however, we turn briefly to the concept of citizenship to reiterate how it has influenced – and been influenced by – this study.

During discussions around the writing of this book, we were frequently reminded that 'citizenship' is a confusing and contested term for both children and adults. As Chapter One has shown, there is a burgeoning literature on citizenship indicating its meaning is subject to much debate and in a constant state of flux and transformation (see, for instance, Cornwall & Coelho, 2007; Isin & Turner, 2002). Equally the term 'citizenship', much like related terms such as 'participation', has become politically contested, appropriated by different ideologies and agendas that attempt to claim it and set it in stone. As such, the notion of 'citizenship' can end up being highly exclusionary, as the term in essence has the power to define who is part of a community and who is not. Given such cautionary status, we should take a critical stance when assessing the ways in which 'citizenship' is used (see Cooke & Kothari, 2001; Rahnema, 1992). With such debates in mind, it is no wonder that children and adults alike find the term confusing.

In the process of carrying out this international comparative research, we have seen that even the term 'citizenship' itself cannot readily be translated into other languages. In Norway, for instance, the research team had difficulty finding a term that was equivalent. In the case of both Brazil and South Africa, societies which have more recently been permeated with the discourse of rights, the notion of citizenship harks back to a divided society where the concept is predominantly associated with being employed, being a 'proper citizen', and which may exclude someone belonging to marginalised sectors of society.

Despite these caveats, the richness of this research endeavour is derived from the ways in which 'citizenship' takes on a local flavour and is talked about by children based on their day-to-day experiences. The children were able to provide numerous examples of rights, responsibilities and citizenship. In doing so, they articulated a nuanced understanding of citizenship. Embedded in this understanding were both commonalities and differences in the ways democratic spaces were experienced. The following section explores some of the common themes that emerged from our study.

Commonalities in Children's Understanding and Experiences of Citizenship

Across all countries, regardless of whether their contexts were more or less likely to allow for active and inclusive notions of citizenship, all children were nonetheless continually looking for authentic opportunities to engage, participate, and contribute as citizens. It was also the case that despite constantly seeking such occasions, children were not inundated with opportunities for authentic participation. Their insights into the nature of rights, responsibilities and citizenship revealed an interpretation from the perspective of exclusion, rather than from direct experience.

From within the children's narratives, however, it is possible to identify expression of a normative model of citizenship grounded in particular political, cultural and symbolic contexts. In this section we explore some of the normative or common themes that emerged in the study before attempting to posit some implications for policy and practice. At this point, it should be noted that this chapter does not afford the latitude to explore implications across all the different domains of children's lives: our comments focus mainly on the place and context where children spend most of their early years – schooling and education. However, we believe our comments below on the importance of critically examining how adults construct their understandings of children should not be limited to education, but can be readily applied to a wide variety of societal contexts where children have the opportunity for democratic participation.

Rights

As we have already described, the children in this study were usually only able to express their understanding of the concept of rights by giving examples. Most could not name particular kinds of rights or provide abstract definitions.

There were mixed findings about whether children understood the concepts of rights, particularly within the younger groups of children – the main difference between the younger and older children being the kind of examples of rights they provided. Some children confused rights with wants (doing what they want to do – for example, going to the movies or watching television).

Despite this, many of the examples of rights given by children revealed several similarities across the different countries, and covered most of the rights in the UNCRC.

1. **Participation Rights**: To have a say, choose friends, be respected, express opinions, be listened to, make choices, to say 'no', be involved in resolving conflict, choose one's own religion, participate in decisions and to have freedom of movement.
2. **Protection Rights:** Protection from bullying by peers, safety at school, home and in the community, freedom from drugs and alcohol, freedom from discrimination and racism, protection from sexual abuse, violence and forced labour, and to be treated fairly.
3. **Provision Rights:** Parental care and nurturance, education, sustenance (food, clothing and housing), healthy environments, recreation/play opportunities, medical care, transport, spaces to hang out, access to employment, access to resources (e.g. equipment at school).

Responsibilities

Across all countries, children emphasised some collective responsibilities, but tended to give examples that were individual responsibilities. The following responsibilities were mentioned by children in most countries:

- Self-care responsibilities: Keeping clean, looking after possessions;
- Family responsibilities: Doing chores, caring for others (siblings or pets);
- Personal moral qualities: Respecting others, being good role models, not telling lies, not taking drugs, not getting drunk, not being noisy, being tolerant;
- Environmental responsibilities: Looking after the environment;
- School responsibilities: Studying/working hard, respecting others (not bullying/teasing), listening to and respecting teachers, following rules;
- Community responsibilities: Not breaking the law, helping the poor or old, being concerned for others, not discriminating against others.

Citizenship

The concept of citizenship seems to have been the most challenging for children to understand and exemplify. Abstract definitions relating to characteristics of society such as democracy or equality were scarce. Generally, citizenship was described as a characteristic which was attached to a person. Citizenship was defined in terms of:

- Personal qualities: Not stealing or hurting others, adhering to laws, respecting others (particularly vulnerable people), being hard working, helping others;
- Membership of a group or organisation;
- Status (because of some characteristic): Owning property, voting, having lived in a country for a long time, being born in a country, age (i.e. adulthood), having a job;
- Having duties, rights and responsibilities.

While children considered that their participation could be valuable and meaningful, they were aware that their agency as young citizens was not the same as adult citizens, and at times the children expressed the need to differentiate between the agency of the child and the adult. In this way, the children appealed to what Lister (2008, pp. 16–17) has described as a 'differentiated universalism' – that is, an expression of citizenship which does not seek to be identical to that of adults, nor aspires to see children possessing exactly the same political and civil rights as adults, but rather seeks acknowledgment that the rights and responsibilities that children do exercise as citizens be recognised and respected.

The above common understandings of children across the six countries provide insight into the way children feel about themselves as citizens. Children see themselves as causally efficacious social agents, who are capable of making a contribution to a democratic society *now* (if given the appropriate support) – yet, at the same time, requiring the protection and nurture of adults.

Beyond these common understandings, we also found differences in children's expressions of citizenship within their own local contexts, and these further contributed to our knowledge of how children understand and experience citizenship. It is to these differences that we now turn.

Differences in Children's Understandings and Experiences of Citizenship

Situating National Historical and Political Contexts

One key difference in the study's findings is the way in which the various national contexts possess distinct historical and political conditions. These may influence the overall social dynamics between groups, such as the marked inequality between social groups in Brazil, the social democratic welfare state model in Norway, the legacy of apartheid in South Africa, the continuing fall-out from Israeli occupation in Palestine, the issue of migration and multiculturalism in Australia, and biculturalism and indigenous issues in New Zealand. Certainly such political climates directly influenced children's understandings and practices of citizenship.

As we have seen in Brazil for instance, persistent inequality led to an acute sense of discrimination by those studying in public schools or belonging to marginalised groups, such as children living on the streets.

To walk into the mall wearing the [school] uniform is like you're naked. They look at you as if you've just got out of jail. (Brazilian young person, Public School)

In such a context, citizenship talk is more often than not about the realisation of how the ideals of citizenship remain elusive. The more extreme example of this is in Palestine, where we see the consequences of violence and the unstable political reality reflected in the way children understood citizenship and rights – which were often related to aspirations for freedom, security and national self-determination:

Rights mean that children like us live securely, safely and peacefully and achieve our independence and security. (Palestinian young person)

And, in South Africa, children aspired to live in an imaginary country which is safe, secure and protects them from crime. They want to be able to:

[not] live in fear of being robbed or raped. Like you must walk freely in the community without worrying about your cell phone or your jewellery. (South African adolescent)

Clearly, such different contexts lead to different aspirations deriving from the concept of citizenship. In the case of Palestine, the very notion of having a viable country still appears as a distant dream. Here the desire to lead a normal life, not subject to the daily dangers of the occupation, expresses the most aspirational aspect of citizenship. In South Africa, children obviously aspired to live in a safe, crime-free society where they would not have to be fearful of robbery or rape. In other countries, children may not mention these factors because they take for granted their safety and the ongoing existence of their country.

While the above cases demonstrate an aspirational notion of citizenship, in more stable and economically developed national contexts we can also see the influence of the political climate on how citizenship is understood. In Norway, the country with the largest percentage of GDP allocated to international aid, we see an internationalist ethos evident in the way some children spoke about citizenship, entailing a concern not only for the national interest but also for helping poorer countries. In developed countries with an increasingly multicultural population, like Norway, New Zealand and Australia, we see a concern with culture and the status of immigrants, and an eagerness to discuss how to recognise citizens of one's own country.

Alongside this direct influence of the national political context is the emergence of specific institutional and policy arrangements that are responsible for citizenship education. For instance, in the case of Australia, significant amounts of federal funding have been allocated for national civics and citizenship education programs. The idea of imparting notions of citizenship which emphasise a particular interpretation of 'being Australian' (including being fluent in English) and teaching of 'Australian values' was an important element of the Howard administration. Yet, as we discuss shortly, we need to be mindful of the ways in which the notion of citizenship is used and applied according to particular ideologies and political agendas, especially in the context of education.

Schooling Differences

The contribution of schools in educating children about democracy and citizenship should not be underestimated (Osler, 2000). At school (as in families), children see citizenship enacted in their daily lives. There is a 'hidden curriculum' at work in how children's rights and agency are respected at school, and whether children are given responsibility and control in their school lives (Taylor, Smith & Nairn, 2001). Another aspect of schooling which affects how children understand citizenship, especially equality of opportunity, is the degree to which school communities are inclusive of students from a range of cultural, socio-economic and ability groups. When children are separated into different institutions by background (for example, in private schools), they may be less tolerant of others who are educated elsewhere. The Brazilian research highlighted differences in perspective and understanding of injustice by children in wealthy private schools and poorer state-supported schools.

There is also the formal curriculum of schools, an issue we have mentioned previously in relation to Australian federal initiatives. In New Zealand, unlike in Australia, there is a National Curriculum[1] for the whole country. This guides curriculum aims, objectives and assessment, and human rights education is an important component of it. Developing understanding about social organisation (including rights, responsibilities, laws and rules) is an important goal of the National Curriculum (both in Social Studies and Health) in New Zealand. There is also a major emphasis in the Social Studies curriculum on respecting indigenous peoples through the Treaty of Waitangi,[2] biculturalism, multiculturalism and gender equity. Teachers in New Zealand are therefore expected to teach children about these issues, and it is thought reasonable to expect children to be aware of them. In New Zealand, participation rights were the most frequently mentioned of all rights across all age groups, at home, at school and in the community. Perhaps this relatively high level of awareness of civil rights amongst children and young people in New Zealand may be partly due to exposure to these concepts at school? The increased visibility recently provided by the New Zealand Government and NGOs to children's rights, as well as extended discussions of child advocacy issues in the media, may have had some influence.

Cultural Differences in Adult/Child Power Relations

Beyond the sphere of influence of the historical, institutional and political climate of each country lies the broader sphere of the cultural and social context, and our findings reflect the culturally specific nature of conceptions of citizenship. For example, it is interesting to note that Brazil was the only country in which adolescents, in talking about rights and responsibilities, openly talked about sexuality, about who is responsible for birth control and about abortion. This openness in talking about sexuality appeared as a strong Brazilian cultural trait. Yet, at the same time, when the children talked about responsibilities for chores in the home, their talk reflected another Brazilian cultural trait, that of *machismo*, as the boys referred to responsibilities like cleaning the house and washing up as distinctly female activities. Parallel with this, the girls complained that the boys did not have to do anything in the home. In this way, our study reinforces the argument made by James (2004) that the ways in which rights are implemented by and for children in their everyday lives varies both within and between cultures.

We can also see that these distinct contexts manifest themselves in particular local dynamics of power relations. For instance, in Norway it is a common experience for children to be encouraged to express their views, even if these opposed those of the teacher, provided this is done 'respectfully'. However, during the research we encountered an instance when children felt hurt that their unfavourable opinion concerning the rearrangement of students and class sizes had not been taken into account, and that change had been effected despite their wishes. This sense of injustice at the whims of adult power occurred in the school context of a developed country in which children's rights and participation have penetrated deeply into curriculum and teaching practices. On the other hand, in the context of Brazil, the sense of injustice in a school setting occurred because of a much more basic sense of deprivation in the school environment itself. As the example highlighted in the research shows, children complained at the lack of toilet facilities in schools, blaming the government for neglect.

Different contexts lead to different configurations of power that are found not only in the institutional level of the school but also in terms of the generational dynamics between children and adults. Citizenship in a democracy involves the sharing and negotiation of world views and the sharing of power, and John (2003) argues that adults' views of the world are the dominant framework for understanding and action, a framework which is linked to controlling children even when it is done in a kindly way. She suggests that in order to learn about power, children need – but rarely have – the opportunity to exercise it. Across the different countries and local contexts, children appeared to experience this power imbalance between the generations.

In some countries, for instance Australia, both parents and teachers appeared more reluctant to embrace wholeheartedly the notion of children's rights and extend to children the power to make some key decisions affecting their lives. This reluctance appears commonplace in some countries that are more wary about government interference within the private sphere, where bringing up a child is seen as a 'natural' sacrosanct space of the 'family'. On the other hand, in countries like South Africa (despite the emphasis children give to obedience) and New Zealand, adults appear much more welcoming of the possibility of children's rights. In the former, this can be partially accounted for by the post-apartheid era's willingness to embrace human rights discourse more generally.

In the latter, as we have already suggested, there is an awareness of children's rights and the value of children's participation at school, community and government level. It is likely that ratification of, and subsequent publicity about, the UNCRC has had an impact in both of these countries.

The example of South Africa reveals interesting local cultural features. Children, as well as teachers and parents, seem to view obedience to authority as an important responsibility of children in home, school and community settings. There appears to be a strong cultural agreement on children's responsibilities to obey laws and follow rules made by adults. However, this emphasis on obedience could possibly be traced to the apartheid government's policies which were maintained through force and also through the formal education system. The education system assisted in perpetuating and entrenching the racist system. In addition, it encouraged obedience and conformity to the ideology espoused by the apartheid state (Harber, 2001).

A major feature of this education ideology (called Christian National Education) was that education should be based on the Christian gospel (Ashley, 1989). Christian National Education was described as 'pernicious and pervasive' (King & Van den Berg, 1991, p. 18) and characterised by a strong belief in Christianity (Ashley, 1989), a strong hierarchical state control of education and schooling (De Jong & Lazarus, 1992), with the child viewed as helpless and needing to be moulded by an authoritative adult (Ashley, 1989). It required acceptance of and obedience to the authority. Being linked to religion, where obedience is such an important concept, provided the backdrop for the further entrenchment of obedience to the apartheid system. Religion has (and still does) played an important role in South African society. This had far-reaching implications insofar as obedience to authority was in a sense legitimised by the link to religion and became embedded in the psyches of generations of parents. Thus the role of adult as authority was reaffirmed and internalised in the home domain. Many parents have been reared and educated under the tenets of this education system and could have (unwittingly) conveyed this to their children.

For many who grew up during the apartheid years, remnants of the apartheid system remain enmeshed in their lives. On the one hand, this is only now beginning to shift with the emphasis on children's rights, and with more progressive parents providing spaces for children to question and express their opinions. On the other hand, children are increasingly also being made aware of their duties and responsibilities towards their families, communities and the state. The new Children's Act includes foundation principles stating that children have these responsibilities.

Yet it is important to note that amongst both children and adults there were differences as to what the ideal balance should be. Children, as well as adults, were ambivalent about children growing up and having more responsibilities. For instance, the young people from Norway claimed that parents '*say that we are going to be like adults, but if we are behaving like adults then they get scared, and then they want us back like kids again*', but on the other hand, they want to have the possibility '*to be a kid as long as I want to*'. There was widespread agreement amongst children that being an adult entailed new and demanding responsibilities, such as having a job, providing for the family and making difficult decisions – actions which not every child looked forward to. Cockburn (1998) warns against treating children as adults and expecting children to be citizens on the same terms. He argues that differences (including those related to age) are to be celebrated, and that children's right to childhood should be respected. Nevertheless, children should have access to citizenship through experiences which build their confidence and agency. As we have already pointed out, children want to have a say and have their opinion respected in matters affecting them.

In the following section, we attempt to draw the threads together of both the commonalities and differences evident in the children's narratives. Listening to the voices of children across the different countries, and in different local social contexts within each country, has led us to propose that while there may well be some common underpinning themes, or, as Lister (2008, p. 17) describes, 'building blocks' of citizenship, there is much to be learned from children themselves about how such building blocks might be re-examined and reshaped in order to better accommodate children and reflect their interests.

Re-thinking Citizenship from a Child's Perspective

(i) Children are Competent

Children's exclusion from the status of citizens – and so from the right to participate in social and political life – is often grounded in arguments about their lack of competence. As suggested in Chapter One, the rhetoric of citizenship for children has traditionally revolved around their future potential, rather than as competent social actors and contributors to their own lives and society in the present. Conceptualising children as agents dependent on nurturance, support and regulation from adults is seen as a contradiction within the traditional models of citizenship, but we would join other researchers (such as: Cockburn, 1998; Davis, 2007) in challenging those models. Indeed, Cockburn points out that putting children in a culture of incompetency and dependency creates a 'Catch 22' situation where children never have the chance to gain experience in decision-making.

Across all countries, children showed us they were social agents, who were able to engage in dialogue and reflection about citizenship and related concepts. The study therefore prompts questions about the ways in which underlying notions of competence, which determine the inclusion of children under the banner of 'citizen', are formulated. In this study, children understood competence across a spectrum that goes from full legal acknowledgement (such as voting age, age of criminal responsibility, legal entitlements of children and so on) to cultural expectations (such as the expectation for children in some places to contribute to keeping the house tidy, or in other contexts to contribute to the household income). As such, the children in this study strongly challenged traditional adult notions of citizenship: far from approaching competence as a pre-requisite of citizenship, the children in this study understood competence as implicit in notions of citizenship. At the same time, their agency and status as social actors did not mean that they were any less dependent on adults for support and nurturance (Alderson, 2000; Cockburn, 1998). The issue of competence and, in particular, the question of which stage in the life-cycle society endows particular rights and responsibilities to its members, is crucial in the debate around children and citizenship. As we shall see, the lack of clarity surrounding this transitional phase, amongst children and adults themselves, is a marked feature of speaking about citizenship.

(ii) Children mainly understand identity and belonging in relational terms (that are sophisticated and nuanced)

In Chapter One, we suggested that belonging to a greater collectivity, and being respected by others, is prominent in talk about citizenship. We further described how belonging is understood in a number of different ways, ranging from more formal and legalistic notions of belonging towards the more subjective and personal. The findings of this study, however, suggest that children emphasise the subjective more than the legal aspect of belonging and that such belonging has a significant role to play in recognising children's sense of identity. Children describe citizenship in relational terms and the ways that individual or particular groups engage in society and its processes and institutions. Their understanding of and engagement in citizenship then appears, not necessarily at the level of an abstract understanding of the democratic systems and institutions of citizenship, but at the level of processes embedded in social relationships and in relationships to their environment. Our research therefore accords with Jans' (2004) view that children's participation at the local level lies at the heart of citizenship: 'The more capacity and connection with groups and/or ideas ... the more one can behave as an active citizen' (Jans, 2004, p. 31).

Inviting children to contribute their own ideas about possible worlds might also help children to construct a sense of citizenship which is meaningful to them rather than remain constrained by normative practice. In our research, asking children about how an imaginary country might be evoked the most interesting and abstract discussion of citizenship. In Australia, for instance, children talked about freedom, peace, democracy, balance and strength while inventing a flag for their imaginary country. Another group talked about representations of co-operation, freedom, peace, and care for the environment and living things. In New Zealand a group of older girls discussing their imaginary country talked about fair ways to divide up land, including who got the best bits (for example, by the sea), and putting in place systems to allow for debate and the resolution of conflict. The success of the imaginary country exercise supports the view that children are active, agentive meaning-makers when encouraged to be so. As Jans suggests 'Children manifest themselves everywhere and throughout history as active meaning-makers' (2004, p. 36). Both opportunities to be socially involved and invitations to discuss and create new ideas about the meaning of democratic concepts are important for children to make sense of citizenship.

Further, children's developing identity is strongly influenced by their agency and voice, and reflective of their attempts to make sense of the world (Pufall & Unsworth, 2004). The children in this study showed how they interpret events in their lives and historical events according to their relationships and interactions with others, and how they 'weave these events and interpretations into personal identities and life stories that are meaningful and significant' (Meacham, 2004, p. 77). This shared sense of identity is reflected deeply in the children's attempts to explain what it means to be a citizen.

In this way, children's sense of identity resonated with insights from socio-cultural theory, which suggests identity is an important aspect of learning that links individuals to their communities and a vehicle that carries experiences from context to context (Bruner, 2003; Holland, Lachicotte, Skinner & Cain, 1998; Wenger, 1998):

> *Building an identity consists of negotiating the meanings of our experiences of membership in social communities. The concept of identity serves as a pivot between the social and the individual, so that each can be talked about in terms of the other.* (Wenger, 1998, p. 145)

(iii) Children participate most authentically when childhood is seen as a site of 'citizenship practice'

Across all countries, children were looking for authentic opportunities to engage, participate and contribute as citizens, and they envisaged childhood as a site of citizenship practice. As we have described above, embedded within children's understandings of citizenship was a conceptualisation of citizenship that valued the importance of relationship and interaction with others. It was also the case that opportunities for authentic participation were 'few and far between'. This is consistent with James' (2007) observation that although the view of children as causally efficacious social agents is now well accepted, problems still remain:

> *The recognition of children as competent social actors is the place from which much contemporary anthropological research with children now sets out. Why is it, then, that – despite the political rhetoric surrounding the commitment to hearing 'children's voices'... little of what children as social actors say is heard outside of the academy?* (James, 2007, pp. 261–262)

Bordenave (1995) suggests that levels of participation tend to increase when people begin to know their reality and reflect and overcome real or apparent contradictions. Participation increases when people begin to anticipate consequences and distinguish cause from effect, inferences from observations, and facts from judgments. The quality of participation also increases when people learn to manage conflicts, clarify feelings and behaviours, tolerate differences and respect opinions. It develops even further when people learn how to organise and coordinate meetings and actions. We can see that such actions involve more sophisticated ways of interacting with our environment and with other people. This research showed that the level of participation also tends to increase when people feel valued and when their efforts and actions are recognised, and when they feel capable of doing, of transforming their environment and the relationships which surround them. The quality of participation also increases when people feel part of a greater collectivity whose objectives and values are regarded as meaningful and profoundly gratifying. The developing skills and competencies around participation identified by Bordenave are most salient to research on citizenship. As a result, the affective aspects of participation, (particularly the sense of belonging, feeling valued and being capable of effecting change) become weighty considerations when thinking about the policy and practice implications of research on children's citizenship.

Our own, and other, research on children's understanding of citizenship suggests that they do not see themselves as experiencing the rich, scaffolded model of participation described above by Bordenave (1995). In many instances, their practice of citizenship is not recognised or respected. Our findings suggest that children are not demanding the equal exercise of rights and responsibilities of adulthood. Nor, indeed, do they expect that adults will support them in their role as citizen children. They do, however, want to be listened to and taken seriously. Like the growing body of literature arguing for recognition of children's citizenship, the children in this study are not, as Lister (2008) says, pursuing the wholesale extension of adult rights and obligations of citizenship, but rather are seeking recognition that their citizenship practices constitute an understanding of children as citizens – albeit in newer ways.

In concluding this section, we propose that the number of major national and international research reports on various policy and curriculum initiatives outlined in Chapter One clearly indicate that post-millennial conceptions of children as citizens are now entrenched in contemporary discourses of childhood. As evaluative reports on the benefits for children, families and communities of many significant policy and curriculum initiatives continue to emerge, a new space for thinking about the citizen child, and childhood as a site of citizenship practice, is opening up. At such a junction, it may be instructive to examine briefly the implications of the findings of this study in light of what is now a considerable body of literature on the subject.

Implications of the Research for Policy and Practice (Institutional Policy-making, Curriculum Design, and Teacher Pedagogy)

Bordenave (1995) argues that we can only learn about participation through participating. This idea appears equally applicable to citizenship. For the children in this study, their status as citizens is assumed, and the idea of childhood as a site of citizenship unquestioned. The issue then becomes whether or not it is possible to accommodate the aspirations of the citizen child within authentic and meaningful citizenship practices, and whether we think it is important to do so.

We suggest that the idea of the 'citizen child', and of childhood as a site of 'citizenship practice', centres around the way we view the child, or the way that 'the child', 'childhood' and 'citizenship' are theorised and practised by researchers, policy makers, parents and those working at the coal-face with children and young people. Children's subordinate status and exclusion from social and political processes is situated in an absence of discourses about children's citizenship which are evident in layers of acquired dispositions or habitus. Across the countries in this study, there was a wide recognition of young people as citizens, yet in limited, mainly passive, ways. On the part of the adults in the study, there seemed to be a limited grasp of the potential of the agency of young people to contribute actively to society.

The more complex notion of children as efficacious social agents who are, at the same time dependent on adults for nurture and support, is embedded within and across children's conceptualisation of their identity as citizens in this study, and is perhaps even more elusive (Alderson, 2001; Cockburn, 1998). While a handful of writers have sought to theorise this nuanced approach to citizenship,[3] there seems to be a paucity of political initiatives, curriculum structures and pedagogical approaches that have the capacity to allow for the complexity of this concept. Given that the idea of research focused on children's voices was certainly not new to the institutions, schools, teachers and parents, clear evidence of policy, curriculum, and pedagogy that could be directly traced to such research/thinking proved to be elusive.

Rethinking Adult Conceptions of Children as Citizens

If we are to take seriously the children's insights into what constitutes citizenship, we suggest that a good place to start is with adult conceptions of children and their citizenship status. Adults' attitudes have an important part to play in recognising and supporting children's citizenship. For children, authentic citizenship practice takes place in relational settings, and as such is dependent to a large degree on the ways in which we as adults recognise and respect the status and voice of children, support and scaffold their citizenship practices, as well as limit, resist or constrain children's citizenship practices. As we mentioned in Chapter One, being a citizen does not naturally emerge alongside biological development, but is instead nurtured by social experiences and interactions with others (Butler, Princeswal & Abreu, 2007; Moosa-Mitha, 2005; Neale, 2004). Such experiences and interactions entail 'progressively more complex patterns of reciprocal activity' (Bronfenbrenner, 1979, p. 60). These complex patterns can be conceptualised as occurring in ever-expanding concentric circles, from the level of the home and relations with close kin, as well as with the local environment (the home, the garden, caring for pets), towards spaces of greater complexity such as schools and the local community. Both the nature of adult constructions, expectations and support for children as citizens, and how children are positioned by adults in their everyday social interactions, are likely to influence how children view themselves in relation to citizenship.

Thus, the implications of this study and the rapidly increasing amount of other research on children and citizenship must begin to reach *beyond* the levels of policy-making, curriculum design, and teacher pedagogy. The real power behind policy, curriculum, and pedagogy is *the set of assumptions that adults hold about children*. Those who work with children and young people themselves need to realise that their actions emanate from a baseline set of assumptions they have about who children are and what they are capable of. Without having explicitly examined the nature of their assumptions about children, childhood and the nature of citizenship, it is simply not possible to identify the key participation opportunities that children really want and need to develop.

> *Although new approaches in the study of childhood and children's everyday lives have opened up a theoretical and conceptual space in which children can speak as participant-observers about their experiences of the world, this is not in and of itself sufficient to ensure that children's voices and views are heard. ... Childhood research must now begin to engage more directly with the core issues of social theory to unleash the political and intellectual promise of positioning children as social actors.* (James, 2007, p. 261)

This is a challenge for childhood researchers to review critically their own concepts and theories and to engage with 'the core issues in social theory' in the construction of concepts and theories from the standpoint of children.

It is therefore vital to have parents, teachers, carers and policy makers (indeed all who interface with children) who can recognise and build upon children's agency, to convey to children how they may engage with and shape their own contexts, in ways that are sensitive to the needs and vulnerabilities of children. We suggest that this means closer attention must be paid to the ways in which those who work with and for children are equipped and encouraged to:

(i) identify key opportunities to facilitate the authentic participation of children;
(ii) scaffold those opportunities so young people can participate at an appropriate and meaningful level, while at the same time building their capacity for increased future participation;
(iii) approach those opportunities in an intentional and reflective way; that is, through the explicit examination of their own assumptions, in order to ensure that their conceptions of 'the child' and of 'citizenship' can be fused into a conceptualisation of the 'citizen child';
(iv) be open to being surprised by what young people and children have to offer – that is that they recognise and develop the ability of children to comprehend quite complex nuances at play in their social situations, and

(v) be explicit about the nature of the concepts associated with children and citizenship, which, as this study has shown, are problematic and contestable.

Re-thinking Pedagogy

However, in positing the above we also argue that this more reflexive approach to working with and for children is just a start! We suggest that further work be undertaken which examines the complexities and intricacies of placing greater value on children as active social and political citizens. This means re-thinking teaching methods and interrogating dominant pedagogical approaches: Do they foster genuine inquiry, critique and reflection? What would staff professional development (or parent education) look like if it were capable of facilitating this sort of explicit conceptual reflection in teachers, parents and others who work with or care for children and young people?

Moreover, in the interest of transparency in policy making and curriculum design, it would be useful if the authors of such could be so bold as to 'nail their colours to the mast' by identifying the theoretical approach underpinning the intention and purpose of the policy.

This is not radical, and is there for the taking if we want it. However, the real issue is deeply entrenched – we are not examining critically enough how we conceptualise children and the ways we engage with them, whether this be in education or some other practice-based context. The real implications may not necessarily lie with the way the children learn, so much as with the way that adults who work with them think about, and therefore engage with, children and young people.

> *In former days, citizenship used to be a static given and the final destination of childhood. Nowadays, within late modernity, citizenship presents itself as a dynamic and continuous learning process. ... (T)his learning process is embedded in the biography and practice of each individual. Because humans are in essence social creatures, their biographical work and their practices are social activities.* (Jans, 2004, p. 40)

We suggest that this study provides only a starting point for further investigation of children's citizenship. The research has many limitations, particularly that of data being collected from one-off focus group discussions.[4] Nevertheless, the study does provide a snapshot of children's constructions of citizenship, which tend to be framed from their personal experiences rather than from any abstract understanding of democracy and society. The challenge for researchers now is to develop ideas about enriching children's understanding of citizenship, and to suggest to teachers, parents and children useful and productive ways of doing so. In socio-cultural terms, adults working with young people need to scaffold children's developing understanding and challenge their existing ideas.

About Childwatch International

Research Network

The Childwatch International Research Network (See www.childwatch.uio.no) is a global, non-profit, nongovernmental network of institutions engaged in research for children. The Network seeks to strengthen child-centred research for the purpose of promoting child rights and improving children's living conditions, well-being and participation around the world. It was founded in 1993 as a response from the research community to the UN Convention on the Rights of the Child. The Convention is the basis for the Network's common agenda and an instrument for changing the focus of research and for ensuring that the perspectives of children are heard.

Childwatch links local, regional and national research efforts to an international research-based knowledge, practice and policy on children's issues. It seeks a more effective and strategic approach to child research globally. Childwatch has unique potential to harness the collective capacity of international child researchers to identify and investigate major questions of global significance in the lives of children.

The Network focuses on critical issues in the lives of children and youth, and their families. It seeks to encourage multi-disciplinary research, policy development and training that promotes the well-being, rights, civic and social participation and full development of children. Childwatch values research about effective and appropriate practices to achieve these goals and research that describes the current condition of children and youth.

The core of Childwatch International is the Key Institutions, which conduct research on children's rights from various perspectives. They are committed to child research with an interdisciplinary approach within a framework of international co-operation. The directing body of the Network is the Board, which gives advice on the Network's overall policy and long-term strategies for its implementation. The Secretariat is an executive, supportive body, headed by the Director of Childwatch International and based at the University of Oslo, Norway. The Business Committee supervises the administrative and financial matters of Childwatch International, and thus provides important support to the Secretariat. The Network is guided by the principles in the Aims and Ethos and Strategic Plan, and in the Governance and Funding documents and their corresponding by-laws.

The Childwatch International Research Network receives its core funding from The Norwegian Agency for Development Cooperation (NORAD). NORAD's child policy is guided by Norway's Development Strategy for

Children and Young People in the South. The funding is channelled through the Norwegian Research Council.

About the Key Institutions and the Authors

Childwatch International is a network of institutions and associations involved in interdisciplinary research on issues relating to children's rights, development and well-being. Key Institutions carry out research on and with children and are committed to a common agenda for promoting children's rights, development and well-being. The Key Institutions have individual profiles, differing histories and backgrounds, scope, size and organisational structures. Representatives of the Key Institutions meet every three years at the Key Institutions meeting to discuss issues connected to Network activities and to develop strategies to pursue application of research to policy and practice and mutual capacity building through collaboration.

Childwatch International provides funding for Key Institutions interested in particular collaborative research projects to meet and to co-ordinate their activities. The Citizenship Study Group is comprised of representatives from six Key Institutions:

1. Australia: Centre for Children and Young People (CCYP)

Southern Cross University, Lismore, New South Wales, Australia
Web site: http://www.ccyp.scu.edu.au

The CCYP was established at Southern Cross University in 2004 and brings together four important strands: an interdisciplinary approach; a focus on research, education and advocacy for children and young people; an emphasis on cross-sectoral partnerships to promote evidence-based policy and practice; and the inclusion and the participation of children and young people. The Centre achieves its aims through:

1. Developing relevant and appropriate inter-disciplinary research.
2. Supporting the provision of education and professional development for individuals and organisations working with children and young people.
3. Engaging with colleagues in the field of child and youth research regionally, nationally and internationally.
4. Collaborating with agencies and organisations concerned with quality service provision for children and young people.
5. Contributing to the development of state and national policies that enhance the well-being of children and young people.
6. Enhancing the participation of children and young people in their families, schools and communities. The Centre engages in a broad range of research and evaluation activities, conferences, seminars, professional development and child and youth participation initiatives.

Associate Professor Anne Graham is the Director of the CCYP, and is also Head of the School of Education at Southern Cross University. Anne's professional and research interests are focused on improved outcomes for children and young people, particularly through education. She developed a loss and grief education program, Seasons for Growth, that focuses on the promotion of social and emotional well-being for children and young people who have experienced significant change in their family due to death, separation or divorce. Anne also has a strong interest in quality teaching and is currently working on an ARC-funded project to develop a model for the professional development of teachers in ICT, based on a metacognitive approach to learning. Anne has recently completed a major study on teachers' views of children's mental health, and is supervising a number of PhD projects that are focusing on the participation of children and young people in both education and family law.

Dr Brad Shipway is a researcher at the CCYP and a lecturer in the School of Education at Southern Cross University in the area of Human Society and Its Environment (also known as Studies of Society and Environment). He has a keen interest in the philosophy of education and critical realism, and supervises postgraduate students in these areas. Brad's current research projects include an investigation into the Spiritual and Religious Development of Young People in Catholic Schools in the Lismore Diocese: A Longitudinal View. This project is examining the factors that shape and influence the religious and spiritual lives of young people aged 12 to 17 years. The study will be undertaken over a period of six years (2005 – 2011).

Robyn Fitzgerald is a researcher and PhD student at the CCYP. She has an education and family law background and has been involved in social and legal research with children since the establishment of the CCYP in 2003. Her research interests include children's participation, rights and citizenship, and the ethical and methodological implications of research with children.

2. Brazil: The International Center for Research on Childhood (Centro Internacional de Estudos e Pesquisas sobre a Infância) – CIESPI

Pontifícia Universidade Católica do Rio de Janeiro, Brazil
Web site: www.ciespi.org.br

CIESPI aims to improve the conditions of low-income children in Brazil, particularly children in urban low income areas, including the slums, through applied research, policy and project development and training. It is a non-profit research centre dedicated to applied research, policy analysis and training about the needs of children, particularly disadvantaged children, and their families. CIESPI's activities include: research and social policy projects, interdisciplinary training for students and professionals, resource centre, project consultation, and print and electronic publications.

Professor Irene Rizzini is a researcher at the Pontifical Catholic University of Rio de Janeiro and Director of CIESPI. She also serves as President of the

Childwatch International Research Network. Irene is the author of several books including: *Globalization and children*; *The art of governing children: The history of social policies, legislation and child welfare in Brazil*; *Disinherited from society: Street children in Latin America*; *The lost century: The historical roots of public policies on children in Brazil*; *Images of the child in Brazil: 19th and 20th centuries*; *Children and the law in Brazil – Revisiting the History (1822–2000)*; *Niños, adolescentes, marginalidad y violencia en América Latina y el Caribe: relaciones indisociables? (Children and youth, marginalization and violence in Latin America and the Caribbean: indissociable relations?)*.

Dr Udi Mandel Butler is a Research Fellow at CIESPI and a lecturer at the Institute of Social and Cultural Anthropology, Oxford University. Udi's research has been with children, adolescents and young adults living, or who have lived, on the streets of Rio de Janeiro. His most recent research with CIESPI looks at young people's perceptions of, and participation in, public action in Rio (NGOs, social movements, politics and citizenship).

Dr Nisha Thapliyal is a Research Associate from the University of Maryland. She completed her doctoral dissertation on social movements in Brazil and has also worked as a social worker and educator with institutionalised and street children in Mumbai, India. Nisha worked with CIESPI during her stay in Brazil and continues to collaborate with the Center as an International Research Associate.

3. New Zealand: Children's Issues Centre
University of Otago, Dunedin, New Zealand
Web site: http://www.otago.ac.nz/cic

The Children's Issues Centre was established in 1995 to address national issues that affect children and young people, and to contribute to improving their well-being, using an interdisciplinary approach. Our research and teaching bring together people from a variety of disciplines, to establish a climate of collaboration and shared research knowledge; and to stimulate new research aimed at improving professional practice and policy development for children and young people. We have four primary roles:

1. Research: We do research which investigates how children's rights are being implemented in New Zealand; which allows children and young people's voices to be heard; which surveys current knowledge about children and young people; which evaluates programmes, policies and practices that affect children and young people.
2. Education: We provide information and continuing education for students, professionals and agencies working with children and young people including seminars, workshops and conferences. We also offer a distance-taught postgraduate Certificate in Children's Issues, a Diploma in Child Advocacy and a Master of Arts degree in Childhood and Youth Studies.
3. Policy and Advocacy: We work with community, professional and

government agencies to develop practices and policies which respect and empower children and young people.
4. Community Resource: We publish a journal – *Childrenz Issues* – and regular reports on our research, and respond to requests for information.

Emeritus Professor Anne Smith is an applied developmental psychologist with a particular interest in social development and in ecological and sociocultural influences on children's development. Anne obtained her PhD from the University of Alberta in 1971 and then lectured in the Education Department at the University of Otago until she was appointed as the inaugural Director of the Children's Issues Centre in 1995. Anne retired from this position in 2006, but remains actively involved with the Centre on a part-time basis. Anne is well known for her research in the field of early childhood education and care. More recently she has been influenced by the UNCRC and the sociology of childhood which highlights the importance of children's own constructions of their experiences. She is currently involved in research on children's participation in a variety of family, legal and community contexts.

Dr Nicola Taylor is a Senior Research Fellow with the Children's Issues Centre. She has a Bachelor of Social Work (Hons) degree from Massey University and a Bachelor of Laws (Hons) degree from the University of Otago. Her PhD thesis explored family members' experiences of Family Court dispute resolution processes. Nicola has worked at the Children's Issues Centre since its inception and also has a part-appointment in the University's Faculty of Law. She has a particular interest in socio-legal research with children, parents and professionals concerning the impact of legal and welfare processes on family life; children's participation in family law proceedings; and children's perspectives on discipline, citizenship and rural childhood issues.

Megan Gollop is a Research Fellow at the Children's Issues Centre. She has a psychology and counselling background, and has been involved in developmental and social research with children since 1990. Megan has worked as a researcher at the Children's Issues Centre since 1996 on a variety of research projects, predominantly relating to socio-legal issues. Her current research interests include: issues for families following parental separation/ divorce, relocation following parental separation, children and young people's perspectives, and family discipline and guidance of children.

4. Norway: Norwegian Centre for Child Research (NOSEB)

Norwegian University of Science and Technology (NTNU),
Trondheim, Norway
Web site: www.svt.ntnu.no/noseb.english/

NOSEB is a national, interdisciplinary centre which started its activities in 1982. It does basic and applied long-term research on children and childhood. The Centre offers an international, interdisciplinary master programme through MPhil in Childhood Studies and a PhD programme in interdisciplinary childhood research.

Through teaching and research NOSEB gives insights to the activities and the conditions of children's adolescence by initiating and carrying out interdisciplinary research projects. NOSEB attaches great importance to international collaboration. The Centre's numerous research conferences is a vital part of this. *Childhood*, the leading journal within the field of childhood research, published in collaboration with Sage Publications Ltd, is another example. NOSEB's international profile is also attended to through the Centre's participation in several research networks and through the fact that it is a key institution in Childwatch International. Furthermore, the Centre is a working place for a whole range of internationally acclaimed child researchers. NOSEB's master and PhD education also has a distinct international profile.

On a national level, NOSEB emphasises the development of the field of child research through participation in networks within similar scientific fields, like geography, social anthropology, sociology, history and pedagogy. The Centre's journal – *Barn* – is an important national and Nordic channel of mediation for this interdisciplinary child research.

NOSEB is organised as part of the Faculty for Social Science and Technology Management and NTNU Social Research Ltd. NOSEB has twenty-five staff members: two professors, five adjunct professors, two associate professors, two researchers, eleven doctoral students and three senior executive officers.

Associate Professor Anne Trine Kjørholt is the Director of the Norwegian Centre for Child Research at the Norwegian University of Science and Technology. Her research interests are discourses on childhood, children's rights, children's perspectives, early childhood education and care. Anne Trine is currently leading three large research projects: Children as new citizens and the best interest of the child; The modern child and the flexible labour market – institutionalisation and individualisation of children's lives; and Children, young people and local knowledge in Ethiopia and Zambia. Anne Trine's publications include: *Childhood as a symbolic space: Discourses on children as social participants in society*, Doctoral thesis, NTNU, 2004; *Beyond listening: Children's perspectives in early childhood services* (co-editor with A. Clark & P. Moss), The Policy Press, 2005; Children as new citizens: In the best interest of the child? (In A. James & A. James (Eds.), *Children as citizens and the politics of childhood in Europe*. London: Palgrave. Anne Trine also recently co-edited a Special Issue of *Children's Geographies* on Global childhoods: Why children? Why now?

Håvard Bjerke is a PhD student at NOSEB. His project is funded by the Norwegian Research Council, as a subproject in the research project Children as New Citizens and the 'Best Interest of the Child' – A Challenge for Modern Democracies at the Norwegian Centre for Child Research, and as part of the international study on Children's Perspectives on Citizenship co-ordinated by the Childwatch International Research Network. Håvard has a Master's degree in sociology, and work experience with Save the Children Norway, Childwatch, and the Norwegian Youth Council. His research interests are children's rights, participation and citizenship.

5. Palestine: Child Research Unit, Al-Quds University

Center for Development in Primary Health Care, AlBireh-West Bank,
P.O.Box 4006, Palestine
Web site: http://www.alquds.edu/

The purpose of the research unit at Al-Quds University is to:

1. Promote child research in Palestine with focus on health and psycho-social issues.
2. Build the local capacity in child research.
3. Advise and develop policy on children's health and development.
4. Promote research networking and co-operation locally, regionally and internationally. The focus of research has been on: Trauma among children; Nutritional status of children; Domestic violence in the family; Immunisation status; Food security in Palestine; Accessibility to health services; Child growth and development; Child participation.

Professor Mohammed Shaheen holds a doctoral degree of public health from the University of Pittsburgh, USA. He is the Associate Professor of Public Health and Dean of the School of Public Health at Al-Quds University, AlBireh-West Bank. Mohammed is also the Director of the Center for Development in Primary Health Care which works on psychosocial and public health projects implemented at the community level. He is one of the vice-presidents of the Childwatch International Research Network. His main research focus is on children's health and well-being (such as psychosocial, nutrition and reproductive health) and on community-based health and development interventions.

6. South Africa: Child and Youth Research and Training Programme (CYRTP)

University of the Western Cape, Cape Town, Republic of South Africa
Website: www.uwc.ac.za

The Child and Youth Research and Training Programme (CYRTP) is a multi-disciplinary programme engaging in research pertaining to children between 0 and 18 years. Our mission is to promote the well-being of children in South Africa by conducting research and disseminating research-based information to inform intervention and policy development for children. The primary functions of the programme are: (i) Research to inform social policy and innovative practices and interventions (ii) education and training of social service professionals and (iii) Internship placements for post graduate research students.

Our work is informed and facilitated through a wide range of partnerships with government, academic institutions, NGO's and CBO's and other child researchers.

Professor Rose September is an Associate Professor in the Faculty of Community and Health Sciences at the University of the Western Cape (UWC), where she heads the Child and Youth Research and Training Programme. She has a PhD degree in social work. She conducts research, publishes, teaches and supervises students and consults with professionals in the areas of social policy research, developmental social welfare services, poverty, child welfare services, early childhood development, youth development and child protection. Her research interests and practice are primarily in social policy research and the utilisation of research as an instrument for transformation – social change and social justice.

Hazel Roberts is a Master's student in Research Psychology and is undertaking an internship year at the Child and Youth Research and Training Programme where she is working on projects concerning citizenship, violence and bullying in schools. Her thesis topic is on the construction of motherhood and how this impacts on the lives of working mothers.

Notes

Preface

1. Childwatch International is an international network of child research centres, co-ordinated in Norway and funded by the Norwegian government.
2. This meeting was attended by Natalie Kaufman and Sue Limber (USA), Jiri Kovarich (Czech Republic), Irene Rizzini (Brazil), Rose September (South Africa) and Anne Smith (New Zealand).
3. The other participants included Natalie Kaufman and Sue Limber (USA), Anne Smith and Nicola Taylor (New Zealand), Ingrid Willenberg (South Africa), Mohammed Shaheen, Ziad Abdeen and Maissa Abu Baker (Palestine), and the CIESPI Research team – including Luciléia Pereira, Marcelo Princeswal, Nisha Thapliyal and Tamo Chattopadhay.
4. Norway was also involved in the study, but the NTNU representatives were unable to attend this meeting. Australia was yet to join the project, but did so shortly after the Rio de Janeiro meeting.
5. New Zealand: Nicola Taylor – New Zealand children and young people's perspectives on citizenship and nation building. South Africa: Ingrid Willenberg – Perspectives on rights, responsibilities and citizenship from children in Cape Town. Norway: Anne Trine Kjørholt, Line Hellem, Gjertrud Stordal & Pernille Skotte – Children as citizens: Perspectives on children's rights and responsibilities in Norway. Brazil: Irene Rizzini – Child and adolescent perceptions on citizenship and their participation in Brazil. Palestine: Maisaa Abu Baker & Mohammed Shaheen – Palestinian school children perspectives on citizenship: West Bank / Jenin Camp. Australia: Anne Graham & Robyn Fitzgerald – Children and young people's perspectives on rights, responsibilities and citizenship in Australia.
6. The other participants were Irene Rizzini (Brazil), Pernille Skotte (Childwatch International), Nicola Taylor (New Zealand), Brad Shipway (Australia), Mohammed Shaheen (Palestine), Rose September and Simone Moses-Europa (South Africa). Apologies were received from Ziad Abdeen (Palestine), Natalie Kaufman (USA), Anne Smith (New Zealand) and Anne Graham (Australia).
7. It was also attended by Anne Graham, Brad Shipway and Robyn Fitzgerald (Australia), Håvard Bjerke (Norway) and Udi Butler (Brazil). Apologies were received from Irene Rizzini (Brazil), Anne Trine Kjørholt (Norway), Mohammed Shaheen (Palestine) and Rose September (South Africa).

3 Australia

1. At the time of writing, proposed changes to the Australian Citizenship Act 1948 were passed by the House of Representatives and were under consideration by the Senate.
2. For example, the Universal Declaration of Human Rights, and the UNCRC.
3. The Australian Council for Educational Research (ACER) conducted surveys of

over 3,000 students, 400 teachers and 150 schools throughout Australia in 1999. Internationally, 90,000 students were surveyed. ACER and the University of Canberra were funded by the Commonwealth Government to organise Australian participation in the international study.
4 Nonumerical Unstructured Data Indexing, Searching and Theorizing software, Qualitative Solutions Research, http://www.qsrinternational.com/index.htm
5 The remaining two parents indicated that they were not sure.

4 Brazil

1 Project Coordination: Irene Rizzini; Researchers: Luciléia Pereira, Marcelo Princeswal; Collaborators: Carla Daniel Sartor, Nathercia Lacerda, Isabela Massa, Alexandra Pena, Tamo Chattopadhay; Intern: Marina Rodriguez de Jesus; Translation: Cristiano Botafogo; Special participation: Nisha Thapliyal and Udi Butler.
2 The term 'menores' (minors) has a negative connotation in Brazil, meaning children and youth who are seen as delinquents.
3 In this book, the child reader can see images of children from other countries and part of the culture and the habits of each country.
4 Names of the schools have been changed to preserve their anonymity.
5 According to data extracted from the website of the Municipal Secretariat of Education of the city of Rio de Janeiro – SME/RJ.
6 According to data extracted from the website of the SME/RJ.
7 According to data extracted from the website of the SME/RJ.
8 The public schools offer lunch for their students at no cost. Everyday they have one menu option, but the adolescents' expressed their desire for having a larger variety of meals.
9 According to data extracted from the website www.cdprio.com.br.
10 According to data extracted from the website http://www.csvp.g12.br/
11 The school develops projects destined for the poor social strata of the population. Many students participate in solidarity actions, like food donation and community work, with the purpose of helping people in need.
12 In Rio de Janeiro, a Social Educator is a person who works with street children. Most are professionals with degrees in human or social sciences and/or adults who lived part of their own lives in the streets.
13 The Rede Rio Criança network comprises 13 Governmental and Non-governmental Organizations that carry out integrated actions, maximizing the care delivered to children and adolescents living in the streets of Rio de Janeiro. Ciespi is part of this network.
14 Any historical data on the moment in this report was extracted from the website http://www.mst.org.br/historico/historia.htm (in Portuguese).
15 We believe that the concept of 'citizenship' is unclear not only to young people. There is also a danger that the word may be used too much, but unreflexively and, as such, becomes meaningless. Some groups repeated the clichés used by politicians and the media to define citizenship, which led us to think that citizenship is not experienced.
16 A group of students that represent the school. The objective of the student councils is to fight for better education both in public and private schools.

5 New Zealand

1   The authors are grateful to Kate Marshall and Philipa Biddulph, who collected data for this research, and to Childwatch International which initiated this project.

6 Norway

1   The Norwegian Centre for Child Research has been responsible for the Norwegian part of the international project. The Director of the Centre, Anne Trine Kjørholt, managed the subproject and participated in drafting the national report from the project in 2005 and this revised chapter. Line Hellem, Pernille Skotte and Gjertrud Stordal were engaged as research assistants and collected the data. They also contributed to the interpretation and editing of the national report. Håvard Bjerke has contributed substantially to this revised chapter, including theoretical perspectives and further interpretation of data. He will extend the original research as part of his current PhD study.
2   Figures from Norway Statistics, 2001–2003.

8 South Africa

1   Since this research study started in 2004 it has benefited from the contributions of a number of researchers: Lead researcher and principal investigator: Prof. R. September; Contributing Researchers (in alphabetical order): Ms Z. Cakata, Ms K. Christiana, Ms S. Moses-Europa, Mr E. Johnson (admin support), Ms K. Kader, Ms Q Kekana, Ms L. Leoschut, Ms F. Peters, Mr S. Savahl, Ms B. Sonn and Dr I. Willenberg.

References

Preface

Doek, J.E. (2008). Foreword. Citizen child: A struggle for recognition. In A. Invernizzi & J. Williams (Eds.), *Children and Citizenship*. Los Angeles/London: Sage Publications.

Lister, R. (2007). Why citizenship: Where, when and how children? *Theoretical Inquiries in Law, 8*(2), 693–718.

1 Children's Citizenship

Alderson, P. (2001). Life and death: Agency and dependency in young children's health care. *Childrenz Issues, 5*(1), 23-27.

Bartlett, S. (2005). Good governance: Making age a part of the equation - An introduction. *Children, Youth and Environments, 15*(2): 1-17.

Ben-Arieh, A., & Boyer, Y. (2005). Citizenship and childhood: The state of affairs in Israel. *Childhood, 12*(1), 33-53.

Bowes, J.M., Flanagan, C., & Taylor, A.J. (2001). Adolescents' ideas about individual and social responsibility in relation to children's household work: Some international comparisons. *International Journal of Behavioral Development, 25*(1), 60-68.

Brannen, J., Heptinstall, E., & Bhopal, K. (2000). *Connecting children: Care and family life in later childhood*. London: RoutledgeFalmer.

Bronfenbrenner, U. (1979). *The ecology of human development: Experiments by nature and design*. Cambridge: Harvard University Press.

Casas, F., Saporiti, A., González, M., Figuer, C., Rostan, C., Sadurní, M., Alsinet, C., Gusó, M., Grignoli, D., Mancini, A., Ferrucci, F., & Rago, M. (2006). Children's rights from the point of view of children, their parents and their teachers: A comparative study between Catalonia (Spain) and Il Molise (Italy). *The International Journal of Children's Rights, 14(1),* 1-75.

Cheal, D.J. (2003). Children's home responsibilities: Factors predicting children's household work. *Social Behavior and Personality, 31*(8), 789-794.

Cockburn, T. (1998). Children and citizenship in Britain: A case for a socially interdependent model of citizenship. *Childhood, 5*(1), 99-117.

Cohen, R. (2001). Children's contribution to household labour in three sociocultural contexts: A Southern Indian village, a Norwegian town, and a Canadian city. *International Journal of Comparative Sociology, 42*(4), 353-367.

Cohen, E.F. (2005). Neither seen nor heard: Children's citizenship in contemporary democracies. *Citizenship Studies, 9*(2), 221-240.

Conover, P.J., Crewe, I.M., & Searing, D.D. (1991). The nature of citizenship in the United States and Great Britain: Empirical comments on theoretical themes. *Journal of Politics, 53*(3), 800-832.

Covell, K., & Howe, R.B. (1999). The impact of children's rights education: A Canadian study. *The International Journal of Children's Rights, 7,* 171-183.
Covell, K., & Howe, R.B. (2000). Children's rights education: Implementing Article 42. In A.B. Smith, M. Gollop, K. Marshall & K. Nairn, (Eds.), *Advocating for Children: International perspectives on children's rights* (pp. 42-50). Dunedin: University of Otago Press.
Covell, K., & Howe, R.B. (2001). *The challenge of children's rights for Canada.* Waterloo: Wilfred Laurier University Press.
Davis, J. (2007). Analysing participation and social exclusion with children and young people: Lessons from practice. *The International Journal of Children's Rights, 15*(1), 121-146.
Davis, J., & Watson, N. (2001). Where are the children's experiences? Analysing social and cultural exclusion in 'Special' and 'Mainstream' schools. *Disability and Society, 16,* 671-687.
France, A. (1998). 'Why should we care?' Young people, citizenship and questions of social responsibility. *Journal of Youth Studies, 1*(1), 97-112.
Freeman, M.D.A. (1996). The importance of a children's rights perspective in litigation. *Butterworths Family Law Journal, 2*(4), 84-90.
Hart, J. (2002). Children and nationalism in a Palestinian refugee camp in Jordan. *Childhood, 9*(1), 35-47.
Heater, D. (2004). *Citizenship: The civic ideals in word history, politics and education* (3rd edition). Manchester: Manchester University Press.
Helwig, C.C., & Turiel, E. (2002). Civil liberties, autonomy, and democracy: Children's perspective. *International Journal of Law and Psychiatry, 25*(3), 253-270.
Hine, J. (2004). *Children and Citizenship.* London: Home Office Online Report 08/04.
Holloway, S., & Valentine, G. (2000). Corked hats and Coronation Street: British and New Zealand children's imaginative geographies of the other. *Childhood, 7*(3), 335-357.
Holzman, L. (1995). Creating developmental learning environments. *School Psychology International, 16,* 199-212.
Howard, S., & Gill, J. (2001). 'It's like we're a normal way and everyone else is different': Australian children's constructions of citizenship and national identity. *Educational Studies, 27*(1), 87-103.
Howard, S., & Gill, J. (2005). Learning to belong: Children talk about feeling 'Australian'. *Childrenz Issues, 9*(2), 43-49.
James, A. (2004). Understanding childhood from an interdisciplinary perspective: Problems and Potentials. In P.R. Pufall & R.P. Unsworth (Eds.), *Rethinking childhood* (pp. 25-37). New Brunswick: Rutgers University Press.
James, A., & Prout, A. (1997). Re-presenting childhood: Time and transition in the study of childhood. In A. James & A. Prout (Eds.), *Constructing and reconstructing childhood: Contemporary issues in the sociological study of childhood* (2nd edition) (pp. 231-250). London: Falmer Press.
Jans, M. (2004). Children as citizens: Towards a contemporary notion of child participants. *Childhood, 11*(1), 27-44.
Jones, E., & Gaventa, J. (2002). *Concepts of citizenship: A review.* Sussex: Institute of Development Studies.
Jonsson, B., & Flanagan, C. (2000). Young people's views on distributive justice, rights and obligations: A cross-cultural study. *International Social Science Journal, 52*(144), 195-208.

Joseph, S. (2005). Teaching rights and responsibilities: Paradoxes of globalization and children's citizenship in Lebanon. *Journal of Social History, 38*(4), 1007-1026.

Kabeer, N. (2005a). Introduction. The search for inclusive citizenship: Meanings and expressions in an interconnected world. In N. Kabeer (Ed.), *Inclusive citizenship: Meanings and expressions* (pp. XIV, 274 s). London: Zed Books.

Kabeer, N. (Ed.). (2005b). *Inclusive citizenship: Meanings and expressions*. London: Zed Books.

Kjørholt, A.T. (2002). Small is powerful: Discourses on 'children and participation' in Norway. *Childhood, 9*(1), 63-82.

Kjørholt, A.T. (2004). *Childhood as a social and symbolic space: Discourses on children as social participants in society*. Doctoral thesis, NTNU, Department of Education / Norwegian Centre for Child Research, Trondheim.

Lee, J.W., & Hebert, Y.M. (2006). The meaning of being Canadian: A comparison between youth of immigrant and non-immigrant origins. *Canadian Journal of Education, 29*(2), 497-520.

Lister, R. (1997). Citizenship: Towards a feminist synthesis. *Feminist Review, 57*, 28-48.

Lister, R. (2007). Why citizenship: Where, when and how children? *Theoretical Inquiries in Law, 8*(2), 693-718.

Lister, R., Smith, N., Middleton, S., & Cox, L. (2003). Young people talk about citizenship: Empirical perspectives on theoretical and political debates. *Citizenship Studies, 7*(2), 235 - 252.

Manning, B., & Ryan, R. (2004). *Youth and citizenship: A report for NYARS*. Canberra: Australian Government Department of Family and Community Services on behalf of NYARS.

Marchant, R., & Kirby, P. (2004). The participation of young children: Communciation, consultation and involvement. In B. Neale (Ed.), *Young children's citizenship: Ideas into practice*. York: Joseph Rowntree Foundation.

Marshall, T.H. (1950). *Citizenship and Social Class*. Cambridge: Cambridge University Press.

Martin, R. (2006). Children's perspectives: Roles, responsibilities and burdens in home-based care in Zimbabwe. *Journal of Social Development in Africa, 21*(1), 106-129.

Matthews, H. (2005). The millennium challenge: The disappointing geographies of children's rights. *Children's Geographies, 3*(1), 1-3.

Mayall, B. (2002). *Towards a sociology for childhood: Thinking from children's lives*. Buckingham: Open University Press.

Melton, G.B. (1991). Socialization in the global community: Respect for the dignity of children. *American Psychologist, 46*, 66-71.

Melton, G.B. (2002). Democratization and children's lives. In N.H. Kaufman & I. Rizzini (Eds.), *Globalization and children: Exploring potentials for enhancing opportunities in the lives of children and youth*. New York: Kluwer Academic / Plenum Publishers.

Melton, G.B., & Limber, S.P. (1992). What children's rights mean to children: Children's own views. In M.D.A. Freeman & P. Veerman (Eds.), *The ideologies of children's rights* (pp. 167-187). Netherland: Kluwer Academic Publishers.

Moosa-Mitha, M. (2005). A difference-centred alternative to theorization of children's citizenship rights. *Citizenship Studies, 9*(4), 369-388.

Morrow, V. (1999). 'We are people too': Children's and young people's perspectives on

children's rights and decision-making in England. *The International Journal of Children's Rights, 7*(2), 149-170.
Nairn, K., & Smith, A.B. (2002). Secondary students' experiences of bullying at school and their suggestions for dealing with it. *Childrenz Issues, 6*(1), 16-22.
Nairn, K., & Smith, A.B. (2003). Taking students seriously: Their rights to be safe at school. *Gender and Education, 15*(2), 133-149.
Neale, B. (2004). *Young children's citizenship. Ideas into practice.* York: The Joseph Rowntree Foundation.
Oakley, A. (1994). Women and children first and last: Parallels and differences between children's and women's studies. In B. Mayall (Ed.), *Children's childhoods: Observed and experienced* (pp. 13-32). London: Falmer Press.
Osler, A., & Starkey, H. (2005). *Changing citizenship: Democracy and inclusion in education.* Maidenhead: Open University Press.
Pufall, P., & Unsworth, R. (2004). *Rethinking childhood.* New Brunswick: Rutgers UP.
Qvortrup, J. (1995). From useful to useful: The historical continuity of children's constructive participation. *Sociological Studies of Children, 7*(1), 49 - 76.
Roche, J. (1999). Children: Rights, participation and citizenship. *Childhood, 6*(4), 475-493.
Ruck, M.D., Abramovitch, R., & Keating, D.P. (1998a). Children's and adolescents' understanding of rights: Balancing nurturance and self-determination. *Child-Development, 69*(2), 404-417.
Ruck, M.D., Keating, D.P., Abramovitch, R., & Koegl, C.J. (1998b). Adolescents' and children's knowledge about rights: Some evidence for how young people view rights in their own lives. *Journal of Adolescence, 21*(3), 275-289.
Scourfield, J., & Davies, A. (2005). Children's accounts of Wales as racialized and inclusive. *Ethnicities, 5*(1), 83-107.
Sinclair, R. (2005). Participation in practice: Matters arising from experience in England. *Childrenz Issues, 9*(2), 31-36.
Smith, A.B. (2002). Interpreting and supporting participation rights: Contributions from sociocultural theory. *The International Journal of Children's Rights, 10,* 73-88.
Smith, A.B. (2007). Children and young people's participation rights in education. *The International Journal of Children's Rights 15,* 147-164.
Smith, A.B., Gaffney, M., & Nairn, K. (2004). Health rights in secondary schools: Student and staff perspectives. *Health Education Research, 19*(1), 85-97.
Smith, A.B., Nairn, K., & Gaffney, M. (2004). Secondary students' involvement in recreational activities at school. *Childrenz Issues, 8*(1), 29-34.
Smith, A.B., Nairn, K., Taylor, N., & Gaffney, M. (2003). Staff and student perspectives on children's rights in New Zealand secondary schools. *Childrenz Issues, 7*(1), 9-16.
Smith, A.B., Taylor, N.J., & Gollop, M. (Eds). (2000). *Children's voices: Research, policy and practice.* Auckland: Pearson Education.
Smith, N., Lister, R., Middleton, S., & Cox, L. (2005). Young people as real citizens: Towards an inclusionary understanding of citizenship. *Journal of Youth Studies, 8*(4), 425 - 443.
Stasiulis, D. (2002). The active child citizen: Lessons from Canadian policy and the children's movement. *Citizenship Studies, 6*(4), 507-538.
Stephens, S. (1997). Editorial introduction: Children and nationalism. *Childhood, 4*(1), 5-18.
Such, E., & Walker, R. (2004). Being responsible and responsible beings: Children's understanding of responsibility. *Children & Society,* 18, 231-242.

Sweetman, C. (2004). Editorial. In C. Sweetman (Ed.), *Gender, development and citizenship* (pp. 2-7). Oxford: Oxfam.
Taylor, N.J., Smith, A.B., & Nairn, K. (2001). Rights important to young people: Secondary student and staff perspectives. *The International Journal of Children's Rights, 9,* 137-156.
Thomas, N. (2007). Towards a theory of children's participation. *The International Journal of Children's Rights, 15,* 199-218.
Torney-Purta, J.V. (2002). Patterns in the civic knowledge, engagement and attitudes of European adolescents: The IEA Civic Education Study. *European Journal of Education, 37*(2), 129-141.
Vygotsky, L.S. (1978). *Mind in society: The development of higher psychological processes.* London: Harvard University Press.
Waldron, F., & Pike, S. (2006). What does it mean to be Irish? Children's construction of national identity. *Irish Educational Studies*, *25*(2), 231-251.

2 Research Methodology

Cresswell, J.W. (1994). *Research design: Qualitative and quantitative approaches.* London: Sage Publications.
Denzin, N.K., & Lincoln, Y.S. (2000). Introduction: The discipline and practice of qualitative research. In N.K. Denzin & Y.S. Lincoln (Eds.), *Handbook of qualitative research* (2nd ed.) (pp. 1-29). Thousand Oaks, California: Sage Publications.
Eisner, E. (1991). *The enlightened eye: Qualitative enquiry and the enhancement of educational practice.* Toronto: McMillan.
James, A. (2007). Giving voice to children's voices: Practices and problems, pitfalls and potentials. *American Anthropologist, 109*(2), 261-272.
MacDougall, C., & Fudge, E. (2001). Planning and recruiting the sample for focus groups and in-depth interviews. *Qualitative Health Research, 11*(1), 117-126.
Madriz, E. (2000). Focus groups in feminist research. In N.K. Denzin & Y.S. Lincoln (Eds.), *Handbook of qualitative research* (2nd ed.) (pp. 835-850). Thousand Oaks, California: Sage Publications.
Mayall, B. (2002). *Towards a sociology for childhood.* Buckingham: Open University Press.
Morrow, V., & Richards, M. (1996). The ethics of social research with children: An overview. *Children and Society, 10*(2), 90-105.
Powell, M., & Smith, A.B. (In press). Children's participation rights in research, *Childhood.*
Robinson, C., & Kellett, M. (2004). Power. In S. Fraser, V. Lewis, S. Ding, M. Kellett & C. Robinson (Eds.), *Doing Research with Children and Young People* (pp. 81-96). London: Open University/Sage Publications.

3 Australia

Archard, D. (1993). *Children: Rights and childhood.* London: Routledge.
Australian Curriculum Studies Association (ACSA). (2003). *Discovering Democracy Forum: Final Report.* Canberra: ACSA.
Davis, J., & Hill, M. (2006). Introduction. In K. Tisdall, J. Davis & A. Prout (Eds.), *Children, young people and social inclusion: Participation for what?* (pp. 1-19). Bristol: Policy Press.
Flekkoy, M.G., & Kaufman, N.H. (1997). *The participation rights of the child: Rights*

and responsibilities in family and society. London: Jessica Kingsley Publishers.

Kaufman, N., & Rizzini, I. (Eds.). (2002). *Globalization and children: Exploring potentials for enhancing opportunities in the lives of children and youth*. New York: Kluwer Academic / Plenum.

Lansdown, G. (2001). Children's participation in democratic decision-making. UNICEF. www.unicef-icdc.org/publications/pdf/insight6.pdf, accessed 25 February 2007.

Limber, S., & Kaufman, N.H. (2002). Civic participation by children and youth. In N. Kaufman and I. Rizzini (Eds.) *Globalization and children's lives*. New York: Kluwer Academic/Plenum.

Lister, R. (2005). Investing in the citizen-workers of the future. In H. Hendrick (Ed.), *Child welfare and social policy: An essential reader* (pp. 449-462). Bristol: The Policy Press.

Mellor, S., Kennedy, K., & Greenwood, L. (2001). *Citizenship and democracy: Students' knowledge and beliefs – Australian fourteen year olds and the IEA Civic Education Study*. Department of Education, Science and Training, Commonwealth of Australia: Canberra http://www.acer.edu.au/research/LSAY/documents/LSA32Lipsig-mumme.pdf.

National Assessment Program for Civics and Citizenship. (2004). http://www.mceetya.edu.au/taskfrce/civics.htm, accessed 27/9/05.

NSW Board of Studies. (1998a). *Human Society and its environment K-6 Syllabus*. Sydney: Board of Studies.

NSW Board of Studies. (1998b). *Human Society and its environment K-6 Units of Work*. Sydney: Board of Studies.

O'Toole, T., & Gale, R. (2006). Participative governance and youth inclusion: The case of youth parliaments. Paper presented at the *Theorising Children's Participation: International and Interdisciplinary Perspectives* conference, 4-6 September, University of Edinburgh, Scotland.

Print, P., & Gray, M. (2005). Civics and Citizenship Education: An Australian perspective. Accessed 16th February, 2007 from http://www.abc.net.au/civics/democracy/ccanded.htm

Smith, A.B. (2002). Interpreting and supporting participation rights: Contributions from sociocultural theory. *The International Journal of Children's Rights, 10,* 73-88.

Smith, A.B., Taylor, N.J., & Tapp, P. (2003). Rethinking children's involvement in decision-making after parental separation. *Childhood, 10*(2), 201–216.

Thompson, M. (2004, March 12). Benchmarks set for share of $31 million. *Sydney Morning Herald*. Accessed 29/9/05 from http://www.smh.com.au/articles/2004/03/11/1078594501154.html?oneclick=true

4 Brazil

Butler, U.M., Princeswal, M., & Abreu, R. (2007). *Cultures of participation: Young people and their perceptions and practices of citizenship*. Research report. Rio de Janeiro: CIESPI; London: Economic & Social Research Council.

Davies, L. (2002). Possibilities and limitations for democratization in education. *Comparative Education, 38*(3), 251-266.

Davies, I., Gorard, S., & McGuinn, N. (2005). Citizenship education and character education: Similarities and contrasts. *British Journal of Educational Studies, 53*(3), 341-358.

Davies, L., & Kirkpatrick, G. (2000). *The EURIDEM Project: A review of pupil democracy in Europe*. London: Children's Rights Alliance.

Flekkoy, M.G., & Kaufman, N.H. (1997). *The participation rights of the child: Rights and responsibilities in family and society.* London: Jessica Kingsley Publishers.

Hart, R. (1997). *Children's Participation: The theory and practice of involving young citizens in community development and environmental care.* London: Earthscan.

Hart, J., Newman, J., Ackermann, L., & Feeny, T. (2003). *Children changing their world: Understanding and evaluating children's participation in development.* Report by PLAN International.

Kaufman, N.H., & Rizzini, I. (Eds.). (2002). *Globalization and children.* New York: Kluwer Academic/Plenum Publishers.

Limber, S., & Kaufman, N.H. (2002). Civic participation by children and youth. In N. Kaufman & I. Rizzini (Eds.), *Globalization and children's lives.* New York: Kluwer Academic/Plenum Publishers.

McCowan, T. (2006). Approaching the political in citizenship education: The perspective of Paulo Freire and Bernard Crick. *Educate, 6*(1), 57-70.

McLaren, P. (1989). *Life in schools.* New York: Longman.

Melton, G.B., & Limber, S.P. (1993). What children's rights mean to children: Children's own views. In M. Freeman & P. Veerman (Eds.), *The Ideologies of Children's Rights* (pp. 167-187). Dordecht: Martinus Nijhoff Publishers.

Morrow, V. (1999). 'We are people too': Children and young people's perspectives on children's rights and decision-making in England. *The International Journal of Children's Rights, 10,* 149-170.

Rizzini, I., & Thapliyal, N. (2006). *Perceptions and experiences of participation of children and adolescents in Rio de Janeiro, Brazil.* Rio de Janeiro: Ciespi & Colorado: University of Colorado Press.

Smith, A.B. (2005). *Research forum on children's views of citizenship: Cross-cultural perspectives - An introduction and overview of results.* Symposium on Children and Young People's Views on Citizenship and Nation Building at *Childhoods 2005* conference, Oslo, Norway, 29 June – 3 July.

Taylor, N.J., Smith, A.B., & Nairn, K. (2001). Rights important to young people: Secondary student and staff perspectives. *The International Journal of Children's Rights, 9,* 137-156.

Tomasevski, K. (2003). *Education denied: Costs and remedies.* London: Zed Books.

Torres, M.A. (2006). Potencial político de la juventud latinoamericana: Notas preliminares acerca de una agenda de investigación para el siglo XXI. In: Irene Rizzini et al. *Niños, adolescentes, pobreza, marginalidade y violencia en América Latina y el Caribe: relaciones indisociables?* Rio de Janeiro: CIESPI/ PUC-Rio, Childwatch International, Save the Children.

UNICEF. (2003). *The State of the World's Children.* New York: UNICEF.

Weithorn, L.A. (1998). Youth participation in family and community decision-making. *Family Futures, 2*(1), 6-9.

5 New Zealand

Action for Children and Youth Aotearoa. (2003). *Children and youth in Aotearoa 2003: The second Non-governmental Organisations' report to the UN Committee on the Rights of the Child.* Auckland: Action for Children and Youth Aotearoa.

Alderson, P. (2000). *Young children's rights: Exploring beliefs, principles and practices.* London: Jessica Kingsley.

Blaiklock, A., Kiro, C., Belgrave, M., Low, W., Davenport, E., & Hassall, I. (2002). *When the invisible hand rocks the cradle: New Zealand children in a time of change* (Innocenti Working Paper No. 93). Florence: UNICEF Innocenti Research Centre.

Child Poverty Action Group. (2003). *Our children: The priority for policy* (2nd ed.). Auckland: Child Poverty Action Group.

Cockburn, T. (1998). Children and citizenship in Britain: A case for a socially interdependent model of citizenship. *Childhood, 5*(1), 99-117.

Cram, F., & Pitama, S. (1998). Ko toku whanau, ko toku mana. In V. Adair & R. Dixon (Eds.), *The Family in Aotearoa New Zealand.* (pp. 130-157) Auckland: Addison Wesley Longman.

Eccles, J.S., & Barber, B. (1999). Student council, volunteering, basketball, or marching band: What kind of extracurricular involvement matters? *Journal of Adolescent Research, 14*, 10-34.

Flekkoy, M.G., & Kaufman, N.H. (1997). *The participation rights of the child: Rights and responsibilities in family and society.* London: Jessica Kingsley Publishers.

Fletcher, A.C., Elder, G.H., & Mekos, D. (2000). Parent influences on adolescent involvement in community activities. *Journal of Research on Adolescence, 10*, 29-48.

Gibbs, A. (1997). Focus groups. *Social Research Update, Issue 19.* Surrey, UK: University of Surrey.

Grover, S. (2004). Why won't they listen to us: On giving power and voice to children participating in social research. *Childhood, 11*(1), 81-93.

James, A. & Prout, A. (Eds.). (1997). *Constructing and reconstructing childhood: Contemporary issues in the sociological study of childhood (2nd edn).* London: Falmer Press.

Joseph, S. (2005). Teaching rights and responsibilities: Paradoxes of globalization and children's citizenship in Lebanon. *Journal of Social History, 38*(4), 1007-1026.

Kaufman, N.H., & Rizzini, I. (Eds.). (2002). *Globalization and children: Exploring potentials for enhancing opportunities in the lives of children and youth.* New York: Kluwer Academic / Plenum Publishers.

Lamborn, S.D., Brown, B.B., Mounts, N.S., & Steinberg, L. (1992). Putting school in perspective: The influence of family, peers, extracurricular participation, and part-time work on academic engagement. In F.M. Newman (Ed.), *Student engagement and achievement in American secondary schools.* New York: Teachers College Press.

Lansdown, G. (1994). Children's rights. In B. Mayall (Ed.), *Children's childhoods: Observed and experienced.* London: Falmer Press.

Law Commission. (2002). *Family Court Dispute Resolution - A Discussion Paper* (Preliminary Paper 47). Wellington: Law Commission.

Limber, S.P., & Kaufman, N.H. (2002). Civic participation by children and youth. In N.H. Kaufman & I. Rizzini (Eds.), *Globalization and children: Exploring potentials for enhancing opportunities in the lives of children and youth.* New York: Kluwer Academic / Plenum Publishers.

Mayall, B. (2002). *Towards a sociology of childhood: Thinking from children's lives.* Buckingham, UK: Open University Press.

Melton, G.B. (1998). The smallest democracy. *Family Futures, 2*(1), 4-5.

Melton, G.B. (2002). Democratization and children's lives. In N.H. Kaufman & I. Rizzini (Eds.), *Globalization and children: Exploring potentials for enhancing opportunities in the lives of children and youth.* New York: Kluwer Academic / Plenum Publishers.

Ministry of Social Development. (2002). *New Zealand's Agenda for Children: Making life better for children*. Wellington: Ministry of Social Development.

Ministry of Social Development. (2004). *New Zealand families today: A briefing for the Families Commission*, Wellington: Ministry of Social Development.

Ministry of Youth Affairs. (2002). *Youth Development Strategy Aotearoa*. Wellington: Ministry of Youth Affairs.

Morrow, V. (1999). 'We are people too': Children and young people's perspectives on children's rights and decision-making in England. *The International Journal of Children's Rights*, 7(2), 149-170.

Nairn, K. (2000). *Young people's participation in their school environments*. Paper presented at the Childwatch International University of Oslo Symposium on Research on Children's Participation in Community Life, 26-28 June, Oslo, Norway.

Piper, C. (2000). Assumptions about children's best interests. Journal of Social Welfare and Family Law, 22(3), 262-276.

Pufall, P., & Unsworth, R.P. (Eds.), (2004). Rethinking childhood. New Brunswick: Rutgers University Press.

Rizzini, I., Pereira, L., Princeswal, M., de Jesús, M.R., & Botafogo, C., (2005). *Young people and civil participation in Brazil*. Paper presented at the Childhoods 2005 Oslo conference, June 29th -July 3rd, Oslo, Norway.

Rizzini, I., & Thapliyal, N., (2005). *The role of schools in the protection and promotion of children's rights in Brazil* (Unpublished paper). Rio de Janeiro, Brazil: International Center for Research and Policy on Childhood (CIESPE).

Shaheen, M., Abu Baker, M., Bany Odeh, K., Dkedek, S., & Abu Ghosh, E. (2005). *Perspective of Palestinian children on rights, responsibilities and citizenship*. Palestine: Center for Development in Primary Health Care, Al Quds University-Child Research Unit.

Smart, C., & Neale, B. (2000). 'It's my life too' – Children's perspectives on post-divorce parenting. *Family Law*, March, 163-169.

Smith, A.B. (2002). Interpreting and supporting participation rights: Contributions from sociocultural theory. *The International Journal of Children's Rights*, 10(1), 73-88.

Smith, A.B. (2005). *Research Forum on Children's views of Citizenship and Nation Building: Introduction and Overview of Symposium on Children and Young People's Views*. Paper presented at the Childhoods 2005 Oslo conference, June 29th July 3rd, Oslo, Norway.

Smith, A.B., Nairn, K., Sligo, J. Gaffney, M., & McCormack, J., (2003). *Case studies of young people's participation in public life – Local Government, Boards of Trustees and the Youth Parliament*. Dunedin, NZ: Children's Issues Centre.

Statistics New Zealand. (2001). *Children: 2001 Census snapshot 13*. Wellington: Statistics New Zealand.

Statistics New Zealand. (2002). *Families and households: 2001 Census snapshot 17*. Wellington: Statistics New Zealand.

Taylor, N.J., Smith, A.B., & Nairn, K. (2001). Rights important to young people: Secondary student and staff perspectives. *The International Journal of Children's Rights*, 9(2), 137-156.

Torney-Purta, J., Lehmann, R., Oswald, H., & Schultz, W. (2001). *Citizenship and education in twenty-eight countries: Civic knowledge and engagement at age fourteen*. Amsterdam, The Netherlands: International Association for the Evaluation of Educational Achievement (IEA).

UNICEF. (2003). *A league table of child maltreatment deaths in rich nations. Innocenti Report Card, Issue No. 5*, Florence: Innocenti Research Centre, UNICEF). Retrieved May 28, 2004, from http://www.unicef-icdc.org
UNICEF. (2005). *Child poverty in rich countries*. Innocenti Report Card No. 6, Florence: UNICEF Innocenti Research Centre.
Vygotsky, L. (1978). *Mind in society: The development of higher psychological processes*. Cambridge, Mass: Harvard University Press.
Weithorn, L. A. (1998). Youth participation in family and community decision making. *Family Futures*, 2(1), 6-9.
Youniss, J., McLellan, J. A., & Yates, M., (1997). What we know about engendering civic identity. *American Behavioral Scientist*, 40, 620-631.

6 Norway

Bartley, K. (1998). *Barnpolitik og barns rettigheter: Avhandling*. Gøteborg: Sosiologiska Institutionen.
Ben-Arieh, A., & Boyer, Y. (2005). Citizenship and childhood: The state of affairs in Israel. *Childhood*, 12(1), 33-53.
Brochmann, G. (2002). Statsborgerskap, medborgerskap og tilhørighet. In G. Brochmann, T. Borchgrevink & J. Rogstad (Eds.), *Sand i maskineriet: Makt og demokrati i det flerkulturelle Norge* (pp. 56-84). Oslo: Gyldendal Norsk Forlag AS.
Casas, F., Saporiti, A., González, M., Figuer, C., Rostan, C., Sadurní, M., Alsinet, C., Gusó, M., Grignoli, D., Mancini, A., Ferrucci, F., & Rago, M. (2006). Children's rights from the point of view of children, their parents and their teachers: a comparative study between Catalonia (Spain) and Il Molise (Italy). *The International Journal of Children's Rights*, 14(1), 1-75.
Cherny, I., & Perry, N.W. (1996). Children's attitudes toward their rights: An international perspective. In E. Verhellen (Ed.), *Monitoring children's rights* (pp. 241-250). New York: Kluwer Law International.
Cockburn, T. (1998). Children and citizenship in Britain: A case for a socially interdependent model of citizenship. *Childhood*, 5(1), 99-117.
Conover, P.J. (1995). Citizen identities and conceptions of the self. *Journal of Political Philosophy*, 3(2), 133-165.
Delanty, G. (2000). *Citizenship in a global age: Society, culture, politics*. Buckingham: Open University Press.
Gibbs, A. (1997). Focus groups. In *Social Research Update*. Issue 19. Surrey, UK: University of Surrey.
Hart, R. (1992). *Children's participation: from tokenism to citizenship*. United Nations Children's Fund, Innocenti Essay No. 4, 19-22.
Haugen, S.P. (1995). *Barn som medborgere. Visjon og virkelighet*. Hovedoppgave. Universitetet i Bergen: Institutt for kunsthistorie og kulturvitenskap.
Helwig, C.C. (1995). Adolescents' and young adults' conceptions of civil liberties: Freedom of speech and religion. *Child Development*, 66, 152-166.
Hine, J. (2004). *Children and Citizenship*. Home Office Online Report 08/04.
Jans, M. (2004). Children as citizens: Towards a contemporary notion of child participation. *Childhood*, 11(1), 27-44.
Kjørholt, A.T. (2001). 'The participating child': A vital pillar in this century? *Nordisk Pedagogikk 2, 21*, 65-81.
Kjørholt, A.T. (2002). Small is powerful: Discourses on children as social participants in contemporary Norway. *Childhood*, 9(1), 63-82.

Kjørholt, A.T. (2004). *Childhood as a social and symbolic space: Discourses on children as social participants in society.* Doctoral thesis, 152. Trondheim: NTNU, Department of Education/Norwegian Centre for Child Research.
Kjørholt, A.T., & Lidén, H. (2004). Children and youth as citizens: Symbolic participants or political actors? In H. Brembeck, B. Johansson & J. Kampmann (Eds.), *Beyond the competent child: Exploring contemporary childhoods in the Nordic Welfare States* (pp. 63-88). Roskilde: Roskilde Universitetsforlag/Samfundslitteratur.
Kjørholt, A.T., & Qvortrup, J. (2000). *Children's participation in social and political change – Western Europe.* Paper presented at the Research Symposium on Children's Participation in Community Settings, arranged by Childwatch International in collaboration with UNESCO and UiO, June 26-28.
Lansdown, G. (1994). Children's rights. In B. Mayall (Ed.), *Children's childhoods: Observed and experienced* (pp. 33-44). London: The Falmer Press.
Lidén, H. (2003). Ungdomsråd – politisk lekestue? In F. Engelstad & G. Ødegård (Eds.), *Ungdom, makt og mening* (pp. 93-120). Oslo: Gyldendal Akademiske.
Limber, S.P., Kask, V., Heidmets, M., Kaufman, N.H., & Melton, G.B. (1999). Estonian children's perceptions of rights: implications for societies in transition. *The International Journal of Children's Rights, 7,* 365-383.
Lister, R., Smith, N., Middleton, S., & Cox, L. (2003). Young people talk about citizenship: Empirical perspectives on theoretical and political debates. *Citizenship Studies, 7*(2), 235–252.
Marshall, T.H. (1964). *Class, citizenship and social development.* New York: Anchor Books.
Melton, G.B. (1980). Children's concepts of their rights. *Journal of Clinical Child Psychology, 9,* 186-190.
Melton, G.B., & Limber, S.P. (1992). What children's rights mean to children: Children's own views. In M. Freeman & P. Veerman (Eds.), *Ideologies of children's rights* (pp. 167-187). Dordrecht, Netherlands: Martinus Nijhoff.
Mikkelsen, R., Buk-Berge, E., Ellingsen, H., Fjeldstad, D., & Sund, A. (2001). *Demokratisk beredskap og engasjement hos 9.-klassinger i Norge og 27 andre land.* Civic Education Study Norge 2001. Institutt for lærerutdanning og skoleutvikling. Universitetet i Oslo.
Morrow, V. (1999). 'We are people too': Children's and young people's perspectives on children's rights and decision-making in England. *The International Journal of Children's Rights, 7,* 149-170.
Moss, P., Clark, A., & Kjørholt, A.T. (2005). Introduction. In A. Clark, A.T. Kjørholt & P.Moss (Eds.), *Beyond listening: Children's perspectives on early childhood services* (pp. 1-16). University of Bristol: The Policy Press.
Moosa-Mitha, M. (2005). A difference-centred alternative to theorization of children's citizenship rights. *Citizenship Studies, 9,* 369–388.
Norway Statistics. (2005). *Tall om barn og unge.* Oslo: Statistisk sentralbyrå.
Ruck, M.D., Keating, D.P., Abramovitch, R., & Koegl, C.J. (1998). Adolescents' and children's knowledge about rights: Some evidence for how young people view rights in their own lives. *Journal of Adolescence, 21(3),* 275-289.
Saporiti, A., Casas, F., Grignoli, D., Mancini, A., Ferrucci, F., Rago, M., Alsinet, C., Figuer, C., González, M., Gusó, M., Rostan, C., & Sadurní, M. (2005). Children's views on children's rights: A comparative study of Spain and Italy. *Sociological Studies of Children and Youth, 10,* 125-152.
Satka, M., & Eydal, G.B. (2004). The history of Nordic welfare politics for children.

In H. Brembeck, B. Johansson & J. Kampmann (Eds.), *Beyond the competent child: Exploring contemporary childhoods in the Nordic Welfare States*. Roskilde: Roskilde Universitetsforlag/Samfundslitteratur.

Schmidt, M.G., & Reppucci, N.D. (2002). Children's rights and capacities. In B.L. Bottoms, M.B. Kovera & B.B. McAuliff (Eds.), *Children, social science and the law* (pp. 76-105). Cambridge: Cambridge University Press.

Sletterød, N., & Gustavsen, T. (1995). *Arti' å lag no' skikkelig, itj bære lego! Evaluering av barn og unges medvirkning i utforming av det fysiske oppvekstmiljøet*. Steinkjer: Nord-Trøndelagsforskning.

Smith, N., Lister, R., Middleton, S., & Cox, L. (2005). Young people as real citizens: Towards an inclusionary understanding of citizenship. *Journal of Youth Studies*, *8*(4), 425-443.

Such, E., & Walker, R. (2004). Being responsible and responsible beings: Children's understanding of responsibility. *Children and Society*, *18*, 231-242.

Such, E., & Walker, R. (2005). Young citizens or policy objects? Children in the 'rights and responsibilities' debate. *Journal of Social Policy*, *34*(1), 39-57.

Therborn, G. (1993). The politics of childhood: The rights of children in modern times. In F. Castles (Ed.), *Families of nations: Patterns of public policy in Western democracies*. Dartmouth: Aldershot.

Torney-Purta, J., Lehmann, R., Oswald, H., & Schulz, W. (2001). *Citizenship and education in twenty-eight countries*. Amsterdam: IEA.

Vestel, V., Ødegård, G., & Øia, T. (2003). *Veien til makta og "det gode liv"? Evaluering av medvirkningsarbeidet blant unge i Porsgrunn kommune*. NOVA – Norwegian Social Research, Rapport 8/2003.

7 Palestine

Alpha International. (2004). *Education for citizenship: A study on civic attitudes and perceptions of twelfth grade students*. Ramallah-Palestine.

Consolidated Appeal Process for the Occupied Palestinian Territories (CAP). (2004, November 11). United Nations Office for the Coordination of Humanitarian Affairs (OCHA).

Defense for Children International. (2007, November 11). *Status of Palestinian Children's Rights*. Palestine section.

Hine, J. (2004). *Children and citizenship*. Home Office Online Report (08/04).

OCHA Special Focus. (2007, August 31). *Israeli-Palestinian fatalities since 2000: Key trends*. United Nations Office for the Coordination of Humanitarian Affairs.

Shaheen, M., & Abdeen, Z. (2004). *PTSD screening among Palestinian Children in the West Bank and Gaza Strip-Ramallah-Palestine*. Al-Quds University, Palestine: Center for Development in Primary Health Care.

UNICEF. (2006, May). *Protecting children during armed conflict*. New York: Child Protection Section, Program Division.

8 South Africa

Ashley, M. (1989). *Ideologies and schooling in South Africa*. Rondebosch: South African Teachers' Association (S.A.T.A).

Brooks, H., Shisana, O., & Richter, A.L. (2004). *The National Household HIV Prevalence and Risk Survey of South African Children*. Cape Town: HSRC Publication.

Casas, F. (1998). Social representations of childhood. In A. Saporiti (Ed.), *Exploring children's rights*. Italy: FrancoAngeli.

Constitution of the Republic of South Africa: Act No. 108 (1996). Cape Town: Government Gazette.
Department of National Education. (2002a). *Revised National Curriculum Statement*. Pretoria: Department of Education.
Department of National Education. (2002b). *Revised National Curriculum Statement Grades R-9 (Schools) Policy: Life Orientation*. Pretoria: Department of Education.
Enslin, P. (2003). Citizenship education in post-apartheid South Africa. *Cambridge Journal of Education, 33*(1), 73-83.
Hart. S., Zeidner, M., & Pavlovic, Z. (1996). Children's rights. In M. John (Ed.). *Children in charge* (pp. 38-55). London: Jessica Kingsley Publishers Ltd.
John, M. (2003). *Children's rights and power*. London: Jessica Kingsley Publishers Ltd.
Mail and Guardian. (2007). *Do South Africans really exist?* April 26 - May 03, pp. 10-11.
Medved, M. (2007, May, 29). Primary schools of crime. *Cape Argus*, p. 1.
Melton, G.B. (1999). Parents and children: Legal reform to facilitate children's participation. *American Psychologist, 54*, 935-944.
Osler, A., & Starkey, H., (1996). *Teacher education and human rights*. London: David Fulton Publishers.
Osler, A., & Starkey, H. (1998). Children's rights and citizenship: Some implications for the management of schools. *The International Journal of Children's Rights, 6*, 313-333.
Osler, A., & Starkey, H. (2005). *Changing citizenship*. London: Open University Press.
Republic of South Africa. (2005). *Children's Act no 38*. Cape Town: Government Gazette.
Rooth, E. (2005). *An investigation of the status and practice of life orientation in South African schools in two provinces*. Unpublished PhD thesis, Faculty of Education, University of the Western Cape.
Saporiti, A. (1998). *Exploring children's rights: Third European intensive Erasmus course on children's rights*. Italy: FrancoAngeli.
September, R. (2005). *Towards the development of child well-being indicators from children's perspectives*. Bellville: Child and Youth Research and Training Programme University of the Western Cape.
Smith, A.B. (2000). *Development as widening participation in sociocultural activities*. Paper presented at the Symposium on Children's Participation in Community Settings. Oslo, Norway.
Spencer, S. (2000). The implications of the Human Rights Act for citizenship education. In A. Osler (Ed.), *Citizenship and democracy in schools* (pp. 19-33). London: Trentham Books Limited.
Verhellen, E. (2000). Children's rights and education. In A. Osler (Ed.), *Citizenship and democracy in schools* (pp. 33-43). London: Trentham Books Limited.

9 Children's Perspectives on Citizenship

Alderson, P. (2000). *Young children's rights: Exploring beliefs, principles and practice*. London: Jessica Kingsley.
Ashley, M. (1989). *Ideologies and schooling in South Africa*. Rondebosch: South African Teachers' Association (S.A.T.A).
Bordenave, J. (1995). *O que é participação?* São Paulo: Brasiliense.

Bronfenbrenner, U. (1979). *The ecology of human development.* Cambridge, Mass: Harvard University Press.
Bruner, J. (2003). Self-making narratives. In R. Fivush & C.A. Haden (Eds.), *Autobiographical memory and the construction of a narrative self* (pp. 209-225). Mahwah, New Jersey: Lawrence Erlbaum.
Butler, U.M., Princeswal, M., & Abreu, R. (2007). *Cultures of participation: Young people and their perceptions and practices of citizenship.* Research Report. Rio de Janeiro: CIESPI; London: Economic & Social Research Council.
Cockburn, T. (1998). Children and citizenship in Britain: A case for socially interdependent model of citizenship. *Childhood,* 5(1), 99-117.
Cooke, B., & Kothari, U. (2001). (Eds.). *Participation: The new tyranny?* London: Zed Books.
Cornwall, A., & Coelho, V. (2007). Spaces for change? The politics of participation in new democratic arenas. In A. Cornwall & V. Coelho (Eds.), *Spaces for Change?* (pp. 1-12). London: Zed Books.
Davis, J. (2007). Analysing participation and social exclusion with children and young people: Lessons from practice. *International Journal of Children's Rights.* 15(1), 121-146.
De Jong, T., & Lazarus, S. (1992). *School guidance and counselling.* National Education Policy Investigation Research.
Harber, C. (2001). *State of transition: Post-apartheid educational reform in South Africa.* Wallingford: Symposium Books.
Holland, D., Lachicotte, W., Skinner, D., & Cain, C. (1998). *Identity and agency in cultural worlds.* Cambridge Mass: Harvard University Press.
Isin, E., & Turner, B. (Eds). (2002). *Handbook of Citizenship Rights.* London: Sage Publications.
James, A. (2004). Understanding childhood from an interdisciplinary perspective: Problems and potential. In P.B. Pufall & R.P. Unsworth (Eds.), *Rethinking childhood* (pp. 25-37). New Brunswick: Rutgers University Press.
James, A. (2007). Giving voice to children's voices: Practices and problems, pitfalls and potentials. *American Anthropologist,* 109(2), 261-272.
Jans, M. (2004). Children as citizens – Towards a contemporary notion of child participation. *Childhood,* 11(1), 27-44.
John, M. (2003). *Children's rights and power.* London: Jessica Kingsley.
King, M., & Van den Berg, O. (1991). *Politics of Curriculum: Structures and Processes.* Pietermaritzberg: Centuar/IEB.
Lister, R. (2007). Why citizenship: Where, when and how children? *Theoretical Inquiries in Law.* 8(2), 693-718.
Lister, R. (forthcoming). Unpacking children's citizenship. In A. Invernizzi & J. Williams (Eds.), *Children and citizenship* (pp. 9-19). Los Angeles: Sage Publications.
Meacham, J. (2004). Action, voice and identity in children's lives. In P.B. Pufall & R.P Unsworth (Eds.), *Rethinking childhood* (pp. 69-86). New Brunswick: Rutgers University Press.
Ministry of Education. (2007). *The New Zealand curriculum.* Wellington: Learning Media Ltd.
Moosa-Mitha, M. (2005). A difference-centred alternative to theorization of children's citizenship rights. *Citizenship Studies,* 9(4), 369-388.
Neale, B. (2004). *Young children's citizenship: Ideas into practice.* York: The Joseph Rowntree Foundation.

Osler, A. (2000). (Ed.). *Citizenship and democracy in schools: Diversity, identity and equality.* Stoke on Trent, UK: Trentham Books.

Pufall, P.B., & Unsworth, R.P. (2004). Introduction: The imperative and the process for rethinking childhood. In P.B. Pufall & R.P Unsworth (Eds.), *Rethinking childhood* (pp.1-24). New Brunswick: Rutgers University Press.

Rahnema, M. (1992). Participation. In W. Sachs (Ed.), *The development dictionary: A guide to knowledge as power.* London: Zed Books.

Taylor, N.J., Smith, A.B., & Nairn, K. (2001). Rights important to young people: Secondary student and staff perspectives. *International Journal of Children's Rights, 9,* 137-156.

Wenger, E. (1998). *Communities of practice: Learning, meaning and identity.* Cambridge: Cambridge University Press.

Author Index

Abdeen, Z. 131
Abramovitch, R. 31, 104
Abreu, R. 63, 181
Abu Baker, M. 97
Abu Ghosh, E. 98
Ackermann, L. 61
Alderson, P. 18, 82, 178, 181
Archard, D. 43
Ashley, M. 149, 165, 176

Bany Odeh, K. 97
Barber, B. 82
Bartlett, S. 33
Bartley, K. 100
Belgrave, M. 83
Ben-Arieh, A. 15, 103
Bhopal, K. 32
Bjerke, H. 99, 169
Blaiklock, A. 83
Bordenave, J. 179, 180
Botafogo, C. 97
Bourdieu, P. 19
Bowes, J. 32
Boyer, Y. 15, 103
Brannen, J. 32
Brochmann, G. 112
Bronfenbrenner, U. 18, 181
Brooks, H. 166
Brown, B. 82
Bruner, J. 179
Buk-Berge, E. 99
Butler, U.M. 61, 63, 169, 181

Cain, C. 179
Casas, F. 31, 126, 148, 167
Cheal, D. 32
Cherney, I. 104, 126
Christensen, P. 20
Clark, A. 101
Cockburn, T. 18, 82, 102, 128, 177, 178, 181

Coelho, V. 169
Cohen, E. 15
Cohen, R. 32
Conover, P. 22, 103
Cooke, B. 169
Cornwall, A. 169
Covell, K. 16, 29
Cox, L. 23, 99
Cram, F. 83
Cresswell, J. 35
Crewe, I. 22

Davenport, E. 83
Davies, A. 26
Davies, I. 62
Davies, L. 62
Davis, J. 17, 21, 43, 44, 177
de Jesús, M. 97
De Jong, T. 176
Delanty, G. 103
Denzin, N. 35
Dkedek, S. 97
Doek, J. 15

Eccles, J. 82
Eisner, E. 37
Elder, G. 82
Ellingsen, H. 99
Enslin, P. 149, 167
Eydal, G. 100

Feeny, T. 61
Fitzgerald, R. 43, 169
Fjeldstad, D. 99
Flanagan, C. 27, 32
Flekkoy, M. 43, 63, 81, 82
Fletcher, A. 82
France, A. 33
Freeman, M. 17
Fudge, E. 35

Gaffney, M. 29, 30, 81
Gale, R. 43, 47
Gaventa, J. 22
Gibbs, A. 84, 104
Gill, J. 24, 25
Gollop, M. 17, 81
González, M. 31
Gorard, S. 62
Graham, A. 43, 169
Gray, M. 44
Greenwood, L. 59
Grover, S. 81
Gustavsen, T. 101

Harber, C.. 176
Hart, J. 22, 27, 61
Hart, R. 61, 102
Hart, S. 167
Hassall, I. 83
Haugen, S. 102
Heater, D. 15
Hebert, Y. 26
Heidmets, M. 104
Hellem, L.. 99
Helwig, C. 20, 32, 104
Heptinstall, E. 32
Hill, M. 43, 44
Hine, J. 23, 104, 131
Holland, D. 179
Holloway, S. 26
Holzman, L. 18
Howard, S. 24, 25
Howe, B. 16, 29

Isin, E. 169

James, A. 17, 18, 19, 20, 36, 81, 175, 179, 182
Jans, M. 16, 17, 18, 19, 102, 178, 183
John, M. 148, 167, 175
Jones, E. 22
Jonsson, B. 27
Joseph, S. 16, 30, 82

Kabeer, N. 22
Kask, V. 104
Kaufman, N. 43, 63, 81, 82, 104
Keating, D. 31, 104
Kellett, M. 35, 36

Kennedy, K. 59
King, M. 176
Kirby, P. 20
Kirkpatrick, G. 62
Kiro, C. 83
Kjørholt, A. 20, 99, 100, 101, 102, 103, 117, 127
Koegl, C. 31, 104
Kothari, U. 169

Lachicotte, W. 179
Lamborn, S. 82
Lansdown, G. 43, 106
Lazarus, S. 176
Lee, J. 26
Lehmann, R. 81, 99
Lidén, H. 100, 101, 117, 127
Limber, S. 28, 43, 63, 81, 104, 126
Lincoln, Y. 35
Lister, R. 16, 17, 18, 23, 24, 43, 44, 99, 104, 172, 177, 180
Low, W. 83

MacDougall, C. 35
Madriz, E. 36, 37
Manning, B. 23
Marchant, R. 20
Marshall, T. 16, 102
Martin, R. 32
Matthews, H. 20
Mayall, B. 17, 35, 81
McCormack, J. 81
McCowan, T. 62
McGuinn, N. 62
McLaren, P. 62
McLellan, J. 82
Meacham, J. 179
Medved, M. 165
Mekos, D. 82
Mellor, S. 59
Melton, G.B. 22, 28, 32, 63, 81, 104, 126, 148
Middleton, S. 23, 99
Mikkelsen, R. 99, 112, 127
Moosa-Mitha, M. 17, 102, 181
Morrow, V. 28, 36, 62, 63, 81, 127, 128
Moss, P. 101
Mounts, N. 82

Nairn, K. 29, 30, 63, 81, 82, 97, 174
Neale, B. 15, 18, 19, 20, 21, 97, 181
Newman, J. 61

Oakley, A. 18
Ødegård, G. 102
Øia, T. 102
Osler, A. 33, 148, 150, 165, 167, 174
Oswald, H. 81, 99
O'Toole, T. 43, 47

Pavlovic, Z. 167
Pereira, L. 97
Perry, N. 104, 126
Pike, S. 24
Piper, C. 97
Pitama, S. 83
Powell, M.A. 36
Princeswal, M. 63, 97, 181
Print, P. 44
Prout, A. 17, 18, 81
Pufall, P. 16, 17, 81, 179

Qvortrup, J. 33, 100

Rahnema, M. 169
Reppucci, N. 104
Richards, M. 36
Richter, A. 166
Rizzini, I. 43, 61, 62, 63, 81, 97, 98
Roberts, H. 147
Robinson, C. 35, 36
Roche, J. 17, 19, 21
Rooth, E. 151
Ruck, M. 31, 32, 104, 126
Ryan, R. 23

Saporiti, A. 31, 104, 126
Satka, M. 100
Schmidt, M. 104
Schultz, W. 81, 99
Scourfield, J. 26
Searing, D. 22
September, R. 147, 166
Shaheen, M. 97, 129, 131
Shipway, B. 43, 169
Shisana, O. 166
Sinclair, R. 21
Skinner, D. 179

Skotte, P. 99
Sletterød, N. 101
Sligo, J. 81
Smart, C. 97
Smith, A.B. 17, 18, 29, 30, 36, 43, 63, 81, 82, 97, 127, 148, 169. 174
Smith, N. 23, 99
Spencer, S. 150
Starkey, H. 33, 148, 150, 165, 167
Stasiulis, D. 16, 18
Steinberg, L. 82
Stephens, S. 24, 27
Stordal, G. 99
Such, E. 33, 126
Sund, A. 99
Sweetman, C. 15, 16

Tapp, P. 43
Taylor, A. 32
Taylor, N. 17, 29, 43, 63, 81, 97, 169, 174
Thapliyal, N. 61, 62, 81
Therborn, G. 100
Thomas, N. 19, 21
Thompson, M. 45
Tomasevski, K. 79
Torney-Purta, J. 22, 81, 97, 99
Torres, M.A. 63
Turiel, E. 20, 32
Turner, B. 169

Unsworth, R. 16, 17, 81, 179

Valentine, G. 26
Van den Berg, O. 176
Verhellen, E. 148
Vestel, V. 102
Vygotsky, L. 18, 98

Waldron, F. 24
Walker, R. 33, 126
Watson, N. 17
Weithorn, L. 62, 81
Wenger, E. 179

Yates, M. 82
Youniss, J. 82

Zeidner, M. 167

Subject Index

A number in **bold** indicates a figure or table. An en dash (–) between two numbers indicates continuous treatment of a topic, a tilde (~) only that a topic is referred to on each page in the range.

abstract understanding 90–91, 97, 98, 158, 170, 171, 178, 183
accent 25, 90
adults
   see also parents; teachers
   advocacy 62, 83, 98, 174; attitudes 19–20, 21, 22, 29, 52, 54–5, 95–6, 100, 102, 119–20, 137, 151, 165~7, 181–3; authority 148, 149, 155, 166, 167, 176; expectations 16, 166; guidance 18, 127; responsibilities 118; source of information 79; support 52, 53, 82, 91, 107, 127, 149, 172, 177, 178, 181; violators of rights 79
age 38, 45, 47, 49, 63, 75, 84, 95, 101, 105~7, 121, 122, 126, 136, 144, 158, 160, 162, 177, 178
agency 16~18, 21, 22, 26, 27, 29, 32, 35, 62, 97, 98, 100, 102, 148, 172, 174, 177~9, 181, 182
alienation 97–8
altruism 81, 94, 97
appearance 76–7, 86, 90, 93
Australia 25, 27–8, 38, **39**, 40, 43–60, 169, 172, 173–4, 175, 178
   Aboriginal children 38; Australian Citizenship Act 44; context 44–5; *Discovering Democracy* 25, 45–8, 60; school curriculum 44–7; *Values Education Framework* 47; *Young People, Big Voice* 47
authenticity 36, 53, 56, 167, 170, 179, 181, 182
autonomy 18, 29, 32, 33, 95, 102, 103, 155, 167

belonging 15~17, 21, 22, 23, 24–7, 28, 34, 43, 52, 81, 103, 114, 156, 161, 163, 178–9, 180
biculturalism 172, 174
Brazil 38, **39**, 61–80, 97, 169, 170, 172–3, 174–5

   context 61; *favelas* 65, 66, 76, 78; *machismo* 175; Movement for Landless Agricultural Workers 38; Movement of Landless Agricultural Workers (MST) 61, 68–70, 77–8; *Statute on the Child and Adolescent* 61, 80; street children 68, 77
Bulgaria 27–8
bullying 30, 86, 87, 89, 92, 94, 107~9, 111, 119, 120, 162, 171

Canada 26, 28, 31
caring 27, 50, 51, 88, 89, 110, 111, 115, 127, 138, 155, 156, 161, 171
cause of floods 72
child development 18
childhood studies 35, 36
Childwatch International 37, 43, 47, 85, 129, 151
citizenship
   aspirational notions of 173; being/becoming citizens 17–18; building blocks of 15, 16, 21, 103; children's understanding of 52–3, 72–3, 90–91, **90**, 98, 99, 103, 112–17, 127, 139, 140–41, 145–6, 157, 160, 167, 171–3, 178~80; education for 33, 43, 44–7, 59–60, 62, 101, 149–50, 151, 173–4; learning about 82, 103; meanings of 15, 17, 23–4, 52–4, 63, 99–100, 102–3, 148–9, 151, 169–70, 177, 181, 183; theoretical models 17, 21, 82, 102, 128
class 17
colonisation 82–3
competence 17–18, 36, 57–9, 82, 100, 102, 120–22, 125, 166, 177–8, 180
confidence 18, 26, 30, 54, 62, 81, 148, 177
contraception 75–6
cultural capital 19

cultural clichés 25
cultural differences 16, 20, 28, 112, 126, 175–7
Czech Republic 27–8

decision-making 16, 21, 29, 32, 171
  Australia 43–4, 52~4, 56; Brazil 61–2; New Zealand 86, 92, 97; Norway 101, 106~8, 110, 112~14, 116, 119, 120–21, 122–5, 128; Palestine 137, 141, 143, 144; South Africa 148, 161, 163, 165~7
democracy 21, 22, 26, 32, 34, 169, 172, 175, 178, 183
  Australia 45~7, 57, 59; Brazil 62, 63; New Zealand 81, 91, 97, 98; Norway 101, 103, 116; South Africa 147~51, 167, 168
dependency 18, 126, 177, 178, 181
'deviant children' 27
dignity 28, 73, 79, 128, 135, 149, 150
disability 17
discourse(s) 17, 19, 24, 27, 34, 103, 180, 181
discrimination 18, 22, 26, 76–8, 157, 159~61, 163, 166, 172–3
diversity 25~7, 36, 59, 64, 151
drugs 78, 88, 92, 109, 154, 155, 171
duties *see* obligations

economic resources 93
education 27–8, 32, 33, 43, 44–7, 59, 60, 71, 76, 86, 93, 101, 106~8, 131, 141, 149–50
egocentricity 28
egocentrism 119
elderly 50, 52, 53, 55, 56, 60, 88, 89, 93, 142, 145
environment 29, 30, 171, 178
  Australia 50, 51, 53~5, 60; Brazil 72; New Zealand 88, 89, 94, 97; Norway 109, 111, 115, 127; Palestine 137, 138–9; South Africa 155~61, 163, 164
equality 16, 17, 21, 49, 106, 117, 140, 144, 149, 168, 171, 174
ethnicity 17, 29, 36, 77, 83, 90, 151–2
exclusion 17, 19, 26, 29, 33, 36, 93, 98, 101, 102, 127, 166, 169, 170, 177, 181
exploitation 33, 80

expressing opinions 18, 20, 28, 34, 171
  Australia 44, 50; Brazil 62, 68, 70; New Zealand 81, 86, 87; Norway 107~9, 117, 123–5, 175; Palestine 136, 140, 143~5; South Africa 148, 149, 154, 158, 160, 176

fairness 33, 46, 74, 89, 116, 154, 160, 178
familiies 30, 32, 33, 116, 175
flags 37, 49, 57–8, **58**, 64, 178
freedom 33, 70, 118, 135, 136, 139~41, 144, 146, 149, 158, 173
friends 30, 32, 56, 87, 91, 92, 106~9, 116, 119, 124, 136, 142, 158, 161, 163, 171

gender 17, 36, 38, 47, 75, 95, 104, 121, 126, 136, 137–8, 140, 144, 145, 151, 160, 174, 175
government 20, 28, 44–7, 49, 71~3, 76, 79, 80, 83, 91, 98, 159, 166, 168, 173~5
growing up/childhood tensions 119, 176–7
guilt 33

habitus 19, 181
homeless children 68, 77, 166
honesty 33, 89, 156, 157
Hungary 27–8

identity 16, 17, 24, 26, 44, 78, 103, 145, 146, 151, 155, 178, 179, 181
imaginary countries 37, 173, 178
  see also flags
  Australia 49, 52, 53, 59, 178; Brazil 64, 73–4, 79; New Zealand 91–4, 97, 178; Norway 121; Palestine 139–40, 143, 145, 146; South Africa 158–60
inclusion 17, 29, 43, 174, 177
independence 106, 116, 120–21, 127, 140, 144
  economic 23; national 135, 136, 144
inequality 61, 71, 77, 79, 80, 83, 140, 172
information 30, 144, 148, 161, 163
interdependence 21
invisibility 16, 19, 115

Ireland 24–5, 28
Israel 32, 129, 130, **130**, 131
Italy 31–2

Jordan 27
justice 73–4, 106, 154, 160, 175
    restorative 23; social 26, 28, 33, 149, 167

language 24, 26, 170
law/legality 28, 45, 50, 56, 61, 63, 90, 91, 94, 103, 112, 127, 146, 156, 157, 160, 166, 178
leadership 54, 56
learning 18, 19
Lebanon 30–31, 82
leprechauns 25
listening/not listening
    by adults 56, 92, 97, 122, 124, 125, 143, 148, 154, 161–4, 171, 180; by children 30, 87, 88, 94, 110, 115, 117, 141, 155, 160, 171

Maori 82–3
marginalised groups 36, 38, 68–70, 76–8, 98, 142, 170, 172
media 27, 28, 34, 78, 137
membership *see* belonging
mentoring 52, 53, 56
methodology 26, 35–40, 47–8, 63–70, 84–5, 97, 98, 100, 104–5, 132–4, 141, 143–4, 151–3
    see also imaginary countries
    consent 38, 48, 84, 85; data collection/analysis 39–40, 48; focus groups 36–7, 38, 47, 48, 63, 65, 67, 69, 84, 85, 95, 103–5, 132–4, 143, 152–3, 183; qualitative research 35, 36, 48, 63; questionnaires/surveys 37–9, 47, 85, 95–6, 153; research questions 40, 103, 151; samples 38–9, **39**, 48, **48**, 65, **65**, 84, **84**, 104–5, **105**, 132–3, **133**, **134**, **153**, 152–3; triangulation 37
multiculturalism 25–8, 90, 172–4

nationality/nationhood 15, 24–8, 34, 43, 44, 54, 59, 135, 136, 141, 173
    diversity 25–7, 44, 59

New Zealand 26–7, 29, 38, **39**, 40, 81–98, 169, 172, 173, 174, 175–6, 178
    Agenda for Children 83, 98; Children's Commissioner 83; Children's Issues Centre 83, 85; context 82–3; family types 83; Maori 82–3; Treaty of Waitangi 82, 174
normative assumptions 17, 20, 21
Norway 38, **39**, 99–128, 169, 170, 172, 173, 175, 176
    attitudes towards children 100; Children's Ombudsman 101; 'citizen' concept 112; context 100, 101, 112; school reform case study 122–5; schools 101; UNCRC 100, 101; Youth Councils 101

obedience 175, 176
    Palestine 137, 138, 145; South Africa 149, 155–64, 166, 167
obligations 15, 21, 24, 28, 34, 44, 50, 52, 71, 82, 137
oysters 159

Pakistan 29
Palestine 27, 38, 39, 97, 129–46, 169, 172, 173
    context 129–31, 144; defence of 137, 142; freedom of movement 129, 135; *Intifada* 129, 135; religion 145; security 135; Separation Wall 129, **130**
parents **39**, 57, 60, 76, 77, 89, 107, 108, 175, 176
    see also adults
    attitudes 95–6, 136; authority 70, 144, 148, 155; expectations 33, 166; listening 56; support 91, 95, 98, 106, 127, 155, 162–3; survey of 37–9, 48, 52, 54–5, 56, 85, 95–6, 153, 162–4; time with children 56
participation 16–18, 20, 21, 23, 24, 30, 34, 178, 179–80, 182
    see also rights – of participation
    Australia 43, 44, 53, 55–7, 59; Brazil 62, 63, 72, 73, 80; New Zealand 81–2, 86–9; Norway 99, 100, 101–2, 103, 113, 115, 118–22, 126; Palestine

141–3; South Africa 148
authenticity of 36, 53, 56, 167, 170, 179, 181, 182; defining 17; resistance to 53
patriotism 54, 55, 157
policy 80, 100, 181–3
politics 121, 122, 127, 130–31, 136, 142, 144, 147, 172, 173
power 16, 33, 45, 62, 94, 148, 149, 167, 175, 182
powerlessness 122, 126
prejudice 71, 76–7, 94

race 17, 26, 27
recognition 16, 21, 34, 180, 181
religion 20, 25, 27, 50, 106, 108, 138, 139, 171
South Africa 145, 155, 156, 158, 176
researchers 35~7, 48, 80, 85, 105, 134, 139, 144, 152
respect 21, 28~30, 34, 171, 172, 175, 178, 180
Australia 43, 50, 51, 53, 54; Brazil 70, 75; New Zealand 81, 86; Norway 127; Palestine 137~9, 141, 145; South Africa 155~64, 166
responsibilities 16, 20, 21, 23, 32–3, 34, 171, 176–7
Australia 44, 50–52, 54~7; Brazil 71–2, 74–5; New Zealand 88–90, 93–4, 96; Norway 107, 109–12, 116, 121, 126; Palestine 137–9, 145; South Africa 150, 155–6, 158, 160, 161, 164, 166
adult/child comparisons 118–22, 126; at home **88**, **89**, **110**, 138; at school **88**, **89**, **110–11**; definition 131; in the community **88**, **89**, **111**, 138; sexual 75–6; tables of 88, 110–11
rights 16, 20, 21, 28–32, 33–4, 170–71
see also United Nations Convention on the Rights of the Child
Australia 44, 46, 49–50, 56, 57, 59, 60; Brazil 61, 70–71, 73~5, 79; New Zealand 82, 85, 86, **86**, 87, **87**, 91~3, 95, 97; Norway 99, 100~3, 105–7, **108–9**, 112, 117–18, 123–6; Palestine 130, 131, 135–7, 144–5; South Africa 147~51, 154–5, 158~63

adult/child comparison 117–18; at home **86**, **87**, **108**, 136, 161, 163; at school **86**, **87**, **108**, 136, 161, 162–3; citizenship 15, 16, 92–3, 148; civil 56, 59, 131, 149, 172, 174; economic 86, 87, 93, 106, 112; human 46, 60, 79, 91, 95, 100, 130, 144, 147~51, 175; in the community 73, **86**, **87**, **109**, 136–7, 161, 163
of association see friends; of participation 16~18, 20, 29, 32, 86, **86**, 87, **87**, 97, 99, 101–2, 103, 106–7, **108–9**, 117, 123–6, 148, 162, 167–8, 170, 171, 174; of protection 18, 29, 30, 56, 86, **86**, 87, **87**, 92, 97, 107, **108–9**, 126, 135~7, 144, 148, 154, 155, 158~63, 166–7, 171; of provision 29, 31, 32, 34, 86, **86**, 87, **87**, 97, 107, **108–9**, 126, 148, 171
to education 29, 32, 49, 50, 70, 86, 93, 106~8, 136, 144, 154, 158, 160, 162, 171; to food 66, 70, 71, 73, 74, 106, 108, 117, 136, 144, 154, 158, 160, 163; to freedom of movement 135, 137, 139, 144, 171; to health 29–30, 50, 71, 73, 86, 92, 93, 161, 163; to peace 135; to privacy 32, 50, 56, 136, 140, 144, 155; to recreation 29, 30, 50, 86, 92, 106~8, 135~7, 154, 155, 158, 160~63, 171; to self-determination 28, 31, 34; to shelter 74, 92, 117, 136, 154, 160; to sleep 50, 71, 158; to space 56, 87, 108, 171; to transport 71, 161, 163, 171; to work 50, 70, 91, 135; universality of 28, 31, 33, 49, 79
rules 25, 51, 53, 56, 70, 73, 88, 89, 93, 94, 96, 109, 112, 115, 116, 139, 155, 156, 161~5, 171, 176
rural/urban differences 78
Russia 27–8

schools 27–8, 29, 30, 44, 174, 175
see also bullying; teachers
Australia 43–7, 54, 55, 56–7, 60; Brazil 61~3, 65–8, 69, 72–3, 76, 77, 79; New Zealand 93, 95; Norway 101, 105, 107, 108, 116, 118, 119, 122–5; Palestine 131, 132–3, 136, 139, 142–3, 144, 145; South Africa

149, 151, 152, 155, 165
curriculum 27, 29, 43, 44–7, 55, 60, 62, 95, 101, 149, 151, 174, 175, 181~3; public/private differences 136, 139, 142~5, 174; reform case study 122–5; student councils 73, 79, 116, 123; uniforms 76, 77, 155, 173
sexual abuse 74, 154, 155, 159, 171
sexuality 75, 175
shame 33, 78
sharing 52, 72, 86, 97, 140
citizenship 15, 16, 44, 93, 158, 179; focus groups 36, 37, 80
skills 18, 23, 45, 55, 98, 103, 180
social networks 16
social reality 17, 67, 137
sociocultural theory 18–19, 21, 179, 183
guidance 18; joint involvement 82; learning 18, 19, 81; scaffolding 57, 98, 180~83
socio-economic status 28, 30, 36, 38
Australia 47; Brazil 76–8; New Zealand 83, 84, 97; Norway 104, 126; Palestine 129, 132, 136, 138, 144, 145; South Africa 152, 160, 166
sociology of childhood 35, 181, 182
South Africa 38, 39, 147–68, 169, 170, 172, 173, 175, 176
African Charter on the Rights and Welfare of the Child 147, 150; apartheid 147~50, 167, 172, 176; Bill of Rights 149; Children's Act 147, 176; Constitution (1996) 147, 149, 151; context 147–8, 151; HIV/Aids 166; poverty 166; *ubuntu* 166
Spain 31–2
status 16, 19, 21, 23, 24, 149
see also socio-economic status
stereotypes 25, 26–7, 90
stress 131
subordination 19
Sweden 27–8

teachers 29, 30, **39**
Australia 45, 48, 52, 54–5, 56, 175; Brazil 70; New Zealand 85, 89, 91, 93, 95–6, 98; Norway 108, 123; Palestine 136, 143~5; South Africa 149, 153~5, 160–62, 176
attitudes 27, 29, 95–6, 123, 160, 161; authority 70, 155; support 30, 91, 95, 98, 161; survey of 37, 38, **39**; UNCRC 57

United Kingdom 26–7, 33
United Nations Convention on the Rights of the Child (UNCRC) 15, 16, 20, 22, 29, 30, 32, 44, 46, 56, 57, 79, 83, 85, 96, 98~101, 107, 130, 135, 144, 145, 147, 148, 164, 176
Universal Declaration of Human Rights 150
urban/rural differences 78
USA 27–8, 40

values 47, 60, 63, 81, 114, 159, 173
violence 29, 30, 74, 86, 87, 92, 94, 98, 111, 147, 159, 171, 173
Palestine 129, 131, 135, 136, 173
voice(s) 16~18, 20, 21, 23, 29, 30, 32, 36, 44, 100, 107, 130, 137, 143, 177, 179, 181, 182
voting 46, 72, 90, 92, 95, 136, 137, 154, 157, 158, 177
Norway 102, 117, 119, 121–2, 125

Wales 26, 28
work 25, 31, 33, 70, 72, 75, 77, 118, 127, 129, 137, 138, 141, 145, 171, 177
community 33, 50, 52, 56, 115, 138, 142; household 32, 75, 88, 110, 155, 161, 175; school 30, 33, 52, 71, 74, 108, 110, 111, 118, 120, 155, 158

youth councils/clubs 101, 116, 137, 142